The United States and the Americas

Lester D. Langley, General Editor

This series is dedicated to a broader understanding of the political, economic, and especially cultural forces and issues that have shaped the Western hemispheric experience — its governments and its peoples. Individual volumes assess relations between the United States and its neighbors to the south and north: Mexico, Central America, Cuba, the Dominican Republic, Haiti, Panama, Colombia, Venezuela, the Andean Republics (Peru, Ecuador, and Bolivia), Brazil, Uruguay and Paraguay, Argentina, Chile, and Canada.

The United States and the Americas

The Dominican Republic and the United States

G. Pope Atkins and Larman C. Wilson

The Dominican Republic and the United States: From Imperialism to Transnationalism

The University of Georgia Press

Athens and London

Set in 10 on 14 Palatino by G&S Typesetters, Inc.
Printed and bound by Braun-Brumfield, Inc.

The paper in this book meets the guidelines
for permanence and durability of the Committee on
Production Guidelines for Book Longevity of the
Council on Library Resources.

Printed in the United States of America

02 01 00 99 98 C 5 4 3 2 1

02 01 00 99 98 P 5 4 3 2 1

Library of Congress Cataloging in Publication Data

Atkins, G. Pope, 1934–
    The Dominican Republic and the United States : from
    imperialism to transnationalism / G. Pope Atkins and
    Larman C. Wilson.
        p.   cm. — (The United States and the Americas)
    Includes bibliographical references and index.
    ISBN 0-8203-1930-9 (alk. paper). — ISBN 0-8203-1931-7
    (pbk. : alk. paper)
    I. United States—Relations—Dominican Republic.
    2. Dominican Republic—Relations—United States.
    I. Wilson, Larman C. (Larman Curtis), 1930–   . II. Title.
    III. Series.
    E183.8.D6A84   1997
    303.48'27307293—dc21   97-30046

British Library Cataloging in Publication Data available

Dedicated to the memory of

Harold Eugene Davis

1902–1988

Scholar, Teacher, Mentor, Colleague, and Friend

Contents

Preface

This book is a general study of the relationships between the United States and the Dominican Republic, from the beginning to the present. We aim to chronicle how connections evolved over time and to analyze why particular characteristics developed in the process, with a balanced treatment from both Dominican and U.S. perspectives.

In consonance with the purposes of the University of Georgia Press series of books on inter-American relations, this volume considers the unofficial transnational cultural and economic interactions along with the official diplomatic political-economic-military relations. Such attention is particularly relevant in the instance of the Dominican–United States association.

The story has been, to a considerable degree, one of a patron-client dependency relationship, but not entirely so or in any simple way. For several reasons, the Dominican Republic has been able to pursue its own objectives and has enjoyed some freedom of action with reference to the United States. It has also had other significant connections, and we acknowledge the roles of other states and non-state entities. Furthermore, the transnational associations, particularly and increasingly since the 1960s, have been a two-way street. While U.S. actors have had an enormous influence on the Dominican Republic in the matters of immigration, economic affairs, drug trafficking, and the concomitant social and cultural consequences, Dominicans have had their own significant impact on the United States in these same areas.

Both of us have had extensive research experience regarding the Dominican Republic, beginning some three decades ago with our doctoral dissertations. We coauthored *The United States and the Trujillo Regime* (1972), a case study of U.S. problems with a Latin American dictatorship, several elements of which have been incorporated into this book. Each of us has independently pursued related topics. These prior efforts and the current one assimilate source materials from both the United States and the Dominican Republic. We have examined numerous archival and research collections, conducted extensive interviews, and made extended visits to the Dominican Republic.

Acknowledgments

We want to take this opportunity to express jointly our appreciation to a number of individuals who provided important assistance in the preparation of this study. In the Hispanic Division of the Library of Congress, Everette E. Larson, head of the reference section; Juan Manuel Pérez, senior bibliographer; and Reynaldo Aguirre, senior bibliographic specialist, located numerous important sources; and Georgette Dorn, director of the Hispanic Division, and Dolores Moyano Martin, editor of the *Handbook of Latin American Studies*, provided both assistance and academic hospitality. Willard Barber, former deputy assistant secretary of state for inter-American affairs, who served during World War II as political officer in the United States Embassy in Ciudad Trujillo, gave us considerable information and insight regarding relations between the United States, Latin America, and the Dominican Republic—and support and friendship for many years. Frank Moya Pons, leading Dominican historian and social scientist, provided, in addition to his vital scholarship, a great deal of advice about sources and discussion of issues. Bernardo Vega Boyrie, economist, former president of the Central Bank of the Dominican Republic, director of *La Fundación Cultural Dominicana*, and since 1997 ambassador to the United States, furnished us with his important series of original archival and analytic publications on the country's relations with the United States. He also supported several of our past projects, which have been reflected in this study.

Sincere thanks are extended to the following people for providing information and other assistance: Marilyn Arnold, Peter Kolar, Anne Langhaug, and Mary Nelson at the U.S. Agency for International Development; Brenda Malveau Freeman at the U.S. Department of Agriculture; Milbrey Jones and John Blake at the U.S. Department of Education; Martin Manning at the U.S. Information Agency; Ramiro A. Solares at the U.S. Information Service; Martha Ellen Davis de Matos,

xiii

Faculty Research Associate at Indiana University (Bloomington); René Fortunato, Dominican film director (two of his videos are cited in the text); Magda Lee Vázquez and Raúl González Díaz, graduate assistants to Larman Wilson; in the American University Bender Library, George D. Arnold, university archivist and head of Special Collections, and Helen E. Ives, reference librarian; and Barbara Breeden, reference librarian in the Nimitz Library at the U.S. Naval Academy.

We single out Lester D. Langley, general editor of the series of books published by the University of Georgia Press of which the present work is a part, for asking us to undertake this project and for his extraordinary patience as we subsequently prepared the manuscript.

Finally, we express our affectionate thanks to our wives, Joan and Olga, for their assistance on the project and for their indispensible personal support and patience.

The Dominican Republic and the United States

Introduction

This book is a study of the political, economic, and social-cultural relations of the Dominican Republic and the United States as they evolved from the middle of the nineteenth century to the mid-1990s. It deals with the interplay of these various dimensions of the association, from both Dominican and U.S. perspectives and in both public and private interactions.

Certain fundamental themes are pursued. From the U.S. perspective, they include interpretation of the rise and fall of the Dominican Republic's strategic importance, the legacy of military intervention and occupation, the problem of Dominican dictatorship and instability, and vacillating U.S. efforts to "democratize" the country.

The United States as a major, metropolitan, industrial, status-quo state has considered its interests to be best served in a secure and stable world. Thus, traditional U.S. policy goals were to exclude as far as possible other foreign presences in the Caribbean and to promote political stability in the area. With the beginning of the twentieth century and the rise of the United States to world power, the Caribbean region was the object of considerable U.S. concern and activity. Over the years the policy issue was not whether regional and individual state security and stability were desirable but rather what was the best means of achieving them.

The United States employed the full spectrum of policy orientations toward the Dominican Republic—coercive and cooperative, and unilateral, bilateral, and multilateral. The instruments and techniques included establishing customs receiverships and forming banking consortia; landing troops and organizing militarily occupations; creating constabularies and training the Dominican armed forces; recognizing or refusing to recognize new governments; granting or refusing to provide foreign assistance (economic, military, and technical); supervising elections; supporting dictators; and promoting democracy and development.[1]

1

The U.S. belief that its intervention or direction was necessary in order to protect its interests was a reflection of a superiority complex and a self-perception of exceptionalism. Analysts who have investigated U.S. decision makers' perceptions of Latin Americans tend to be struck by the persistence of negative stereotypes and paternalistic attitudes. This impression has been especially relevant to U.S. contacts with the circum-Caribbean, with particular overtones regarding the special characteristics of the Dominican Republic. U.S. officials tended to believe that Dominicans were incapable of governing and managing their own political and financial affairs. This belief resulted in a number of stereotypes that persisted in U.S. public and official images of Dominicans.[2]

A number of private U.S. citizens and U.S.-based companies, church groups, foundations, and international voluntary organizations to varying degrees affected and influenced the Dominican government and society. On occasion some of them cooperated with and supported policies of the U.S. government, but most of the time they pursued their own commercial, economic, educational, humanitarian, or religious objectives.

In the post-Cold War era, traditional security concerns and their connection to Dominican stability greatly decreased in importance, while the issues of Dominican democratic transformation and economic well-being rose to top priority. Consequently, the actions and influence of the U.S. government decreased while those of the private sectors increased. This increase was particularly true of U.S.-based private business and commercial influence, especially in the dynamic and expanding Industrial Free Zones.

From the Dominican viewpoint, the essential themes involved foreign policy ends and means adopted from a position of relative weakness, ambivalent love-hate views toward the United States, emphasis on economic interests and the movement of Dominicans between the two countries, international political isolation, the adversarial relationship with neighboring Haiti, the legacy of dictatorship, and the uneven evolution of a Dominican-style democratic system.

The Dominican response to the U.S. presence took different forms, but all of them were those associated with a small and weak state in the shadow of a major power. In the earlier period, the United States was viewed with great suspicion. Later, in response to mounting U.S. economic and political penetration, and especially military intervention and occupation during World War I into the 1920s and the landing of troops in 1965, Dominicans reacted with a combination of harsh criticism, xenophobia, and appeals to international law. The response was manifested in Dominican literature and folklore with the recurrent theme of the search for freedom from foreign interference and control. The theme in the nineteenth century also pertained to European states. A version of it was always directed toward Haiti; in recent years it emphasized population pressures and the fear that Haitians would racially and culturally transform Dominican society.

Another manifestation of the Dominican reaction was stressing the importance of international law, especially as it respected state sovereignty and the principle of nonintervention. After 1933 these aspects of international law were also strongly expressed legal tenets of the Inter-American System. Most Dominican governments, however, found it necessary to accommodate the economic and political realities of their U.S. relations. They were also adept at manipulating the United States.

A major source of weakness on the part of the Dominican Republic, in addition to its "smallness" and location within the U.S. sphere of influence, was its own political system. The history of the Dominican Republic has always been marked by personalism, until the mid-1960s by dictatorship punctuated with political chaos and instability, and since then by a mix of civilian authoritarianism and partial democracy. Instability and lack of economic development initially led to European and later U.S. military intervention and domination in other respects.

Although after the turn of the century the U.S. government and private companies were the most significant foreign influences in the Dominican Republic, certain other states and private groups were important in Dominican society. Relations with Haiti were always significant and troubled—and often affected U.S.-Dominican relations. These other foreign interests are also considered in this book.

Special attention is given to international social-cultural developments. Some analysts of international relations view the cultural aspect as a "fourth dimension" in interstate affairs accompanying security, politics, and trade.[3] In any event, we view culture in a broadly defined way, its meaning taken from both the humanities and the social sciences. In the former sense, culture refers to things of the intellect and the arts, and in the latter instance it is extended to mean learned behavior (attitudes and values) shared by and transmitted to societal members. International cultural relations allude to how the sum total of the ways of living associated with a nation or society are transmitted beyond its own boundaries. The process of transmission may be formal or informal and promoted under either public or private auspices. This definition will be applied by discussing how culture and the cultural dimension affected and conditioned economic and political relations between the United States and the Dominican Republic. Formal intergovernmental cultural exchanges and programs and the activities of private cultural exchange organizations were important. But of considerably more significance were the dramatically increasing transnational relations between the two countries, which were a mix of governmental and (probably more important) nongovernmental transactions.

In the Dominican-U.S. relationship, the social-cultural element had a mutual and major transnational impact. Analysts referred to the consequences of U.S. influence as the "Northamericanization" of the Dominican Republic and the reciprocal Dominican impact as the "Dominicanization" (a special part of the larger "Caribbeanization") of the United States. The former expression first arose in the 1950s and then referred to the continuing nature of and effects on Dominican society. The latter phrases were evident in the 1960s and achieved broader currency from the 1980s into the 1990s. A third dimension, the "Dominicanization of the Dominican Republic," was pursued by long-time President Joaquín Balaguer (1966–78, 1986–96) as a way to counter U.S. cultural penetration by stressing the Spanish legacy (the ideology of *hispanidad*). Dictator Rafael Trujillo (1930–61) had initiated the process in the 1930s and pursued it thereafter as a way to counter his fears of Haitian penetration; Balaguer also included this element in his conception of Dominicanization. This notion, however, denied the African roots of the vast majority of Dominicans and a long suppressed countercultural movement along these lines had considerable success after its revival in the 1960s. Racism connected to xenophobia toward Haiti was a persistent Dominican phenomenon and problem.

Transnational linkages received great impetus in the early 1980s with the rapid, momentous, and related increases in three phenomena. First was the movement of Dominicans back and forth between their homeland and the United States. Second was Dominican economic dependency on the United States as a function of structural imbalances in the Dominican economy exacerbated by the "debt crisis." Third was the international trafficking in illicit narcotics, with the United States a major market and Dominicans both at home and in the United States participating in the transporting and marketing of drugs.

The combination of U.S. foreign policy and the private economic and commercial impact on the Dominican Republic indicates the accuracy of the description of the U.S. relationship as one of "suprasovereignty" and the Dominican Republic as an "unsovereign state."[4]

1 Colonial and Nineteenth-Century Foundations

Much of the history of the Dominican Republic has been characterized by chaos, dictatorship, and foreign domination. This unfortunate legacy was rooted in the three-century Spanish colonial period and reinforced during the complex half-century road to independence in 1844; it was carried forward in the rest of the nineteenth century (and beyond).

The domination of foreigners and the paradoxical Dominican acceptance of and resistance to that domination is a pervasive theme of Dominican international history. Among the important actors were individuals, including private U.S. citizens and some officials, seeking personal gain. The U.S. government had some interest in what was to become the Dominican Republic as early as the beginning of the eighteenth century but did not become a major presence until after the U.S. Civil War ended in 1865. Then the United States took an essentially imperialist attitude, characterized by a mixture of strategic-political and economic motives with an overlay of cultural arrogance.

Cultural relations as we know them today did not exist between the Dominican Republic and the United States during this time. But cultural attitudes among U.S. officials shaped perceptions of the Dominican Republic that reinforced negative stereotypes and paternalism. These attitudes stemmed from the combination of the popular U.S. view of Latin American culture, a strategic outlook on the circum-Caribbean, and an estimation of the Dominican Republic itself.

The Spanish Colonial Experience

♣ The island today comprising the Dominican Republic and Haiti was visited by Christopher Columbus in 1492 during his first voyage. He called it *La Española* (Little Spain), a name later evolving as Hispaniola. Short-lived settlements were established on the northern Atlantic coast beginning in December 1492. In 1496 the city soon to be called Santo Domingo was founded as the colonial capital, situated on the southern Caribbean coast at the mouth of the Ozama River. It was the first permanent European settlement in the New World.

Colonists were brought in and the Spanish-American empire was begun. Spanish objectives from the beginning were to found in Hispaniola a mining and farming colony that would send gold to Spain and provide a base for further exploration and conquest.[1] Many Spaniards were attracted to Spain's first American colony during the early years and it developed rapidly. By 1514 gold and silver mines had been established (although little was found and they were soon exhausted), cotton and sugar planted, roads built, and thirteen towns founded; the colonial population stood at about sixty thousand people. Hispaniola owed its early importance to the lucrative sugar trade with Europe, which established the base for the Dominican economy that has persisted to the present day.

Hispaniola served as the initial point of departure for the *conquistadores* as they expanded the empire to more valuable American domains. Once the Spanish moved on to conquer Mexico and then Peru, and Spanish interest was diverted to the mainland, Hispaniola became depopulated, with people leaving for other colonial centers. The island fell into decay, becoming a neglected, poverty-ridden, isolated backwater of the great Spanish-American empire. By 1570 the economy was stagnant and the population reduced by about half, to no more than thirty-five thousand people (including the slaves). A brief resurgence of relative prosperity and population increase occurred in the eighteenth century but Hispaniola remained poor in comparison with the other Spanish-American colonies.

Spain experimented with and developed colonial institutions during its three-century rule in Santo Domingo. That rule was harsh, evolving into a system based on political and religious authoritarianism, a slave economy and economic exploitation by the mother country, and a rigidly hierarchical society. Regionalism emerged early, forming another persistent reality of Dominican political life. The colonial government in Santo Domingo exercised little control over the interior, where plantations were virtually autonomous entities. The northern city of Santiago de los Caballeros, the urban core for the fertile Cibao Valley, became the country's economic center and resisted political control from Santo Domingo.

Black African slavery was an important economic and social element of the colonial system. The native Arawak Indians were virtually eliminated within a half century of the Spanish arrival as a result of brutal maltreatment, disease, and suicide. Numbering about four hundred thousand in 1492, in 1819 the Indian population was reduced to less than three thousand and by the 1540s it had virtually vanished.[2] Beginning in the 1520s, Spain brought slaves from Africa to replace Indians as laborers in the mines and fields. They became the preponderant portion of the population.

The Caribbean Sea was transformed into a Spanish lake after Columbus's voyages and organization of the lands under the Spanish crown. Attracted by the circum-Caribbean's apparent mineral and agricultural wealth and its strategic value in the evolving colonial competition in the New World, other European powers eventually challenged Spain's control. As part of the Caribbean competition, France, England, and the Netherlands sought to conquer or otherwise acquire Hispaniola. The island was also frequently attacked by pirates and privateers.

Spain nevertheless controlled Hispaniola until French buccaneers took over part of the west coast in 1630. French settlers arrived soon thereafter. Spain finally ceded the western third of Hispaniola to France in the Treaty of Ryswick in 1697, thus establishing the basis for the later national divisions between Haiti and the Dominican Republic. The treaty did not precisely delineate the border between Spanish and French Hispaniola, leading to continual controversy between Spain and France and, later, the Dominican Republic and Haiti. French planters made their colony of Saint-Domingue the most prosperous agricultural economy in the Caribbean, with the sugar, coffee, and tobacco plantations worked entirely by black slaves brought from West Africa.[3] Active trade was carried on between the Spanish and French sections of Hispaniola. U.S. commercial interest in Hispaniola was first indicated in the early eighteenth century when North American trading vessels sailed the West Indies.

The Road to Independence

The movement for independence in Spanish-speaking Hispaniola was a half-century process characterized by changing foreign masters. The slave revolt against France in the western part of the island led to the creation of independent Haiti in 1804 and subsequent Haitian ambitions to control the entire island. From the outbreak of the French Revolution in 1789 until the founding of the Dominican Republic in 1844, a complex period ensued in which the Spanish portion of Hispaniola was, in turn, ceded to France (1795), returned to Spanish control (1809), declared independent (1821), occupied by Haiti (1822), and again declared independent (1844).[4]

Haitian slaves, under the leadership of Pierre Dominique Toussaint L'Ouverture, partly inspired by the ideas of the French Revolution of 1789, revolted in 1791 against their French masters. They were initially supported by Spanish and British forces and by Dominicans who, opposing the French colonists in the west, backed Spain's war effort against France in Europe. The situation changed in 1794 when a new French government abolished slavery in its colonies; Toussaint consequently made common cause with France against Spain. Spain was no longer able to administer effectively its far-flung American empire, in which Santo Domingo was of low priority, and France forced it to transfer ownership of its portion of the island in the Treaty of Basle (1795). France then appointed Toussaint as governor of the entire colony; Spanish-speaking Dominicans predictably resisted his authority. France, for its part, was preoccupied with revolution at home and war in Europe and never consolidated its rule. In 1798 Toussaint led Haitian troops into the Spanish-speaking territory and eventually gained control. Among other things he ordered the freeing of slaves; the Dominican upper class fled in large numbers to other Spanish colonies. At this time Haitians outnumbered Dominicans by more than five to one (some 520,000 people to about 100,000).

Napoleon Bonaparte, who in 1802 had taken dictatorial power in France, was unhappy with Toussaint's independent position. In that year Napoleon sent a military expedition to Hispaniola, commanded by his brother-in-law, General Charles Leclerc, to assert French authority. The French forces defeated Toussaint and, in the process, occupied the entire island. The French then perpetrated an infamous act of betrayal: they allowed Toussaint to retire but, having second thoughts, then arrested and sent him to prison in France, where he died within a year in 1803. Haitians continued their struggle under the leadership of Jean Jacques Dessalines, declared their independence, defeated the French forces (with the help of yellow fever), and, in 1804, established the Republic of Haiti on the western third of Hispaniola. The French defeat included the death of Leclerc and the loss of fifty thousand soldiers.

By the time of Haitian independence, U.S. considerations were complex and ambiguous: the United States desired commercial relations with Hispaniola, which it thought would be enhanced by independence (France had placed an embargo on U.S. trade); yet it had to deal with the precedence of a slave revolt in terms of its own slavery question at home. In April 1799, the United States and Great Britain had signed an agreement "to prevent dissemination of dangerous principles among slaves held in territories belonging to the respective countries and to open up intercourse with the islands." At about the same time, a U.S. consul was appointed to facilitate trade through Haitian ports, and the following year, in 1800, the United States sent warships to blockade the southern ports in support of Toussaint.[5]

After Haitian independence in 1804, Spanish-speaking Dominicans on the rest of the island remained technically under French authority, but Haiti and Spain also sought control. Great Britain aided Spain first in driving out Haitian forces and then in winning the old Spanish colony back from France. Dominicans themselves rebelled against both France and Haiti and proclaimed loyalty to Spain and the anti-Napoleon junta. Once Haiti and France were expelled, Dominicans asked Spain anew to exercise colonial administration over their part of Hispaniola.

From 1809 to 1821 Santo Domingo was again a Spanish colony. Slavery was reimposed and some of the Dominican elite returned. But Spain again showed little interest in its possession. Ferdinand VII, restored to the Spanish throne in 1814, reverted to harsh colonial policies. Conditions continued to deteriorate until 1821 when, after years of guerrilla warfare, disillusioned and resentful Dominican patriots declared independence from Spain (joining most of the rest of Spanish America in doing so) and ejected the Spanish governor. Even then Dominicans were hesitant to go it alone. They petitioned Simón Bolívar to join the newly independent South American Republic of Gran Colombia (a union that later divided into Venezuela, Colombia, and Ecuador). Within weeks of the Dominican declaration of independence from Spain, however, Haitian armies again invaded.

In Haiti, Dessalines had been assassinated in 1806. A power struggle among several competitors had ensued until 1818, when Jean Pierre Boyer took uncontested power as president, a position which he held until 1843. In February 1822, Boyer marched his army into Spanish Santo Domingo, with little resistance from Dominicans, and declared the entire island united under rule from Port-au-Prince. The Haitian occupation lasted for twenty-two years until 1844. The period is often viewed as the principal cause of the racial, social, and political antagonism that even today continues to separate Dominicans from Haitians. The occupation by Haiti established a continuing fear, enmity, and hostility toward the neighboring nation. Positive elements may also be pointed out, however, such as the ending of slavery.

During the occupation Haitians perpetuated their own racial views, which they had acquired while subjected to the French colonial black slavery plantation system in St. Dominique. After the successful uprising ended French control in 1804 (there were about five hundred thousand slaves on the island), black Haitian racial attitudes were both antiwhite and antimulatto.[6] Once the Haitian occupation began, these attitudes were reinforced, and an effort was made to "darken" the eastern part of the island—as well as to weaken Roman Catholicism. In order to alienate the clergy, starting in 1824 Haitians promoted the immigration of African-American Protestants. About five thousand left the United States, coming mainly from Philadelphia and New York City and settling in the Samaná area.

The principal international questions for the United States and European nations had to do with the recognition of Haitian independence and commercial relations. Great Britain extended recognition in 1826; France finally did so in 1838. The United States, however, did not accord recognition even when it was doing so throughout the rest of Latin America. Governmental instability was hardly a ground for inaction, since President Boyer remained in office for twenty-five years. The reason was the sensitive slavery question.[7] The violent end of slavery in Haiti and its later abolition from the rest of the island were viewed by proslavery elements in the United States as intolerable precedents.

The Boyer regime envisioned a significant trading relationship with the United States and formally petitioned for its recognition. President James Monroe referred the application to the Senate where it met an unfavorable response because of Southern senators' vehement opposition. After 1830 the development of the abolition movement in the United States led to increased interest in the recognition of Haiti, but the United States continued to refuse recognition. According to Luis Martínez-Fernández,[8] in the United States the "Africanization scare" and North-South rivalry meant continued U.S. refusal to recognize Haiti until after the issue was resolved by the U.S. Civil War. The United States nonetheless carried on commercial relations.[9]

The United States adopted a politically paternalistic and culturally negative attitude toward the other Americas early in the evolution of inter-American relations, while the Dominican Republic was following its unique and tortuous path to independence. The initial U.S. perception of Latin America, however, was part of the "Western Hemisphere idea," the concept of a special relationship between the United States and the other Americas due to their geographic, political, economic, social, and moral separation from the autocratic Old World of Europe. As a result of its own successful independence movement and creation of a constitutional, representative political system, the United States ex-

pressed strong criticism of Europe's corrupt, royal, and hierarchical political systems and rigid class order of privilege based on birth and
wealth. But the United States also developed a superiority complex
about its institutions, values, and opportunities in the New World. The
disapproving evaluation of Latin Americans also began in the early
days of inter-American relations. John J. Johnson, in a study of the
struggle for independence in Spanish-America, analyzes the shift in
U.S. views from a pro-insurgent perspective in the early part of the independence movement to one of disdain for Latin American culture
and institutions by 1830.[10] Thus, by the time of Dominican independence in 1844 the negative view was well-established.

In this context, U.S. relations with the island of Hispaniola were be-
deviled by U.S. attitudes of cultural superiority, prominently including
religious and racial elements. The United States considered itself to be
exceptional also as a white, Anglo-Saxon, Protestant nation, an attitude
that particularly and adversely affected its relations with the Dominican Republic, where the vast majority of inhabitants were black and
mulatto, Hispanic, and Roman Catholic. As a result of these views, and
with the divisive issue of the institution of black slavery in the United
States, recognition of the Dominican Republic (and Haiti) was not forthcoming until after the U.S. Civil War. The racial aspect of this equation
was shared by the white Spanish-American elites (*criollos*) in the Dominican Republic. They were antiblack and anti-Haitian, attitudes that
they made synonymous, and they had paternalistic and disdainful attitudes toward blacks and mulattoes in their own country.

The strategic-cultural context of interests and values had motivated
President James Monroe in 1823, in what later came to be the Monroe
Doctrine, to declare that the Americas were off-limits to further colonization. The United States, however, was not able to back Monroe's principles with power against the numerous European interventions, including intervention in the Dominican Republic, until after the end of
the Civil War.

Spanish Santo Domingo finally revolted against Haitian rule. Dominican nationalists, led by Juan Pablo Duarte, founded a secret revolutionary society in 1838 called *La Trinitaria*. The revolutionary forces

ended the occupation, ejected the Haitians, and on 27 February 1844 declared the independence of the Dominican Republic for the second time.

The Early National Period, 1844–1859

Dominican national history from the "Restoration of Independence" in 1844 through the rest of the nineteenth century was characterized by dictatorship, chaos, and foreign intervention. Duarte and *La Trinitaria* had intended the Dominican Republic to be just that—a republic—but their purpose was quickly betrayed by power rivalries among competing upper-class factions allied with military strongmen. Duarte and his followers were exiled shortly after independence in 1844. Thereafter politics were dominated by *caciques* and *caudillos*—local and regional strongmen, who were both military and political figures. They ruled by means of shifting alliances, bribery, treachery, armed force, imprisonment, exile, and assassination. Intense regionalism continued after independence and was especially strong in the northern Santiago city–Cibao valley region, the nation's agricultural economic heartland. Consequently, politics were the result of the combination of intense regionalism and localism, *caciques* and *caudillos* indulging their political ambitions, and the prevalence of strong personalities over institutions. Dominican presidents by and large were military men presiding over corrupt and violent dictatorial regimes. The struggle among strongmen for supremacy resulted in constant plotting, revolts, counterrevolts, and frequent changes of presidents and constitutions.[11]

During the struggle for independence, according to Harry Hoetink, being Dominican in the sense of cultural identity transcended racial identity.[12] This attitude receded, however, once independence was gained in 1844. Because of the scarcity of inhabitants and the need for skilled artisans, farmers, and workers, in 1847 the Dominican government passed an immigration law; over the years many others followed. Although the laws stressed admission of educated and skilled people and those with wealth, a concern about race was also included. As a result, immigrants included those from Puerto Rico, the Canary

Islands, Europe (particularly Italy and Spain), and Arabs from the Middle East.[13] At the same time, Dominicans were fully aware of the importance of race in U.S. policies. For example, in 1844 Dominican special envoy José M. Caminero pointedly emphasized to U.S. Secretary of State John C. Calhoun that in the Dominican Republic whites largely held political power; he claimed that of the country's total population of two hundred thousand, half were white (a gross exaggeration) and two-thirds of the remainder were mulatto.

The Dominican Republic's international history followed closely with the political and personal fortunes of the individuals who dominated Dominican politics. At first generals Pedro Santana and Buenaventura Báez alternated in power; they or their personal choices were the presidents. The Santana-Báez rivalry brought fraudulent elections and a series of revolts around the country. Santana tended to dominate until his death in 1864; Báez lived until 1882, achieving the presidency five times and being overthrown on each occasion.

A basic recurring theme in the Dominican foreign orientation was the effort to exchange sovereignty for security under a foreign protector. At independence Dominicans had no experience or traditions of self-government and the basis for continuing authoritarian rule had been established. When the last Haitian garrison was evicted in 1844, the nation was torn by the issue of whether it should be a free republic or seek the protection of some foreign state. Duarte and his associates had stood for independence; the generals, fearing Haiti and seeing possibilities for personal gain, favored some kind of protectorate status. Dominican presidents approached France, Spain, the United Kingdom, and the United States. Such probings were particularly prevalent during the Haitian dictatorship of Faustin Soulouque (1847–59) because of his repeated military attacks on Dominican territory. In addition, the Dominican Republic suffered increasingly from the international consequences of its internal financial mismanagement. Foreign interests, both governments and individuals, became deeply involved in the chronic intrigue of Dominican politics.

In 1844 President Santana, after unsuccessfully seeking European assistance, dispatched Special Envoy José M. Caminero to the United

States to ask for its recognition and a treaty of friendship and commerce. U.S. President James K. Polk (1845–49) responded in February 1845 by sending a special agent to the Dominican Republic, who submitted a favorable report on the situation there. Polk also sent Navy Lieutenant David D. Porter as special agent, and he arrived in Santo Domingo in May 1846. Porter's report emphasized Samaná Bay as an important location for a U.S. naval base and discussed the country's rich natural resources that would yield handsome profits if properly exploited. With the commencement of war with Mexico in 1846, however, the United States set aside both reports.

Dominican presidents, frustrated by U.S. inattention and faced with Haitian incursions, approached France and Spain. Although neither European state was anxious to annex such a chaotic entity, President Polk became alarmed about the possibility of a European protectorate. He appointed a commercial agent to the Dominican Republic in order to have an observer on the scene, carefully pointing out that the appointment did not imply recognition. The United States regularly sent commercial agents to the Dominican Republic thereafter; they carried out the functions of representation and reporting in lieu of a formal diplomatic presence.

In August 1848 General Santana resigned as president and was succeeded by General Manuel Jiménez. A Haitian army crossed the border in March 1849 and on 19 April a secret session of the Dominican Congress adopted a resolution requesting the French government to declare a protectorate over the Dominican Republic in return for ownership of Samaná Bay. The congressional majority was strongly influenced by Báez, Santana favored Spanish protection, and Jiménez suggested annexation to the United States. For its part, the United States was fearful of British designs on Samaná Bay. In August 1849, Báez succeeded Jiménez as president, inspiring U.S. efforts also to be directed at countering the new government's pro-French tendencies.

As it turned out, the problem of Haitian-Dominican relations dominated the attention of outsiders for the next three years. Haiti had refused to recognize Dominican independence and Emperor Soulouque threatened invasion to restore Haitian control over the entire island.

Great Britain took the lead in trying to effect peace between the uneasy neighbors; its goal was to convince the Dominican Republic to remain independent rather than be annexed to any outside state. On 22 February 1850, the Dominican government addressed identical notes to the United States, France, and Great Britain, urgently soliciting their joint mediation. All three agreed to act as third parties to restrain Faustin, and for the next two years they exerted pressure on him in favor of a conciliatory policy. In 1852 they abandoned the policy of joint mediation and resumed the rivalry for advantage.

At this point two colorful U.S. personalities entered the Dominican scene—unscrupulous adventurers, entrepreneurs, and imperialists who were to appear and reappear as central characters in the Dominican drama for the next eighteen years. In November 1853 Secretary of State William A. Marcy appointed General William A. Cazneau as special U.S. agent to visit the Dominican Republic and report on conditions there. Cazneau, born and educated in Boston, had been a land speculator in Texas, where he participated in the independence movement, thus acquiring his military rank. He went to the Dominican Republic on a temporary mission but decided to establish permanent residence there. Cazneau was joined by his friend and fellow Bostonian Colonel Joseph W. Fabens, who had also gained his military rank in the Texas independence struggle.

U.S. President Franklin Pierce (1853–57) authorized Cazneau, who had developed good personal relations with President Santana, to negotiate a treaty, which in effect offered U.S. recognition of the Dominican Republic in return for possession and control of a tract of land on Samaná Bay. President Pierce wanted a naval station in the Dominican Republic as part of his design to acquire Cuba. But a supporting resolution, introduced in the Senate on 23 May 1854, was sharply opposed by anti-imperialist members led by Senator Charles Sumner of Massachusetts and supported by certain newspaper and public opposition to Caribbean expansionism. Leading Dominicans also resisted, some of them opposed to any foreign concessions and others preferring the patronage of one or another European state. Santana remained favorably disposed to the United States but his fear of a Haitian invasion induced him to heed protests from the mediators, France and Great Britain, about a U.S. naval base at Samaná Bay. Cazneau complained that his negotiations were being jeopardized by the activities of a young officer of the U.S. Army Engineer Corps, Captain George Brinton McClellan (later of U.S. Civil War fame). McClellan was surveying the Bay of Samaná without Dominican permission to determine the best site for a naval station. On 5 October 1854, Cazneau concluded a treaty of amity and commerce with the Dominican Republic. Although it did not mention Samaná Bay or a naval base, the French and British consuls so vigorously protested that the Dominican government did not ratify it.

Báez returned to power in October 1856 and continued to express hostility toward the United States. But the threat of revolution forced Báez to resign, and on 31 January 1859 Santana was again installed as president. President James Buchanan saw an opportunity to inaugurate an imperialist policy. On 7 April 1859 he appointed Cazneau as special agent to the Dominican Republic again to take up the plan of a naval station at Samaná. In that year Cazneau and Fabens also tried to secure a land grant from President Santana in order to launch a project for the encouragement of emigration from the United States to the Dominican Republic. The beginning of the U.S. Civil War and Spain's annexation of the Dominican Republic, both in 1861, deferred both the official and personal plans.

Spanish Recolonization, 1861–1865

Santana continued to seek for his country an economic *patrón* and military protector against Haiti. On a personal level he desired prosperity and political power against Báez's opposition. In 1861 Spain accepted Santana's invitation to reannex the Dominican Republic. Other outside states were unwilling or unable to stop the arrangement: both France and the United Kingdom were exhausted by the Crimean War, and the United States was on the verge of civil war.

Spain resumed its colonial rule on 18 March 1861.[14] Queen Isabella II was proclaimed protector of Santo Domingo. She appointed Santana to serve as governor with the title of captain-general and provided the support of Spanish troops brought from Cuba. But Spain manipulated the island's affairs for its own profit, a Spanish bishop imposed reforms on local priests, and the best government appointments were reserved for Spaniards. Santana resigned as captain-general in 1862 after serious disagreements with Spanish officials, and he died two years later. He was replaced by a Spaniard who provoked even more protests.

Dominicans and Spaniards both justified the Spanish annexation of the Dominican Republic (1861–65) on the grounds of defending Dominican culture, religion, and racial purity (*limpieza la sangre*) against Haiti; and protecting the Dominican-Spanish church from encroachments by U.S. Protestants (Spanish government and church officials suppressed them to the extent that the Samaná congregation wrote a letter to President Abraham Lincoln protesting their treatment). At the same time, Dominicans serving in the Spanish army complained bitterly about the discrimination they suffered under Spanish officers.

William H. Seward became secretary of state to President Lincoln in 1861. He strongly opposed the European presence in the Caribbean, but the approach and outbreak of the Civil War forced U.S. inaction other than general protestations. During the four years of Spanish recolonization, resident U.S. business interests arranged understandings with Spanish officials. The United States continued to maintain a commercial agent in Santo Domingo. Cazneau and Fabens tried to capitalize on the U.S. Civil War by offering refuge to those who wanted to escape the turmoil and find economic opportunities in the Dominican colony. In 1862 they organized the American West India Company, with New York investors serving as trustees and officers, and acquired access to border lands near Haiti. The scheme failed, as most of the U.S. participants died in the Dominican Republic or returned home.[15]

In 1863 a Dominican underground insurrection, known as the War of the Restoration, was directed against Spanish colonial rule. On 14 September 1863 the rebels again proclaimed Dominican independence and named General José Salcedo president of a provisional government. They sent a special agent to the United States seeking assistance, but Seward maintained U.S. neutrality. The provisional government then attempted to come to terms with Spain, to the consternation of certain Dominican generals. General Salcedo was assassinated, and on 25 March 1865 General Pedro Antonio Pimentel succeeded him as provisional president. In the meantime, the Dominican *caudillos* united their personal armies and, with the unusual help of Haiti, pressure from the United States (coincident with the termination of the Civil War), and the effects of yellow fever (which killed some nine thousand of the twenty-one thousand Spanish soldiers in the country), they defeated the Spanish army. On 3 May 1865, the Spanish Cortés annulled the annexation, and Queen Isabella ordered the withdrawal of Spanish troops. Dominicans thus realized their national independence for the third time.

Dominican Insecurity and the Annexation Issue, 1865–1872

Dominican foreign policy orientations toward the United States, Haiti, and European states after 1865 were primarily influenced by domestic political and economic concerns. After the Spanish departure, Dominicans resumed their intense political rivalries, which were accompanied by severe economic crises. Plots, counterplots, rebellion, and revolutionary activity were almost constant, with occasional respites. During this period all Dominican presidents pursued schemes for surrendering Dominican sovereignty to the United States. The opposing Dominican political alliances had their counterparts in Haiti, complicating the endemic Dominican-Haitian conflict to include mutual factional support. Dominican leaders were also wary of European interests and actions and regularly played them off against the United States. Policy initiatives on the part of all actors were disrupted by chronic Dominican political instability.[16] Luis Martínez-Fernández argues that in cultural terms the "endemic annexationism of the Dominican elite manifested itself in a profound cultural disorientation and the proclivity to imitate foreign patterns of behavior and material culture."[17]

By this time U.S. hemispheric policy had come to be concentrated on the actions of external great powers, so that Latin Americans were of secondary or peripheral consideration.[18] When they did confront Latin Americans themselves, U.S. officials adopted a paternal attitude. They were reluctant to relinquish predominance in the region, especially in the Caribbean area, and tended to assume that Latin Americans were incapable of managing their own governmental and financial affairs. This perception, along with continuing turmoil in the Dominican Republic and the threat of European control of the island, often at the invitation of Dominicans themselves, helps to explain the ready acceptance by some U.S. presidents to consider Dominican offers of annexation. Such perspectives were reinforced with the negative appraisal of Latin American political culture and a self-evaluation of the United States as a superior civilization.

General Pimental, provisional president from 25 March to 13 August 1865, was forced out in favor of General José María Cabral. He, in turn, was compelled to give way to Buenaventura Báez, who was inaugurated as president for the third time on 8 December 1865. Báez had protested the Spanish annexation, but after it became a reality he had lived in Europe with the honorary rank of field marshall in the Spanish army and a subsidy from the Spanish crown. He had resigned his emoluments once the end of Spanish rule was in sight, eventually returning to the Dominican Republic to recapture his political fortunes. Báez's partisans were established in the *rojo* party. His old nemesis General Santana was dead, but other vociferous opponents were loosely organized in the *azul* party. Strong *azul* personalities battled for leadership among themselves—the principal ones were Generals Cabral, Pimental, Federico de Jesús García, and Gregorio Luperón (who enjoyed the greatest public esteem). The *azules* had little in common other than mutual opposition to Báez, yet they remained united for two decades.

By the time of the Spanish reoccupation, the Dominican Republic had become a dual and divided society, with the north and the south based on different economic and social structures. These different bases helped determine the interests of the leading political parties, the *azules* and the *rojos*. The north, in particular the city of Santiago de los Caballeros and the fertile Cibao Valley, was a rural and mercantile society of small landowners. They engaged primarily in the raising of tobacco, which they exported by way of Puerto Rico to the Virgin Islands and Germany. The *azules* represented the interests of the tobacco growers and small landlords. In the south and southeast—Santo Domingo and the surrounding provinces—large cattle ranches and forests were found, although the major economic base was the exportation of cacao to the Virgin Islands, Curaçao, and Great Britain. This area supported the *rojos*. For many years this economic-political division amounted to two separate and virtually independent countries. In the 1860s, however, the situation began to change with the collapse of the cacao market and the increased importance of sugar. As the Cuban struggle for independence became more violent, increasing numbers of Cuban sugar entrepreneurs departed for the Dominican Republic. Dominicans had grown sugar since the earliest colonial days, but the major investments and large scale production occurred at this time. The Cubans introduced the latest sugar mill technology and sugar growing and processing skills, and the Dominican Republic was soon a leading producer and competitor in the world market. This industry was concentrated near the Santo Domingo area and in the eastern provinces and became the essential base for the larger Dominican economy.[19]

With the end of the U.S. Civil War, President Andrew Johnson (1865–69) and Secretary of State Seward (who remained in his position after Lincoln's assassination in 1865 until 1869) adopted an expansionist policy toward the Caribbean. According to Sumner Welles, Seward was primarily concerned with restoring the Monroe Doctrine after the damage it had suffered during the Civil War.[20] To this end, he sought to acquire a Caribbean naval base to deter European expansion in the region, and he was inclined toward securing Samaná Bay as a U.S. naval station. Seward worried about similar French designs on Samaná and about British attempts to neutralize the area. He wanted either to lease or, preferably, to purchase the Samaná peninsula.

Within six months after Báez's inauguration, General Cabral emerged from the rivalry among *azul* leaders and seized the presidency, where he remained for almost two years (28 May 1866 to 31 January 1868). The United States recognized the Dominican Republic on 17 September

1866. At Seward's urging, President Johnson nominated Cazneau to be the minister resident in the Dominican Republic. But Senator Sumner, chairman of the Senate Foreign Relations Committee, vigorously opposed the nomination because of Cazneau's unsavory reputation, his support of the Confederacy during the Civil War, and his denunciation of northern leaders (including Seward). President Johnson withdrew the nomination.[21] The United States sent a commercial agent to Santo Domingo and the Dominican Republic a consul-general to New York.

President Cabral expressed interest in negotiating a treaty of amity and commerce as well as an agreement for a U.S. loan. Secretary Seward continued to seek the lease or sale of territory around Samaná Bay so as to establish a fortified naval station. In January 1867, Assistant Secretary of State Frederick W. Seward, son of the secretary of state, went as special agent to the Dominican Republic authorized to conduct negotiations and to conclude a convention. He was accompanied by Vice Admiral David D. Porter, who twenty years earlier as a lieutenant had visited the country on behalf of President Polk. The U.S. proposals inspired serious disagreement within Cabral's cabinet and strong opposition by a significant minority in the Dominican Congress. Worried that Báez would use an agreement as the basis for revolution, Cabral announced that since Dominicans had adopted an article in their post-Spanish-occupation constitution prohibiting the sale of national territory, they could offer only a limited leasing arrangement. The United States was not interested and the U.S. delegation returned home in May 1867. A commercial treaty was ratified by both parties.

The unpopular negotiations damaged Cabral's standing and inspired the opposition to increase its attacks. His problems were compounded by events in Haiti. During the U.S.-Dominican negotiations, Haitian President Fabré Geffrard, with whom Cabral had an arrangement to prevent Dominican revolutionary actions in the frontier area, had been overthrown by General Silvain Salnave, who, in turn, was colluding with Báez. Cabral tried to deal with Salnave. On 27 July 1867 after the Dominican-U.S. negotiations had been suspended, the Dominican and Haitian governments signed a convention providing, among other things, the mutual obligation to discourage revolutionary activities and to maintain the integrity of their respective territories and not "cede, pledge, or alienate in favor of any foreign power either the whole or any part of their territories." Salnave continued to support Báez, however, so Cabral refused to ratify. Cabral then approached Seward about renewing negotiations. Seward was skeptical because of past experience and offended by the aborted treaty with Haiti, but he assented.[22] On 21 January 1868 terms were agreed to in which the Dominican Republic granted the United States a lease to territory in Samaná Bay in return for payment in cash and munitions. On the same day Cabral was overthrown by pro-Báez elements and the treaty went unratified.

A junta of three revolutionary generals governed from 31 January to 2 May 1868, when Báez was inaugurated president for the fourth time. He remained in office for more than five and a half years, until 31 December 1873. Báez continued a friendly disposition toward the United States, at least partly attributable to the efforts of Cazneau and Fabens, who exploited Báez's interest in personal monetary profit. Báez proposed that the United States assume a protectorate over the Dominican Republic and take possession of Samaná Bay as a first step toward annexation, perhaps as a state in the union. This proposal went well beyond Seward's ideas but he took it up.[23]

In the meantime, Báez made ruinous contracts with London banks. In 1868 English bankers agreed to a loan of about $3,750,000 but paid over little of the proceeds received from the sale of Dominican Republic bonds. In 1869 a lending group headed by Hartmont and Company agreed to a loan of £420,000 and provided for an advance to be raised by the sale of Dominican government bonds. Báez claimed the object was to construct highways and railroads but the proceeds in fact redeemed part of the outstanding Dominican paper currency and the rest went to the personal accounts of certain members of the government.

In 1868 Báez granted a contract to Cazneau and Fabens to conduct a geological survey of Dominican mineral resources in return for concessions of large tracts of land. They launched the Santo Domingo Company to finance the project, with New York capitalists William L. Halsey, Cyrus McCormick, Ben Holliday, John Young, and Samuel L. Barlow as sponsors. Cazneau and Fabens also acquired a charter for a

National Bank of Santo Domingo and enlisted the support of the Spofford, Tileston and Company investment house and of other New York entrepreneurs. The bank began operations in 1870 in Santo Domingo. The Dominican government conceded other valuable holdings to Cazneau and Fabens, including frontage on the most valuable part of Samaná Bay. Fabens went to Washington to represent Báez (and his partnership with Cazneau) in the Samaná negotiations. The two men calculated that, with their holdings and activities, conclusion of the annexation project would bring them great wealth. Cazneau also expected to be named the first U.S. territorial governor. On 9 December 1868 President Johnson included in his annual message to Congress a passage in which he proposed U.S. annexation of both Haiti and the Dominican Republic. The U.S. House of Representative tabled a resolution to that effect by an overwhelming vote of 126 to 36.

President Ulysses S. Grant (1869–77) vigorously but unsuccessfully pursued the attempt to annex the Dominican Republic. Secretary of State Hamilton Fish had opposed U.S. expansionism but acquiesced in the Dominican project. Imperialism was supported by influential people for different reasons. One group, led by Cazneau and Fabens, was comprised of business people who wanted to exploit the resources of the Dominican Republic. They were allied with a corrupt coterie around President Grant who primarily sought personal wealth in the colonial enterprise. Another circle had a basically strategic-political orientation (not devoid of economic overtones), seeing the Dominican Republic and Samaná Bay as a defense outpost for a future transisthmian canal.

In August 1869 President Grant sent his private secretary, General Orville Babcock, as U.S. commissioner to the Dominican Republic. Babcock had been one of Grant's aides-de-camp when he commanded the Armies of the United States during the Civil War. On 17 July 1869 Babcock, accompanied by Fabens and other interested persons, sailed to Santo Domingo on a steamer owned and operated by Spofford, Tileston and Company, financiers to Cazneau and Fabens who had become the agent for the Hartmont loan. The party was joined in Santo Domingo by Cazneau, who escorted the Babcock mission during its entire ten-day visit. On 4 September 1869 Babcock and Dominican Foreign Minister Manuel María Gautier signed a preliminary protocol of agreement for annexation. A few weeks later, on 29 November 1869, Dominican and U.S. representatives signed two agreements in Santo Domingo. The principal one was a treaty for the annexation of the Dominican Republic as a territory of the United States. The United States agreed to remit one hundred thousand dollars in cash to the Dominican government and fifty thousand dollars worth of armaments, and the Dominican Republic pledged to cancel the Hartmont loan contract. The second agreement provided, in the event the U.S. Senate rejected the treaty of annexation, for the ninety-nine-year lease of Samaná Bay. On 10 January 1870, President Grant sent the treaties to the Senate for advice and consent.

Luperón and Cabral vigorously opposed annexation, which they linked with their plans to overthrow Báez, with the financial support of foreign resident merchants who opposed annexation. The revolutionaries also played the Haitian card: in January 1870 Cabral captured President Salnave, in league with Báez, and turned him over to General Nissage Saget, allied with the Dominican revolutionaries. Saget executed his rival and assumed the Haitian presidency. Báez ordered a plebiscite in the Dominican Republic that, on 19 February 1870, overwhelmingly ratified the treaty. Báez had made clear that any opposition would meet with severe penalties.

President Grant put great pressure on Republican senators, who were in the majority in the U.S. Senate, to vote for the treaty. But on 15 March the Committee on Foreign Relations, chaired by Senator Sumner, defied the Republican leadership and reported adversely. On 24 March debate began on the Senate floor. Sumner, who enjoyed considerable influence with his colleagues, delivered the principal opposition speech. He argued that Dominican annexation would lead to more possessions in the Caribbean, provoking conflict with Europeans states; further European interventions in an independent Dominican Republic were unlikely; the United States would face extreme violence in the Dominican Republic as a result of annexation because most Dominicans had no desire for it; and annexation would unjustly "impair the predominance of the colored race in the West Indies." [24] The last point reflected Sumner's view that annexation of the Dominican Republic would also require the annexation of Haiti (Sumner had been a leading New England abolitionist). Sumner also understood that the stimulus for annexation came from Báez's ambitions and the machinations of Cazneau, Fabens, and some members of Grant's staff. U.S. public opinion did not favor annexation, and even some members of Grant's cabinet were opposed. The vote was finally taken on 30 June and resulted in a twenty-eight to twenty-eight tie, far short of the two-thirds of those senators present and voting required for approval.

Thus the annexation issue faded, despite the president's protestations and attempts to revive it. Grant managed the removal of Sumner from his committee chairmanship; Cazneau and Fabens left the Dominican stage; and in 1874 Báez was overthrown for the fourth time.

Dominican Instability and U.S. Detachment, 1872–1882

In 1873 President Báez faced growing discontent in the Cibao, where leaders of the *Partido Rojo* had decided he no longer effectively represented their interests. Generals Cabral, Pimentel, and Luperón continued to lead the opposition *Partido Azul*. In November 1873 Báez's former ally, General Ignacio María González, governor of Puerto Plata, led a plot against Báez that included members of both parties. In January 1874 they forced the president into exile. González tenuously held power for only two years (from 2 January 1874 to 21 February 1876), unable to reconcile the diverse party interests. González cancelled the Samaná Bay Company concession because of default on payments. He negotiated a provisional treaty with Haiti but it failed to establish the frontier.[25]

The six years following the overthrow of González in February 1876 were characterized by constant plotting among generals and important civilian figures, numerous revolutions, elections, and interrupted presidencies. In sum, nine presidencies were organized as follows: from 29 May to 5 October 1876 by Ulises Francisco Espaillat, a non-partisan

Santiago-born civilian intellectual aristocrat supported by Luperón, in office for slightly more than four months until his overthrow (he died shortly thereafter); for forty days from 5 October to 27 December 1876, again by General González, who ruled until he was forced out; for about fourteen months from 27 December 1876 until 2 March 1878 by Báez for the fifth time, until his dictatorial rule fomented a coup that ousted him; from 3 March to July 1878 by a provisional government; from July to 2 September 1878 by González for the third time, following a confused election; from 2 September 1878 to 26 February 1879 by another provisional government; from 27 February 1879 to 5 December 1879 by General Cesáreo Guillermo, who forced his own election and maintained power with a strong dictatorship for slightly more than eight months; from 6 December 1879 to 1 September 1880 by General Gregório Luperón, who resided in and governed from his native Puerto Plata and appointed his ally General Ulises Heureaux as his representative in the Santo Domingo capital; and from 1 September 1880 to 1 September 1882 by Padre Fernando Arturo de Meriño, a distinguished but authoritarian public figure, Luperón ally, and Báez enemy, who was elected and served his full two-year constitutional term.[26]

In such a dysfunctional system foreign policy was of low priority and ineffective. Some tentative and weak efforts were made to adjust foreign debts and concessions and reduce the accompanying political entanglements.

In the 1870s and 1880s, the modern sugar plantation system was introduced by Cubans fleeing from the independence wars in their homeland. Sugar became the major industry in the Dominican Republic, a development creating a great demand for sugarcane cutters. Consequently, thousands of black workers were recruited from the British, Danish, and French Caribbean colonies (they were pejoratively called *cocolos*) and from Haiti. This influx, which the "elite-white" Cibao region landowners and press widely criticized on racial grounds, altered the social pyramid in such a way that the base became mainly black and unskilled. The cutting of sugarcane became the most demeaning work, one reserved for *negros* (meaning Haitians). Many of the workers from the British West Indies, who were better educated than their counterparts from elsewhere in the Caribbean and could speak English with those U.S. owners of sugar plantations and mills, gained a higher status and were called *negros blancos*.[27]

The Heureaux Dictatorship, 1882–1899

General Ulises "Lilís" Heureaux dominated Dominican politics for seventeen years from his election to the presidency in 1882 until his assassination in 1899.[28] Heureaux created a brutal dictatorship, although he began his tenure seemingly headed in a different political direction. On 1 September 1882 following duly held elections, General Heureaux, then thirty-seven years old, was inaugurated president for a two-year term. He and his vice president, General Casimiro Nemesio de Moya, had been supported by both President Meriño and General Luperón, consequently enjoying considerable popularity and hope for political peace and economic prosperity. Heureaux's inauguration was only the second occasion in which power had been passed according to the constitution (the other had been from Báez to Santana in February 1853). Thus the dictatorial outcome was particularly disappointing to Dominicans seeking democratic political development.

Heureaux's father and mother were former slaves from Haiti and the Virgin Islands, respectively. Heureaux himself was well-educated, shrewd, courageous, unscrupulous, energetic, and self-indulgent. At the age of eighteen he had fought in the War of Restoration against Spain. He had attracted the attention of General Luperón, whom he thereafter served and, as protégé, gained considerable rewards in terms of military rank and political position. At Luperón's urging President Meriño had appointed Heureaux minister of interior and police.

In 1882 both Luperón and Meriño had strongly supported Heureaux's candidacy for president. As the 1884 elections approached, however, Heureaux maneuvered to break up the unified leadership of his own *azul* party, the major constraining element on his ambitions, by successfully playing the several strong personalities off against each other. He sought especially to undermine the influence of his long-time patron, General Luperón. His actions split the party and inaugurated (after much electoral fraud) Heureaux's candidate for president, General Francisco Gregorio Billini.[29] But Billini, inaugurated on 1 September 1884, was more independent and less submissive than Heureaux had anticipated. Heureaux managed his removal through a vicious rumor campaign that inspired an insurrection serious enough to cause Billini to resign on 16 May 1885. Billini was replaced by Vice President General Alejandro Woss y Gil, who willingly submitted to Heureaux's will. Heureaux easily won the elections of July 1886, but he had to deal with a serious revolutionary challenge that forced the postponement of his scheduled inauguration for five months, until 6 January 1887.

Heureaux then constructed an unrelenting tyranny that relied on an effective spy system, a large personal army, systematic corruption, and terror and cruelty. He co-opted numerous former and potential opposition leaders with government appointments and outright bribes. If these methods failed, he readily resorted to arrest, exile, and assassination. In 1889 Heureaux ordered the constitution amended to ensure his continuation in office for life. His despotic rule created many enemies, and much of his efforts went into suppressing the numerous revolts and plots.

Dominican foreign policies under Heureaux, like those of his predecessors, were closely connected to domestic Dominican politics and his personal concerns. He spent heavily on projects such as building roads, bridges, and railroads, putting in telegraph lines and public utilities, and establishing a national bank. Generous concessions for these undertakings were awarded to foreign entrepreneurs, many of whom were U.S. citizens, but they often were adventurers who did not fulfill the contracts. Heureaux used considerable public funds to bribe the caudillos and other political figures, pay his personal spies, and maintain his lavish style of life. He demonstrated shrewdness in the way he, as leader of a small, poor country, played off the United States and European states against each other.

Heureaux also followed tradition in the matter of the Samaná Bay, appealing to certain external states' strategic calculations to exploit the region as a Dominican financial asset. During his first presidency,

Heureaux informed both the United States and France that Samaná was available. He told the United States that he preferred to revive the lease to the defunct Samaná Bay Company of San Domingo, but he signed an agreement with the French interests (they included Ferdinand de Lesseps). The lease was to become valid with the successful construction of the Panama Canal, but that project failed. A deal with the Samaná Bay Company fell through because the company could not raise adequate financing.

Heureaux was deeply involved in the struggle for political power in Haiti. He supported General Florville Hippolite's effort to overthrow President General Légitime, who in turn permitted Dominican General Casimiro N. de Moya and his followers to organize against Heureaux in Port-au-Prince. Heureaux reached an agreement with President Légitime under which de Moya and his colleagues were expelled from Haiti, and they signed a treaty providing that each government would maintain strict neutrality regarding the internal politics of the other. Légitime was nevertheless overthrown. Heureaux then came to a personal understanding with President Hippolite (1889–96), after which Heureaux had the upper hand in the relationship. He successfully pressured Haiti for payments in return for his neutrality or secret support and bribed Haitians to assure their neutrality in Dominican politics.

The fact that the United States maintained dual Dominican-Haitian diplomatic representation, with the mission located in Port-au-Prince, was a matter of great resentment in the Dominican Republic. In 1889 the U.S. government acceded to Heureaux's insistence for separate representation and appointed a chargé d'affaires to Santo Domingo. President Benjamin Harrison appointed Frederick Douglass, the famous black civil rights leader, who arrived on 23 February 1890.

Douglass's changing position on the earlier annexation issue is worth noting. He had been appointed in 1871 to the U.S. commission of inquiry to consider adding the Dominican Republic to the United States. At the outset Douglass did not favor the proposition, although he was torn between his loyalty to President Grant and the Republican party and his admiration for Senator Sumner, who adamantly opposed annexation. Douglass changed his position, however, after an eight-week visit to Santo Domingo. His observations led him to conclude that the Dominican people, if U.S. citizens, would greatly improve their miserable condition, which he attributed to their absentee landlords, past civil wars, and slavery. (In 1871 the National Convention of Colored Men in the United States voted in favor of annexation.) Douglass later supported U.S. expansionism toward the general Caribbean area.[30]

Heureaux sought trade agreements with the United States. In 1885, during the last weeks of the administration of Chester A. Arthur (1881–85), a convention was concluded revising the U.S.-Dominican Commercial Treaty of 1867, providing for a degree of free-trade reciprocity. But President Cleveland withdrew it from the Senate soon after assuming office. In 1891 President Heureaux persuaded President Benjamin Harrison (1889–93) to revive the treaty. An instrument was concluded on 4 June 1891 and later ratified under which the United States gave free entry to certain Dominican products (notably sugar, molasses, coffee, and hides) and the Dominican Republic granted free entry to U.S. products in twenty-six classifications. President Harrison then determined to press vigorously for the lease of Samaná Bay and secret negotiations were undertaken.

Protests over the trade treaty and Samaná negotiations immediately came from Europe, certain Dominican interests, and Haiti. Britain, France, Germany, and Italy were angered over the exclusive most-favored-nation portion of the reciprocity agreement. They threatened reprisals with restrictive tariffs against Dominican cacao and tobacco; planters in the Cibao threatened to revolt if the threats were carried out. News of the secret Dominican-U.S. negotiations over Samaná leaked out, intensifying domestic opposition to Heureaux. Haiti vociferously expressed official outrage. Heureaux denied that such negotiations were going on (they had been suspended). The European governments jointly issued an ultimatum demanding that Heureaux abrogate the commercial treaty. In July 1892 the United States agreed to Heureaux's appeal to modify the treaty enough to satisfy the Europeans; the Samaná talks were not resumed.

Dominican external indebtedness continued to increase under Heureaux. In 1887 he sent General Generoso de Marchena as his agent to

Europe to secure more financial assistance. The major problem was opposition by the bond holders of the outstanding Hartmont loan. Although the Dominican Republic in 1869 had received only the initial
installment of about $150,000 and the following year canceled the loan
contract, the Hartmont syndicate nevertheless had issued bonds in the
London market totaling £750,000. In 1872 the loan had gone into default, with the British government insisting that no further lien be
placed on Dominican revenues until the bondholders' interests had
been satisfied. De Marchena secured a secret contract from Westendorp
and Company of Amsterdam. Under it the Dominican government was
to issue thirty-year gold bonds for £770,000, of which about 38 percent
was to pay off the Harmont loan and Dominican domestic indebtedness, with the remainder held by Westendorp (after generous payments
to Heureaux and de Marchena). The loan was secured against Dominican customs revenues. Westendorp, authorized to collect and administer all customs duties, was to receive payments on the loan and reim-
burse its agent's expenses and commissions (which turned out to be
about 30 percent of total revenues) before turning over remaining funds
to the Dominican government. The contract was ratified on 26 October
1888 and the Westendorp agent took over on 1 November.

About two years after the Westendorp loan, Heureaux persuaded the
company to approve a second one and issue fifty-six-year bonds total-
ling £900,000. The loan was secured by a mortgage on a railroad to be
built from Puerto Plata to Santiago and a second lien on customs revenue involving substantial additional annual charges. Heureaux soon
spent the proceeds of the loan, while customs revenues were insufficient to service the two bond issues. Westendorp refused Heureaux's
application for another loan.

Heureaux then arranged for assistance from a group including John
Wanamaker, postmaster general in the Harrison cabinet, and New York
financiers Smith M. Weed and Charles W. Wells. They organized and
headed a syndicate called the San Domingo Improvement Company of
New York. In May 1892 the company bought up the claims of Westendorp, which was glad to divest itself, at a fraction of the real value of
the bonds, and extended further credits to Heureaux. The Improvement

Company assumed direction of the customs collection arrangement. In mid-1893 Heureaux contracted further indebtedness with the company, raising the total Dominican receivership obligation to sixty-six years.

Heureaux faced complications in his 1892 reelection that were due to Haitian involvement. General de Marchena declared his electoral candidacy and simultaneously plotted to overthrow Heureaux, but Heureaux used his spy system to subdue the conspiracy and easily won the elections.[31] Heureaux arrested and imprisoned de Marchena and a year later had him shot. In the meantime, General Ignacio María González, implicated in the de Marchena plot, resigned as Heureaux's minister of foreign affairs. González, supported by several generals from the Cibao, attempted his own coup d'état. Haitian President Hippolite provided money and allowed a rebel advance through Haitian territory. But Heureaux's forces defeated the invaders and the Haitian president asked for a peaceful settlement. The Holy See arbitrated and helped settle the dispute.

For two years, from mid-1893 to September 1895, Heureaux confronted a serious problem with the French government. The French syndicate holding the concession for the Banque Nationale de Domingue had been badly compromised by its participation in the de Marchena plot. (De Marchena, European-oriented and opposed to U.S. influence, had advocated a plan for a European syndicate to convert and take over the Dominican Republic's entire internal and external indebtedness, as well as to lease and fortify a part of Samaná Bay.) The French syndicate continued its anti-Heureaux campaign when he refused to repay a loan. Heureaux's agents physically removed Dominican public funds, all of which, according to the concession agreement, were deposited in the bank. The situation was complicated in November 1894 with the murder of French citizens in Santo Domingo and Samaná. France asked Spain to arbitrate, threatening, if Heureaux refused, to blockade Dominican ports. The San Domingo Improvement Company, realizing such action would interfere with its collection of customs and payments on its loan, supported Heureaux's appeal to the United States for assistance. President Cleveland interceded through the U.S. ambassador in Paris. But Heureaux refused the French demands while the French Caribbean Fleet anchored off the Dominican coast, and the United States sent warships to the Dominican harbor. France agreed to negotiate with Spanish mediation. The San Domingo Improvement Company provided Heureaux with additional funds, and Heureaux agreed to include in the new arrangement the formerly French-owned National Bank concession. By September 1895 the San Domingo Improvement Company was firmly in control of Dominican customs revenues, the Dominican National Bank, and outstanding bonded obligations.

The End and Aftermath of Dictatorship

Numerous Dominican exiles, often operating from Cuba, Puerto Rico, and Venezuela, conspired against Heureaux's regime. Among them were two personalities who would figure prominently in Dominican politics for the next thirty years: General Horacio Vásquez and Juan Isidro Jiménez. Vásquez, a cousin of the late General González, had participated in the unsuccessful 1892 revolution and the abortive 1893 invasion from Haiti with Generals Luperón and de Moya. He had gone into exile in Puerto Rico and formed the Revolutionary Council of Youth (*Junta Revolucionaria de Jóvenes*). They eventually returned to the Dominican Republic and went underground, joined by Vásquez's cousin, General Ramón Cáceres.

Juan Isidro Jiménez, a wealthy merchant in exile in France, pursued his own plans. The junta had invited Jiménez to join its conspiracy but he refused, having his own presidential ambitions. He organized an invasion force that included other prominent Dominicans and in June 1898 landed in the Dominican Republic. Heureaux's forces repulsed them and Jiménez fled to Cuba.

After three years of unsuccessful attempts to overthrow Heureaux, the junta led by Vásquez decided to assassinate him.

On 26 July 1899 Ramón Cáceres and sixteen-year-old Jacobito Lara shot Heureaux dead in the Moca town center. They had taken Heureaux's guards by surprise and escaped in the confusion. That night,

General Vásquez and his small band entered Moca and proclaimed the revolution.

Heureaux's assassination began a period of political disorder that culminated in U.S. intervention. The Vásquez-Jiménez competition for power led to a succession of weak compromise presidents, constant plotting, and violent changes of government through coups and counter-coups. Each government borrowed money from abroad; foreign creditors, many of them citizens of major European powers, insisted on repayment and called on their governments to support their claims. The bonded indebtedness became so oppressive that those governments threatened military invasion. To forestall these eventualities, the United States, in the name of the Monroe Doctrine, took control of the Dominican economy in 1905, signaling a new era of U.S.-Dominican relations that included military as well as economic tutelage.[32]

2   United States Imperialism

The principal international themes during the period from about 1900 to 1930 were U.S. domination of and direct intervention in Dominican political, economic, and military affairs and efforts by the United States to extricate itself from such explicit involvement. The United States emerged at the turn of the century as a global great power and adopted imperialist policies toward the circum-Caribbean. The Dominican Republic was a small, weak, politically and economically chaotic country located in the U.S. sphere of influence and one of the major targets of U.S. actions. Those actions were primarily interventionist, involving a U.S.-directed customs receivership established in 1904, periodic military and electoral intervention, and military occupation and governance from 1916 to 1924. In the aftermath of the occupation, Rafael Trujillo rose to power through his position as commander of the Dominican National Police, a body created by the United States during the occupation, and established his dictatorship in 1930. U.S. actions toward Trujillo were hesitant, pursued in the early stages of an evolving policy of nonintervention. Thus, during the first three decades of the twentieth century, certain enduring characteristics of the U.S.-Dominican relationship were established, rooted in changing and ambiguous power relations.[1]

U.S. Interventionism

General Caribbean policies of the United States developed as part of the aftermath of the 1898 war between Spain and the United States and U.S. acquisition of canal rights in Panama. The primary U.S. objectives in the Caribbean were the prevention of further foreign (European) influence and force and the maintenance of political stability in the sub-regional states.

37

U.S. intervention became the logical culmination of the new imperial mentality and concomitant goals. Since at least the 1870s, certain U.S. leaders had visualized the Dominican Republic's potential strategic and economic value to the United States, but not until the turn of the century and the rise of the United States to great power status did U.S. officials adopt thoroughgoing imperial orientations. An essential part of U.S. policy making was to secure the Caribbean approaches to the new Panama Canal. Part of that problem was the Dominican Republic's overwhelming financial obligations to European creditors, which posed the possibility that European governments, in the process of enforcing the pecuniary claims of their citizens, would establish a military presence in the Caribbean and challenge U.S. control of the canal.

The war with Spain produced a wave of expansionist nationalism in the United States and strategic calculations by its officials that had profound consequences for the circum-Caribbean, prominently for the Dominican Republic. Prior to the emergence of the United States as a new world great power, signalled by its military victory over Spain in 1898, strategic calculations were sporadic and speculative. This attitude changed in the late nineteenth and early twentieth centuries, with the thinking of U.S. Navy Captain (later Admiral) Alfred Thayer Mahan occupying center stage. Mahan brought together the nascent policy thinking into a fully argued theory of "national destiny" and balance of power, based on concepts of international commerce and sea power in the changing international and Caribbean contexts.[2]

Mahan's argument, which strongly influenced U.S. Caribbean policies for many years to come, centered on the relationship of mercantilist imperialism and sea power to national security and "progress." The Caribbean area was crucial in Mahan's global design and was one of the main subjects of his writing. He strongly advocated the construction of an isthmian canal as essential to U.S. welfare. But he warned that such a canal would have great strategic importance since the Caribbean Sea would become a great shipping thoroughfare attracting the commercial interests of European states backed by their strong navies. Thus, for the United States to construct a canal without also controlling the entire Caribbean area would be a disaster for its own vital interests. Such control required not only building a strong navy and controlling and fortifying the canal but dominating the entire Caribbean in order to command the approaches to the canal. The Dominican Republic loomed large in this strategic calculation.[3]

The United States intervened in six Caribbean countries, including the Dominican Republic, in pursuit of its post-1898 policies in the Caribbean area. Intervention was soon justified by the Roosevelt Corollary to the Monroe doctrine, articulated by President Theodore Roosevelt in 1904 as a general policy principle. It was prompted by the contemporary situation in the Dominican Republic and in light of a recent European military intervention in Venezuela. Roosevelt's statement, made in his annual message to Congress in 1904, referred to three European powers blockading Venezuela in order to enforce their financial claims and The Hague Court's ruling in their favor. The rationale of the corollary was that, in order to keep Europeans out of the Western Hemisphere (specifically, the Caribbean area), the United States must correct the fiscal irresponsibility of the local states and maintain political order through the exercise of an international police power. According to this theory, European governments would have no legal basis to intervene if the United States assumed the task of bringing about Caribbean fiscal responsibility and political stability. That is, the United States would intervene in order to prevent European intervention. The Dominican Republic, in which European states seemed on the verge of forcefully asserting the financial rights of their nationals as in Venezuela, was the first state to bear the brunt of the corollary. Thus, an important extension of the Monroe Doctrine underlay U.S. actions toward the Dominican Republic until the late 1920s, when the United States took the first steps to liquidate imperialism.

In the meantime, the administration of President William Howard Taft (1909–13) added the practice of "dollar diplomacy." Secretary of State Philander C. Knox encouraged U.S. entrepreneurs to make capital investments and extend loans in the Caribbean region, notably in the Dominican Republic. This private capital investment then led to the landing of U.S. Marines during times of default or disturbance to protect U.S. property and lives.

President Woodrow Wilson, inaugurated in 1913, increased the number of U.S. interventions and further justified them in terms of a democratic credo. The Dominican Republic was again a principal target of the enlarged U.S. interventionist theory and practice. Wilson believed that Caribbean political instability, dangerous to U.S. security, was caused by lack of progress toward constitutional democracy. As a policy matter he assumed that democracy could be imposed from outside. He reasoned that the United States, as the most democratic and powerful American state, had the political and moral duty to foster democracy in the Caribbean, by force if need be.

The chaotic Dominican Republic was a likely target for U.S. imperialist policies, first in terms of the Roosevelt Corollary and then dollar diplomacy and the Wilsonian dogma. In fact, the first application of the Roosevelt Corollary occurred in the Dominican Republic in 1905, an instance of fiscal rather than military intervention, when the United States established a customs receivership. In sum, the United States administered the most important aspects of the Dominican economy in order to satisfy foreign creditors' claims and forestall European intervention to collect them. Armed intervention followed in 1916, with military occupation and government lasting until 1924, during which the Wilsonian democratic conviction was applied.

An important element in U.S. policy making and execution was the role of the United States Navy. Richard Challener emphasizes the "world view" of the U.S. military services as a primary influence on U.S. policy toward the Caribbean from the war with Spain in 1898 until the outbreak of European war in 1914, especially that of the Navy imbued with Mahan's ideas. The Navy's General Board, with specific reference to Mahan's prescriptions, strongly favored building the canal and creating a string of permanent bases in the Caribbean. The Dominican Republic's location made it especially important in the latter regard. As early as 1903 the board, fearful of a German naval presence in the Caribbean, advocated gunboat diplomacy and recommended some sort of permanent naval presence in the Dominican Republic and Haiti. The General Board had a special strategic interest in Samaná Bay; in 1903 the U.S. Navy sent a mission of two of its officers to discuss the matter with Dominican political leaders. The Navy had been an early advocate of U.S. control of Dominican customs (which it proposed to oversee), even before Roosevelt had overcome his reluctance to assume the responsibility. Navy officials also saw a naval dimension to dollar diplomacy; while they were highly concerned with and intolerant of the constant political disorder in the Dominican Republic, the "cardinal sin" in their view was Dominican interference with the customs receivership. The General Board expressed great concern about the tangled Dominican finances that, by providing a pretext for European intervention, posed a threat to U.S. strategic interests. It devised a plan to seize the Dominican Republic in case of a European war. In late 1916, shortly before U.S. entry into World War I, the board concluded that proper protection of the Caribbean required direct control of Samaná Bay and requested that it be authorized to exercise such oversight.[4]

U.S. cultural arrogance noted in the previous chapter continued into the period covered in this one. The official view of U.S. superiority and Latin American inferiority was clearly and forcefully articulated in the Roosevelt Corollary. While it was primarily a strategic power statement, it also said that "chronic wrongdoing, or an impotence which results in a general loosening of *the ties of civilized society*, may in America . . . ultimately require intervention *by some civilized nation*"— in the Western Hemisphere, Roosevelt said, the United States might be forced, "in flagrant cases of such wrongdoing or impotence, to the exercise of an international police power" (emphasis added).

Establishment of the Customs Receivership

The U.S. action to administer Dominican international finances was first prompted by Dominican internal disorder and international financial arrears. Dominican political life in the latter part of the nineteenth century, characterized by turbulent domestic politics, *caudillismo*, and foreign commercial influence, was continued into the twentieth. The five years following the assassination of President Ulises Heureaux in 1899 were confused and tumultuous. The discord was attributable primarily to the continuing struggle between the two leading personalist political groups: the *horacistas,* supporters of General Horacio Vásquez, popular hero of the struggle against Heureaux; and the *jimenistas,* followers of Juan Isidro Jiménez. The strife during this period was indicated by more than 70 percent of government budgets devoted to military expenditures so as to suppress rebels, and by two joint U.S. Navy–European military interventions in 1903. The first was in concert with Germany and the second with France and Italy. They were intended to protect foreign nationals and consulates.[5]

The Dominican government's default on bonds, among other unmet obligations, nearly resulted in intervention by Europeans demanding payment and threatening to use force. The Dominican Republic had borrowed money from European creditors so extensively that payments would have required the great majority of national income; they were not made. In 1903 and 1904 European governments, on behalf of their nationals, again threatened to collect the debt payments by force (debts were owed to investors from France, Belgium, Germany, Italy, and Spain, as well as the United States). At the same time a combined Anglo-French-German military expedition was doing just that in Venezuela, an action that lent urgency to the Dominican issue.

U.S. nationals also complained about their situations. The San Domingo Improvement Company had acquired the holdings of a Netherlands corporation in 1892, and in an agreement with the Dominican government took over customs collections; after loan servicing and expenses the remaining proceeds were paid to the government. In 1901 the Dominican government repudiated the arrangement, and the company appealed to the U.S. government for support. Negotiations between the company and the Dominican government led to a settlement that was incorporated into a U.S.-Dominican protocol, signed on 31 January 1903, that stipulated Dominican payments to the company. The agreement provided for an arbitration board to fix the details of payment (which was subsequently done); and, in case of failure to pay, for a U.S. financial agent to take over certain customhouses and carry out the award. The Dominican government made no payments. On 21 October 1904 a U.S.-appointed financial agent took over the Dominican customhouse at Puerto Plata. In response, France threatened to seize the customhouse at Santo Domingo, and Italian creditors appealed to their government to demand payment of their claims.[6]

President Theodore Roosevelt, in order to forestall European intervention, arranged with the Dominican government to take over all of the customhouses and to act as receiver for the bankrupt country, obliging the Dominican Republic to entrust the collection of customs duties to U.S. officials. The two governments signed a protocol on 4 February 1905 and submitted it for approval to their respective legislatures. But determined opposition in the U.S. Senate delayed the measure to the extent that the Senate adjourned without acting on it. President Roosevelt then put the treaty provisions into operation as an executive agreement and *modus vivendi* with Dominican President Carlos F. Morales (whose government had been inaugurated on 19 June 1904). Under this arrangement the United States collected Dominican customs revenues for the next two years, applying 55 percent of the receipts to debt service and remitting the remainder to the Dominican government.[7]

Dominican Politics and U.S. Demands, 1905–1916

The Dominican political scene temporarily changed soon after the inauguration of the new receivership arrangement. General Ramón Cáceres became the dominant political figure and then assumed the presidency. In 1899 Cáceres had been one of the principals in the conspiracy to assassinate President Heureaux, and one of the two members who actually shot the dictator to death. He led his own political group thereafter and was vice president in the Morales government. By the end of 1905, President Morales had lost control to Cáceres's dominant influence and in 1906 Cáceres forced Morales out of office and into exile. President Cáceres was able to crush several rebellions and, for the first time in Dominican history, to pursue a government-led program of development and modernization. Of particular import was his expansion of the primitive public works program; he contracted a U.S. engineer to supervise the building of the country's first highways and promoted public ownership of utilities. He also allowed foreign entrepreneurs to amass large sugar enterprises. During the Cáceres administration, Dominican-U.S. relations were relatively harmonious. President Roosevelt saw the Dominican Republic as a stable entity amenable to U.S. tutelage, and President Taft and Secretary Knox perceived the relationship as a model for dollar diplomacy.[8]

The customs receivership was put on a bilateral treaty basis. After President Roosevelt and the U.S. Senate agreed to a compromise, another convention was signed with the Dominican Republic on 8 February 1907; this time the Senate gave its consent. The Dominican government ratified the instrument in May and the treaty went into effect on 25 July. It provided for a general settlement to be reached with foreign creditors. The customs receivership was to continue as long as bonds were outstanding. Debts were to be paid with a loan from the United States, to be serviced out of future customs collections. The floating of a bond issue of twenty million dollars was to be devoted exclusively to paying the long-dormant accounts and financing Dominican public works projects. The U.S. right to intervene in defense of its agents was continued. The treaty remained unchanged until it was superseded by a second convention in 1924 (the arrangement then lasted until 1941).[9] The Dominican Republic's financial condition improved considerably.[10]

The eastern part of the Dominican Republic completed its "economic revolution," in which sugar replaced traditional agriculture. By 1910 sugar constituted the major export, dominated the economy, and was the leading beneficiary of foreign investment. The change resulted in Santo Domingo in the south (with a population of twenty-one thousand) coming to the fore as the economic as well as political capital and replacing the domination of Santiago de los Caballeros (population fourteen thousand) in the north. Internally the country was not self-sufficient in foodstuffs. Wealthy Dominicans and foreign entrepreneurs pushed small farmers off their land and large numbers of immigrants, mostly Haitians and black British West Indians, came to labor on the sugar plantations. The immigrants existed in the most primitive of conditions, and most other Dominicans lived in extreme poverty. The new wealthy sectors were merchants, shippers, and foreign entrepreneurs, joining the existing wealthy landholders.

Cáceres's innovative government was ended on 19 November 1911, when an assassin shot him to death. It should be noted that both Juan Isidro Jiménez and Horacio Vásquez had remained in exile abroad and refused to take any part in the coup d'état.[11] The period following Cáceres's assassination until the U.S. military intervention on 5 May 1916 was characterized by factional strife, intermittent civil wars, and short-term presidencies.

Soon after Cáceres's death, the chief of the army, Alfredo Victoria, forced the Dominican Congress to elect as president his uncle, Senator Eladio Victoria.[12] The latter took office on 27 February 1912, serving at the will of his nephew. Vásquez returned to the Dominican Republic and organized a rebellion; his followers, the *horacistas*, were joined by those of the powerful rebel *caudillo*, General Desiderio Arias. Severe government repression and a particularly bloody civil war followed. Arias gained control of the customhouses along the Haitian border and the United States seriously considered military intervention under the provisions of the 1907 Customs Convention. In September President Taft sent a commission to Santo Domingo in order to negotiate an end to the civil war. President Victoria resigned and a provisional government, led by Archbishop Adolfo Alejandro Nouel, took office on 30 November 1912. It was charged with the specific task of organizing free elections within one year. Arias immediately defied the government, and four months later Nouel resigned. The Dominican Congress elected Senator José Bordas Valdez as provisional president to organize elections. But Bordas, after taking office on 14 April 1913, acted to ensure that, by whatever means, he would remain president.

Six weeks before Bordas became provisional president, Woodrow Wilson had become president of the United States on 4 March 1913. He developed policies toward the Dominican Republic that began with electoral intervention, evolved into military intervention, and ended with occupation of the country and creation of a U.S. military government.

The Wilson administration's policy was first directed by Secretary of State William Jennings Bryan, whose recommendations lay behind what became known as the "Wilson Plan."[13] That plan evolved to include five elements: (1) a U.S.-supervised election of a new Dominican president and subsequent U.S. support and protection for him; (2) a reordered Dominican financial system under continued U.S. administration; (3) the appointment of the U.S. comptroller as a permanent official financial adviser within the Dominican government; (4) the appointment of U.S.-designated director of public works in the Dominican government; and (5) the creation of a Dominican national guard under the command of U.S. military personnel to replace the existing Dominican armed forces. In the case of the Customs Convention, U.S. officials saw policy as having failed in the aftermath of the Cáceres assassination because its successful functioning, as conceived by the Roosevelt administration, required stable and progressive Dominican politics and public policies.

In September 1913, Vásquez went to war against Provisional President Bordas but the U.S. minister in Santo Domingo negotiated an end to the insurrection. The United States forced Bordas to accept the appointment of a U.S. comptroller to supervise public expenditures and the customs receivership continued to deliver funds to the Dominican government. Presidential elections were agreed to, but they were not held as scheduled. Consequently, in July 1914, the internally divided *horacistas* again rebelled (Arias was a leading promoter of the uprising); they were joined by *jimenistas* and *vidalistas* (followers of *caudillo* Luis Felipe Vidal) and intense fighting ensued. The United States sent another commission to the Dominican Republic that forced the contenders to agree to a truce under threat of military intervention. In sum, the commission refused to recognize Bordas and demanded fair elections.

The commission presented the first elements of the Wilson Plan. The rebels were to lay down their arms and agree to the selection of a provisional president (if they did not do so the United States would choose the president and back him in office by force). The new president would organize a government to hold elections that the United States would supervise. The newly elected government would be accepted by all parties and supported by the United States. The three principal Dominican parties accepted the conditions (in addition to the *jimenistas* and *horacistas* the group now included the *velazquistas*, followers of Federico Velásquez). Bordas resigned and the parties selected Ramón Báez (son of the prominent nineteenth-century political personage Buenaventura Báez) as provisional president with the task of organizing elections within three months. Báez took office on 27 August 1914 and elections were held on 25 October. Jiménez, supported by Velásquez, won the presidency, and Vásquez accepted the results. Jiménez took office on 5 December and named a multiparty cabinet. Velásquez was named finance minister; Arias, who enjoyed a strong position within the *jimenista* party, was appointed minister of war with control of the armed forces.[14]

The United States then required President Jiménez, in order to continue to receive its support, to appoint two U.S. nationals to his government. In one instance it demanded that the extant position of U.S. comptroller be converted to a permanent official position, and in the other the creation of the post of director of public works. When the Dominican Congress rejected the U.S. demands, the United States instructed the comptroller to supervise delivery of customs revenues to the government as well as all public expenditures. The United States also further insisted on the creation of a national guard under the direct command of U.S. military personnel, to replace the existing Dominican armed forces then under Arias' control. President Jiménez refused.

When the *horacista* generals rebelled, the United States threatened to send troops to restore order and renewed its demands for appointment of a permanent comptroller and a director of public works and for military reform. The government and opposition leaders then actually joined together to reject the U.S. demands and protest foreign interference in Dominican internal affairs. At about the same time, on 15 April 1916 Minister of War Arias revolted against the president with elements of the armed forces loyal to him. The U.S. minister failed to negotiate a settlement between Jiménez and Arias (he had been instructed to favor Jiménez) and called for marines to protect the legation. The Dominican

Congress, under pressure from Arias, impeached Jiménez. With civil war again threatened, President Wilson accepted the recommendation of Secretary of State Robert Lansing (the former counselor of the State Department who had recently succeeded Secretary Bryan) for military intervention in the Dominican Republic; the United States then publicly announced that such action would occur in order to preserve both public order and the Jiménez government. The first contingents of U.S. Marines landed on 5 May 1916; on 29 November the United States proclaimed its occupation and the creation of a military government, which remained for more than eight years until 18 September 1924.[15]

U.S. Intervention, Occupation, and Military Government

The U.S. intervention occurred in 1916 in the face of the failure of the Wilson Plan, armed political strife in the Dominican Republic, and continued receivership difficulties—all in the context of acute U.S. concern with the intensification of the war in Europe. President Wilson's military intervention was not immediately undertaken to establish constitutional government or to reorder the financial and military systems but to stabilize a turbulent political and economic situation within a worsening world situation. He had threatened military intervention more than once but, as Challener notes, the military occupation took place only after the European war had become the "overriding concern."[16] Once the occupation began, however, civil action was undertaken to create a democracy-supporting political, economic, and social infrastructure. It was later argued that the Wilson Plan, in both its political and financial elements, had failed because such fundamental social restructuring required more intense U.S. control—the U.S. military presence provided the authoritative environment in which the United States could impose stability and reform. The United States engaged in public works designed to improve transportation, communications, educational, health and sanitation, and agricultural facilities;

supervised elections aimed at promoting constitutional government; and reorganized and trained Dominican armed forces with the intent that a professional and nonpolitical military body would maintain order and protect constitutional governments after the U.S. occupation ended. In retrospect the public works development was a success but the political-military elements represented naive hopes.

On 7 May 1916, two days after the first U.S. troops landed in the Dominican Republic, President Jiménez resigned, despite the military action in his favor. On 12 May Rear Admiral William B. Caperton arrived in Santo Domingo and assumed direction of the operation as more marines landed. They easily took control of the capital, but Arias and his men withdrew to the northern city of Santiago. Marine units, under the command of Colonel Joseph H. Pendleton, deployed off the northern city of Puerto Plata and moved inland. With some fighting against insurgents along the way, they arrived at Santiago on 6 July. A military encounter was avoided when Arias arrived at an agreement with Caperton to cease resistance.[17]

On 25 July the Dominican Congress elected well-known physician Francisco Henríquez y Carvajal as interim president for six months. This development was unfortunate from the U.S. point of view, since the pro-Arias congressional faction strongly influenced President Henríquez. In addition, Henríquez, who had promised not to seek his own election, expressed his intent to run in the U.S.-supervised elections that were being considered. Furthermore, Henríquez and U.S. officials quarreled over the way customs revenues were being handled. In fact, the United States refused to recognize the provisional president on the grounds that Dominican treaty obligations were not being fulfilled and refused to do so unless a new treaty was signed. The United States demanded that such a treaty grant the United States the authority to collect and disburse all moneys, authorize appointment of a U.S. financial adviser, and establish a Dominican constabulary force commanded by U.S. officers. Henríquez said he would accept the financial advisor but rejected the other demands. U.S. financial agents then refused to remit any funds to the unrecognized Dominican government.[18] Bruce Calder says that in using the threat of nonrecognition in order to gain financial control and establish the constabulary, the United States treated Henrí-quez with the same disdain they had for Dominican politicians in general, despite his experience, education, patriotism, and honesty.[19]

President Wilson took Secretary Lansing's advice to escalate U.S. involvement and ordered outright occupation. More U.S. troops landed, and a military government was declared. Marine personnel strength reached a high of 3,007 in February 1919; it stood at 1,076 in March 1924 when the withdrawal began.[20]

On 29 November 1916 U.S. Navy Captain (later Rear Admiral) Harry S. Knapp, who had succeeded Rear Admiral Caperton, issued a proclamation from the Santo Domingo harbor declaring the Dominican Republic under U.S. military jurisdiction. The statement charged the Dominican government with "repeated violations" of the financial provisions of the receivership treaty and failure to maintain domestic order. The proclamation said ingenuously that the United States had no intention to destroy Dominican sovereignty but to restore and maintain order and carry out the terms of the 1907 convention. It announced that the U.S. military government, under the Department of the Navy, would assume complete control of Dominican finances and direct administration of most government functions.[21]

U.S. rule was not carried out through puppet presidents as was being done in Haiti, where U.S. military occupation and governance had begun the previous year. The military government suspended the Dominican Congress, prohibited political party activity, and took away Dominican civil and political liberties; strict press censorship was maintained during most of the occupation. Since no Dominican cabinet members and few other government officials would serve in or even cooperate with the foreign regime, administrative positions were filled by U.S. officers to supervise Dominican personnel. Exception was made of the judiciary; the Dominican Supreme Court remained. Dominican courts continued to dispense ordinary justice except for cases involving U.S. military personnel or Dominican resistance to the military government, which were tried by U.S. tribunals. In any event, the military government had ultimate executive, legislative, and judicial authority.[22]

Thus the "subterfuge was maintained that this was 'an independent state under temporary occupation.'"[23]

The "essentially judicial mind" of Rear Admiral Knapp, the recently promoted first military governor, for a time tempered the impact of foreign control and inspired a temporary Dominican "spirit of tolerance" toward military officials that allowed for a modicum of friendly relations.[24] This tolerance changed rapidly to resentment, however, when Knapp was superseded in 1919 by the authoritarian Rear Admiral Thomas Snowden, who utterly lacked Knapp's diplomatic qualities. The military government became virtually a foreign dictatorship.

Serious general problems in U.S. policy implementation were evident. Bruce Calder stresses the lack of consistency in U.S. policy because of competition and fragmentation among three executive departments (State, War, and Navy), the war in Europe, and the subsequent world war. Consequently, U.S. policy tended to be an ad hoc process on the part of the military government in the Dominican Republic. The quality of U.S. military personnel declined after the United States entered World War I in 1917. The best officers and men were sent to Europe, leaving more inefficient and often racially prejudiced ones assigned to the occupation forces. Especially those marines from the segregated South transplanted their views and made distinctions between "darker" and "lighter" Dominicans in the way they treated them.[25] U.S. military people came to symbolize U.S. rule in the Dominican Republic; thereafter, continuing to the present era, Dominicans have commonly assumed that in their case the U.S. armed forces acted independently from civilian officials and dominated policy decisions. Problems were also evident in the State Department. Lester Langley points out that State Department officials dealing with the Caribbean were mostly political appointees who generally lacked experience in the region and rarely acquired the language, knowledge, or skills expected of professional diplomats; Wilson's first minister to the Dominican Republic, James M. Sullivan, "was both incompetent and corrupt."[26] The situation improved in the 1920s when Sumner Welles and Dana Gardner Munro, both skillful career diplomats whose writings are cited in this chapter, gained influence on U.S. policies in the Caribbean. Yet

Welles (who helped arrange the withdrawal of U.S. troops from the Dominican Republic in 1924) revealed his own negative racial biases in his lengthy history of that country.

U.S. Objectives and Actions

The military government had several clear priorities. In military and police affairs, it was determined to disarm the populace, pacify the country, bring local *caciques* and regional *caudillos* under control, and establish a professional and apolitical military establishment. The military government initiated organization of a national armed force, paralleling its pacification and disarmament programs and efforts to enforce political unification of the provinces through governmental reform, civic action projects, and denial of armed force to the *caudillos*. The idea was to centralize, professionalize, and depoliticize the military. In the economic and social arenas, the government sought infrastructure development. With regard to the political system, it supervised a political campaign and national elections toward the end of the occupation period. In the long term a democracy was to be established through free elections, the constitution protected by the reformed and restructured national police force, and the populace pacified through a combination of disarmament and improved economic and social conditions.

U.S. civil action emphasized social and economic improvements. It resulted in significantly improved educational, transportation, communications, agricultural, health, and sanitation facilities. Modern roads, bridges, piers, wharves, schools, and health facilities were constructed and expanded. The postal service and telephone and telegraph systems were reorganized and upgraded. Financial, judicial, and military reforms were vigorously pursued.

U.S. Marines finally achieved pacification and disarmament with forcible searches and seizures. Their efforts proceeded rapidly in urban centers but more slowly in rural areas. Resistance movements arose throughout the country, with guerrilla fighting being especially serious in the eastern provinces of Seibo and Macorís. Disarming the populace was a difficult undertaking, especially in a country where possession of firearms was not only common but a status symbol. Nevertheless, a reported fifty-three thousand firearms were collected during the first eighteen months of the occupation.[27]

Rural violence also included traditional banditry, which was a continuing problem in certain outlying areas. Because of the relative inefficiency of the newly formed constabulary, the marines assumed responsibility for combating the bandits. They perhaps exaggerated the threat in order to justify greater restrictions on the populace, labeling as "bandits" any elements who opposed the United States in a hostile manner. This exaggeration seems to be indicated by the limited number of combat casualties during a period of more than eight years: five officers and ten others killed, and five officers and fifty others wounded.[28] Pacification efforts took on new intensity in late 1921 and early 1922 when a U.S. withdrawal was being contemplated, and a systematic drive was launched to finish off banditry in the eastern district.[29]

The Wilson administration and the military government did not pursue Taft's dollar diplomacy. Langley points out that both Wilson and Bryan had been highly critical of the resort to "predatory capital in the tropics" and would use public moneys to finance U.S. policy purposes.[30] Calder takes the same view, arguing that while economic imperialism was a factor in broad hemispheric policies, official support for U.S. business and investments in the Dominican Republic was negligible. He points out how the military government successfully resisted pressures brought to bear by certain U.S. interests (such as the United Fruit Company) for favorable and special treatment in the Dominican Republic. A partial exception was the sugar industry; some laws were designed to favor U.S. companies but others had the opposite effect.[31]

Development of Public Forces

The organization and training of Dominican armed forces, of special interest to the United States and of singular consequence for Dominicans after the U.S. departure, requires particular analysis. It should be emphasized again in this context that the occupation coincided with

U.S. participation in World War I. One of the military government's first acts was to authorize creation of a new national constabulary, trained by the U.S. Marines, to replace the old Dominican forces (army, navy, Republican Guard, and Frontier Guard). Originally called the Guardia Nacional Dominicana (GND), the constabulary was in effect a national police force, and in June 1921 its name was changed to Policía Nacional Dominicana (PND). By that time it had replaced all other military organizations; a decree dated 15 September 1922 declared the PND to be the only national armed force charged with the maintenance of public order.[32]

Progress in creating a national force was slowed by opposition from an alliance of provincial governor-*caudillos* and landholding elites. The former feared erosion of their regional authority by a national force and the latter that it would undermine their local power. Prior control over the armed forces had been divided between the national president and provincial governors, with the president responsible for financial support but the governors in command of the military forces and rural police in their provinces. The governors had, in effect, private armies that supported their political positions. They also had a vested interest in civil strife: the more disorder in their jurisdictions, the more public funds they were entitled to receive from the national government and the more authority they had to force men into military ranks (for a period up to four years).[33] The landholding elite also strongly opposed a U.S.-created constabulary and a truly national military or police force, and they allied with the governor-*caudillos* over the matter.

Development of an officer corps presented some special difficulties. Upper-class officers in the existing forces resigned their commissions, and elite families refused to allow their sons to become officers in the new organization. They considered service under the occupying foreigners who had undermined their power a traitorous act. To help solve the initial officer shortage, the U.S. Congress passed a law in 1917 permitting U.S. Marines and certain other U.S. citizens to accept commissions in the constabulary. Marine officers were scarce during World War I, however, and few of them were interested in such appointments.

As a result, most of the marine-supplied constabulary officers were sergeants and corporals. In addition, many other officers were U.S. citizens who had served in the old Dominican Frontier Guard or other police agencies.[34] These measures were temporary, however, and the problem of creating a Dominican officer corps remained.

With the impossibility of attracting educated upper-class Dominicans to the officer corps, commissions went to the emerging middle class and the lower strata of Dominican society, including men drawn from the ranks to receive officer training. These people were seeking economic security, social advancement, and, perhaps, personal and political power. They were also motivated by their antipathy toward the upper classes. U.S. Marines founded the Haina Military Academy in order to provide professional training for Dominican nationals and a systematic source of regular officers. The first class, made up of veteran Dominican police officers, arrived in August 1921 for a five-month training course. Thereafter, classes of cadets entered and upon graduation were commissioned second lieutenants. Thus Dominicans of even humble origin, both blacks and mulattoes, were able to join the constabulary, move up through the ranks, attend the academy, and climb the economic and social ladder as commissioned officers in a class-conscious society. Traditional elites remained disdainful of and hostile to the constabulary long after the U.S. departure and continued to refuse commissions. The social composition of the officer corps set at its establishment has remained essentially the same to the present day.

No serious problems existed in recruiting enlisted personnel whose ranks consisted entirely of Dominicans. They continued to be drawn from the poor and mostly illiterate lower classes, attracted to the regular pay and guarantee of bunk, board, and medical care. Some of them were former members of the old armed forces; others were new recruits, many of them former rural guerrillas and bandits who had been pursued by the marines. They received a two-month standardized course run by U.S. Marines at two training centers, one established alongside the military academy at Haina for the southern district and another at Santiago for the northern district.

Liquidation of Intervention

The military intervention and occupation were highly unpopular in the Dominican Republic and increasingly so throughout the other Americas and in the United States itself. Considerable publicity, much of it adverse, was given the U.S. military governments in the Dominican Republic and Haiti. The U.S. Senate appointed a special committee to hold lengthy hearings on the military occupations from mid-1921 to March 1922.[35] They revealed incompetent and harsh treatment of uncooperative Dominicans, including careless shootings, assaults, arbitrary arrests, unjust imprisonment, and even torture. Both U.S. officers and enlisted men were cited, some of whom also engaged in extortion. The latter apparently were a minority and when discovered were tried in military courts. A young poet, Fabio Fiallo, was jailed for denouncing the United States; the case was widely publicized and anti-U.S. sentiments ran high throughout Latin America. In fact, the U.S. military occupation prompted a wave of anti-U.S. publications, some polemical tracts and others in the form of novels and short stories. The reaction also resulted in a great revival in the popularity of José Enrique Rodó's *Ariel* (first published in the Dominican Republic in 1901) and his portrayal of the United States as Caliban.

In December 1920, with the Dominican intervention an issue in the U.S. presidential campaign, the Wilson administration said it intended to withdraw U.S. troops as soon as Dominican political stability and constitutional government were achieved. Opposition candidate Warren Harding promised to take similar action. In mid-1921, President Harding appointed Sumner Welles, formerly head of the division of Latin American affairs in the State Department, to be the U.S. commissioner to Santo Domingo to negotiate agreements for ending the U.S. intervention.

The first conciliatory step was the removal of Admiral Snowden, the uncelebrated military governor who, according to Sumner Welles, had established a foreign military dictatorship that boasted about its complete control and suppression.[36] Rear Admiral Samuel S. Robison replaced Snowden. In sharp contrast to Snowden, Robison was more open to Dominican sensitivities.

The change of command was followed by bilateral conferences held in Washington, beginning in early 1922, to negotiate a plan of withdrawal. The Dominican negotiators, representing the major Dominican political factions, included Francisco Peynado, Velásquez, and General Vásquez; Secretary of State Charles Evans Hughes officially represented the United States. Numerous Dominican objections that the United States was insisting on too much continuing control over Dominican affairs were finally overcome, and a program of U.S. withdrawal was agreed upon, known as the Hughes-Peynado Plan. Dominicans were to select immediately a provisional government to administer executive departments, carry out constitutional reforms, and hold general elections. The Dominican National Guard was to become the Dominican National Police, and marines would pass control to the provisional president. The provisional government would appoint delegates to negotiate an agreement with the United States recognizing the bond issues of 1918 and 1922 and confirming that the 1907 convention would remain in force as long as bonds remained unpaid. Once the Dominican Congress approved the convention and a president was elected and inaugurated, U.S. military forces would depart.[37]

A provisional government was organized, and on 21 October 1922, Juan Bautista Vicini Burgos, a wealthy sugar planter nominated by the Dominican negotiating team, was installed as provisional president. Plans were made for a national electoral campaign and elections, but they were postponed because of persistent wrangling among the various Dominican political groups. Negotiations for a new receivership convention proceeded, and on 27 December 1924 an instrument was signed revising and superseding the 1907 treaty. It authorized a new bond issue of twenty-five million dollars to pay off other outstanding loans and provide ten million dollars for "public improvements"; until this loan was paid the Dominican national debt could not be increased except with U.S. agreement. Administration by a U.S.-appointed general receiver continued as before. Strong opposition in the Dominican

Congress was surmounted and the convention was approved; ratifications were exchanged on 24 October 1925.[38]

In the meantime, a political campaign was finally organized (Sumner Welles played a central role in overcoming partisan disagreement on the rules), and national elections were held on 15 March 1924. General Vásquez, who was Welles's preferred candidate, was elected president over Francisco Peynado. Vásquez was backed by a coalition of Dominican parties called the *Alianza*, which also gained majorities in both houses of congress. A special assembly then met and drafted a new constitution, completing its work in June. On 13 July 1924, President Vásquez was inaugurated. Marine units began leaving immediately after the inauguration; the last departed on 18 September 1924. For the first time in eight years and four months, no United States occupation forces were present in the Dominican Republic.

The Impact of Military Occupation

The United States left the Dominican Republic with a newly elected government, a professionally organized and trained national police force, apparent internal stability, and a reasonably good financial position (official U.S. reports said the public debt had been reduced from RD$12 million to RD$3.5 million, although disagreement exists about the accuracy of these figures and the amount of the reduction). Considerable material progress had been made since 1916 in school construction and teacher training, health and sanitation, public administration, and communication and roads. Calder, however, makes a distinction between the survival after the U.S. withdrawal of education and public health projects on the one hand and public works on the other. He says that public works were at the peak of development in 1924, and although the departure of U.S. personnel was detrimental, the following Dominican government provided the funding required to ensure relative effective operations. Public works during and after the occupation not only had sufficient U.S. funding but Dominican support as well, whereas the other programs initiated by the United States without Dominican support were much less successful.[39]

Little political development accompanied the significant economic achievements, however, since few Dominicans had taken part in governing their country. By 1924 the *Policía Nacional Dominicana*, with its modernized and centralized force and the disarmed Dominican populace, had a monopoly over arms and munitions. Marvin Goldwert plausibly asserts that the chasm between democratic possibilities and political realities undermined the idea of a nonpolitical constabulary from the outset.[40]

The eight-year military occupation had a profound impact on the Dominican economy and society and on political and military affairs. U.S. control forced political and military integration on a national basis for the first time. But the foreign presence, wielding arbitrary power, engendered considerable opposition and strong anti-U.S. bitterness. Nationalist upper-class elites were especially incensed over the undermining of Dominican sovereignty. They considered U.S. occupation an affront to the Dominican nation and resented the undermining of their own political power. While U.S. military-directed public works resulted in certain social and economic progress and a procedural democracy was established, political and social reform were absent, leaving the democracy without substance. In the short run, the United States achieved its objectives in that the Dominican Republic was stabilized. Only six years after the end of the military government, however, democracy gave way to a long-term dictatorship.

The Rise of Trujillo and the Revolution of 1930

The constabulary force caused a shift in the locus of political power, especially when Rafael Leonidas Trujillo y Molina gained command and control. Trujillo's career is the leading example of the social mobility offered a mulatto by commissioned service in the PND. He was born in 1891 in the village of San Cristóbal, near Santo Domingo city.

During the period of U.S. military occupation he began his rise to power. He was among the members of the first class to enter the Haina Military Academy, doing so in August 1921 as a provisional second lieutenant; he graduated in December and thereby confirmed his rank. (Prior to the establishment of the Haina academy, Trujillo had applied for a commission, which he had received on 11 January 1919.) He worked hard to ingratiate himself with U.S. officers and earned a reputation for intelligence and efficiency. Trujillo was promoted to major in March 1924, at about the time U.S. forces began to withdraw. In December of the same year, President Vásquez promoted him to lieutenant colonel and assigned him as chief of staff of the National Police, headquartered in the capital city. Within a year, Vásquez promoted Trujillo to colonel and named him commander of police. In 1927 Vásquez reorganized the police as the Dominican National Army and placed Trujillo in command with the rank of brigadier general.[41]

President Vásquez had been elected to a four-year term in 1924, after which he was ineligible to succeed himself. In 1927, however, Vásquez called a constitutional convention that supported his ambition by approving an amendment, of dubious constitutional validity, continuing his tenure to 1930. He later announced his intention to be a candidate in the presidential elections scheduled for 15 May 1930.

On 23 February 1930, just three months before the elections, an insurgent movement disgruntled with the president's maneuvering was initiated in the northern city of Santiago de los Caballeros. Little more than a week later, the revolutionaries succeeded in overthrowing Vásquez, who was then seventy years old. The U.S. legation in Santo Domingo mediated negotiations between the government and the revolutionaries, and through its efforts an armistice was arranged and a settlement reached between the Vásquez and Estrella forces. Rafael Estrella Ureña, the young lawyer who led the uprising, was named to act as provisional president pending the scheduled elections.[42]

After the Vásquez government was overthrown, the United States had to decide whether to recognize a government established by *golpe de estado*. The official trend of thought was set early in the affair. U.S. Minister Charles B. Curtis deplored the methods that led to the ap-

pointment of Estrella Ureña as provisional president because an unde-
sirable precedent was being established, but he did not openly object to
the arrangement. The State Department concurred and informed the
legation that the United States would continue "normal friendly diplomatic relations" with Estrella Ureña's government.[43]

General Trujillo's activities as commander-in-chief of the national
army had been largely responsible for the success of the revolution. Although Trujillo conspired with the rebels, he succeeded in concealing
his role from all outsiders until the fall of Vásquez had been assured. In
fact, during the revolution General Trujillo had assured Minister Curtis
that he and the army were loyal to President Vásquez. Curtis later reported that Trujillo had in fact repeatedly betrayed the Vásquez government, shipping arms to the revolutionaries in Santiago and being in
league with Estrella Ureña from the very beginning. Curtis was convinced that without Trujillo's support the revolt could not have succeeded and probably would not have been undertaken in the first
place.[44] While Curtis had reluctantly accepted Estrella's government,
the endorsement of Trujillo was another matter. Because Trujillo had
betrayed the government and lied to the U.S. legation, Curtis thought it
"highly desirable that General Trujillo be not nominated on the list of
any party" for the May 1930 elections. Curtis even informed Estrella
that under no circumstances would he recommend the recognition of
a government led by Trujillo.[45] In fact, a provision of the agreement
between Vásquez and Estrella said that in the elections no restrictions
as to candidates would be imposed except that neither Vásquez's vice
president, José Dolores Alfonseca, nor General Trujillo would run.
Estrella Ureña asked Curtis to reinforce the agreement by publicly declaring that the United States would not recognize a Trujillo government should he be elected president. The State Department's telegram
to Curtis rejecting Estrella's request shortly before the election is significant enough to quote extensively:

> We feel that through scrupulously avoiding even the appearances of inter-
> fering in the internal affairs of the Dominican Republic our relations with
> Santo Domingo have been put on a very sound basis in the 5 years since

the withdrawal of the military occupation. . . . Your view that it is most unfortunate that the head of the army should use that position for his own political advancement and as a means of obtaining the Presidency is concurred in by the Department. The Department would be willing for you to talk personally, confidentially and in the most friendly manner with Trujillo, urging on him as your personal advice the damage which he will do to the political development of the Dominican Republic by being a candidate rather than by using his power to guarantee free and fair elections. . . . Any duress through a public statement would defeat the ends we are seeking. While the Department hopes that you will be able to persuade Trujillo not to be a candidate, yet it realizes the great difficulty of bringing it about and should you not succeed and Trujillo be elected it is most important that you should not impair in any way your relationship with him. . . . For your strictly confidential information the Department desires you to know that it expects to recognize Trujillo or any other person coming into office as a result of the coming elections and will maintain the most friendly relations with him and his Government, and will desire to cooperate with him in every proper way.[46]

To the surprise of no one, including Curtis, Trujillo sought (and obtained) the presidency. Trujillo was elected through coercive campaign techniques and fraudulent electoral procedures. After attaining the office, he established a regime that was to last more than three decades. Trujillo built a brutal, militarist, personalist, and absolute dictatorship. Dominican politics were completely dominated by his personality; his control over Dominican affairs was virtually total, whether he was officially president or not. Any hopes the United States had that the results of its intervention would be the establishment of representative democracy were utterly destroyed.

Was the United States responsible for the rise of Trujillo? Some critics have charged that the U.S. military occupation, instead of preparing the Dominican Republic for democracy, allowed Trujillo to establish his dictatorship.[47] The United States was at least indirectly responsible for Trujillo through its training of him and establishing the constabulary that became his source of power but, after the U.S. occupation was ended, President Vásquez was responsible for bringing Trujillo to the capital and promoting him until he was head of the armed forces. The fact that Trujillo was admitted to the marine-organized and commanded constabulary and regularly promoted does not necessarily make the United States accountable for his subsequent dictatorship. Certainly the United States did not intend for the Dominican armed forces to be used as an instrument for overthrowing constituted government or for maintaining a military dictatorship.

After 1924 the United States remained aloof from Dominican domestic affairs for six years, indicating that Trujillo's military power was further derived from the elected president rather than the United States. Vásquez compounded his error of trusting and promoting Trujillo by abusing the system that had elected him, thus weakening his own position and the system itself. Given the prior Dominican political record, it cannot be assumed that without the police force, or in the absence of U.S. intervention, Trujillo or another ambitious strong man would not have found alternative routes to power.

The United States can be criticized for failing to understand the Dominican political process and for believing that an efficient police force could be organized without becoming the instrument of a future faction or *caudillo*. The rise of Trujillo as a power-seeking strong man was consistent with the Dominican past. The crisis surrounding the election of 1930, precipitated by President Vásquez's attempt to violate the constitution and succeed himself and manipulated by Trujillo to get himself elected president, was a Dominican affair. During the crisis the U.S. minister urged Trujillo not to run and attempted to get firm pledges that he would not do so; Trujillo ran, and won, in spite of these pressures.

The United States was also criticized for not opposing Trujillo after the revolution and fraudulent election of 1930, and for recognizing his regime. The Trujillo case is a prime example of the dilemmas created with the emerging U.S. nonintervention policy—noninterference meant dealing with dictators. U.S. endeavors indicate that the United States did not want Trujillo to run in the 1930 presidential contest, but once elected it reluctantly recognized him. It seems unlikely that a U.S. refusal to recognize the Trujillo government, or a persistent bargaining for reforms, would have had any real effect on Dominican politics. The United States had few alternative choices short of further intervention. Any sort of military intervention in order to preempt Trujillo's rule was out of the question as a policy alternative; the political price would have been too high to violate Dominican sovereignty again. The United States had withdrawn its forces in 1924 partly in response to the increasing unpopularity of its occupation—in the Dominican Republic and the rest of Latin America and within the United States—and the realization that it was exacerbating inter-American relations in general. Furthermore, the U.S. Congress was scaling back on expenditures for these military operations, so that policy was significantly shaped by national budgetary considerations.

These were the logical outcomes of U.S. interventionism and the Dominican context in which U.S. policies were operating. In our view, valid criticism must, therefore, grow out of disagreement with the broader U.S.-Caribbean imperialist orientation decided upon in the first place. That experience tells us that the United States cannot force adoption of its model of representative democracy. The United States may assist in developing some structures and practices through cooperative means and even through limited coercive influence to see to it that certain rules of the game are observed, but democratic development first and foremost requires effective domestic (Dominican) leadership.

3   The Trujillo Regime, Nonintervention, and World War II

In the 1930s Rafael Trujillo established and consolidated his dictatorship, and during World War II he took advantage of the world crisis to make himself useful to the United States. During this beginning of the era of Trujillo, the United States faced the dilemma posed by a commitment to representative democracy in Latin America and an interest in the maintenance of political stability, conditions that U.S. officials did not necessarily see as complementary. This difficulty came to the fore after the United States accepted the principle of nonintervention as the cornerstone of the Inter-American System and as an important part of its own policies in the 1930s.

Consolidation of the Trujillo Dictatorship

By the end of 1931 Trujillo's own Dominican Party (PD) was the only legally functioning political group. His reelection in 1934 was uncontested. He was succeeded in 1938 by his hand-picked candidate, Jacinto Peynado. When Peynado died in 1940, Vice President Manuel de Jesús Troncoso became president. During this time the government continued under the aegis of General Trujillo. In 1942 Trujillo again ran unopposed for reelection. In 1940 Trujillo had unctuously declared that although he "declined to continue in the executive position that the unanimous will of my people was offering," he nevertheless did not refuse the obligation that he had contracted with his "conscience in 1930 to keep a constant watch for the well-being of the Republic."[1]

Trujillo established an absolute dictatorship and ruled for thirty-one years. Until near the end he dominated all political and other aspects of the country and built a financial empire. His personalist leadership involved astuteness and skill, combined with megalomania, greed, and brutality. Trujillo controlled the armed forces (which were his primary basis of power), the church, and communications media. His official PD was the only political party allowed for most of his dictatorship and interest associations were beholden to him.

Trujillo embellished himself with all the trappings of honor and glory. In 1933 the Dominican Congress raised his rank to generalissimo and later voted him the title of "Benefactor of the Nation." In 1934 he was awarded an honorary doctorate from the University of Santo Domingo. In 1936 Santo Domingo, the oldest city of European origin in the New World, was renamed "Ciudad Trujillo." The dictator held at least forty different official titles, including "Chief Protector of the Dominican Working Class," "Genius of Peace," "Father of the New Fatherland," "Liberator of the Nation," "Protector of Fine Arts and Letters," and "The First and Greatest of the Dominican Chiefs of State." This adulation increased with the passing years; one source estimates that 1,870 monuments to Trujillo were erected in Ciudad Trujillo alone, public buildings carried the sign "God and Trujillo," and a hospital the slogan "Only Trujillo cures you."[2]

Bases of U.S. Policy

Two related factors underlying U.S. policy must be considered: (1) the legacy of U.S. intervention in Latin America and the consequent Latin American demand for and U.S. acceptance of the principle of nonintervention as the prerequisite for inter-American cooperation; and (2) the long-standing policy goals of maintaining stability and preventing foreign control—by European creditors, Nazi Germany, and the Soviet Union.

From its earliest relations with Trujillo beginning in 1930, the United States was careful to avoid any overt intervention in Dominican affairs such as had marked its actions for the preceding quarter century. The inter-American principle of nonintervention was formally adopted by the American states in 1933, making it illegal for one American state to interfere in the affairs of others. The principle was confirmed in 1936, when the corollary of consultation among the American states on matters of mutual concern was agreed to. The United States subsequently found itself consulting about chronically bad intra-Caribbean international relations in which the Dominican government was involved within the framework of the Inter-American System.

While the new policies were applauded by advocates of nonintervention, they were criticized by those who objected to the lack of U.S. pressure placed on dictators such as Trujillo.[3] Indeed, as a policy matter, nonintervention carried with it the necessity of dealing, even if gingerly, with Latin American dictators. The United States defended itself against the criticism that nonintervention in Dominican affairs constituted support of a vicious dictator. Some critics felt that in the early 1930s the United States should have pressured Trujillo to reform his government. A few years prior the United States had been criticized for intervening in and violating the sovereignty of the Dominican Republic; now nonintervention was being attacked on the grounds that it permitted and even supported the continued existence of Trujillo.

During the early 1930s when Trujillo was first consolidating his power the real nature of his regime had not yet manifested itself. Furthermore, the United States, in response to increasing Latin American and domestic opposition to its intervention in other American states, was moving toward accepting the principle of nonintervention as a basis for policy. The United States pledged adherence to nonintervention at the 1933 Seventh International Conference of American States in Montevideo, where it signed the Convention on the Rights and Duties of States, but the Senate consented with a reservation. In 1936 the United States joined in reiterating acceptance of the principle by signing the Additional Protocol Relating to Non-Intervention at the 1936 Inter-American Conference for the Maintenance of Peace in Buenos Aires, which it subsequently ratified without reservation. Thus the United States had no legal basis to interfere unilaterally against Trujillo by way of coercive military, political, or economic instruments, despite any objections to his governmental policies or practices. The nonintervention principle was the *sine qua non* for inter-American cooperation.

With the rise of the totalitarian threat around the world in the late 1930s, antidictatorial elements were disillusioned with the paradoxical posture of the Good Neighbor and continued to insist that pressure be applied against Trujillo and other dictators. When Trujillo arrived in Washington for a state visit on 6 July 1939, Carleton Beals, chairman of the Committee for Dominican Democracy, sent a telegram to President Roosevelt calling attention to the "inappropriateness of endorsing home grown dictators" such as Trujillo while condemning the European variety.[4]

The Customs Receivership

After Trujillo came to power in 1930, the most immediate continuing issue for the next ten years was the U.S.-administered customs receivership. An astute contemporary observer in 1936 accurately described the receivership as "both the closest link and the greatest potential source of friction" between the United States and the Dominican Republic.[5]

After 1930 the customs arrangement was informally revised in several respects, which modified provisions of the 1924 treaty. Following his inauguration on 15 August 1930, Trujillo faced staggering national problems, resulting primarily from the worldwide economic depression and worsened by a hurricane on 3 September that devastated the capital city of Santo Domingo. Trujillo soon devised his own refinancing plan to lighten the burden of external debt, expressed in the Dominican Emergency Law of 23 October 1931. Even though the law violated the 1924 convention, the United States announced that it was "not disposed at this time to take any action other than to continue to follow with close attention and care, the developments in the Dominican Republic." Eventually the Dominican financial condition improved, the

Emergency Law was repealed as of 1 September 1934, and the receivership was restored to its original status.[6]

Meanwhile, another readjustment of the Dominican Republic's foreign obligations was in the making. In August 1934, a Dominican proposal to readjust its foreign obligations was approved by the State Department and the Foreign Bondholders Protective Council, which had been established under the auspices of the U.S. government to provide a forum whereby bondholders could present their petitions for amelioration of the terms of the original obligations. The agreement provided that maturities for the two outstanding bond issues were to be extended from 1942 and 1940 to 1962 and 1970, respectively. U.S. supervision of customs collections was to continue until 1970 and amortization payments to be reduced. The United States commended the Dominican government for its "spirit of cooperation" and expressed the hope that "adjustments of a similar nature might be made with other Latin American countries that are in default on their foreign bonds."[7]

Despite these friendly accommodations, the United States and the Dominican Republic began to dispute the spending of the customs revenues. The U.S. minister in Ciudad Trujillo summed up Dominican calculations as follows: "From the Dominican Government's standpoint, the real issue was not considered to be the question as to what particular proposed expenditures of the Dominican Government required the consent of the United States, but rather the necessity of consultation of the United States at all regarding any of the Dominican Government's financial matters outside the scope of the external funded debt now outstanding."[8]

Beginning in 1936 and for some four years thereafter, bilateral negotiations sought to revise, replace, or abrogate the 1924 convention.[9] During this period, the Dominican government argued that: the existence of the receivership conformed neither with the "new way of life" of the Dominican Republic nor with the spirit of the Good Neighbor Policy; the 1924 treaty was an obstacle to the economic development of the Dominican Republic, since conditions were so different from those of the past; and the arrangement was offensive to Dominican sovereignty and conflicted with the new Pan-Americanism being promoted by the United States that stressed nonintervention. The U.S. government countered that it was obligated to uphold the bondholders' interests; but, it said, with assurance that the rights of bondholders would be respected, it would welcome the termination of the receivership in accordance with its policy of noninterference in Latin American domestic concerns.[10]

The U.S. minister in Ciudad Trujillo recognized that the two governments were attempting to achieve mutually conflicting objectives and admitted that the 1924 convention was "anachronistic." He could see no advantage "in keeping up the fiction" that the two governments behaved in accordance with the treaty, even though he was "well aware that the fiction remains a solace to a considerable body of informed opinion, not to mention the bondholders and floating-debt creditors."[11] During a visit to the United States in 1939, Trujillo stated that negotiations to end the "vexing and anachronistic" customs receivership, which constituted intervention in internal Dominican affairs, had "failed in the face of an imperialistic attitude" by the United States. Nevertheless, the Dominican Republic would continue "to be a good and sincere friend of the United States."[12]

The negotiations provided an example of Trujillo's control of Dominican policy even when he was not the formal head of state. With great candor President Peynado and Foreign Minister Roberto Despradel at one point informed Minister R. Henry Norweb that negotiations on the treaty had been suspended until Trujillo's return from a visit to Washington and that renewed conversations would depend entirely on his views. It was clear to Norweb that "no one in the Dominican Republic will touch the Convention question pending the return of General Trujillo."[13]

The United States was beholden to the bondholders under the treaty's binding provisions as long as they were in force. Nevertheless, the receivership had been originally established to prevent European intervention, and the Trujillo dictatorship had removed any further occasion for intervention by achieving financial stability and public order. Thus

the United States found it difficult to justify the continuation of the arrangement when the Good Neighbor Policy stressed nonintervention.

Despite their fundamental differences, both sides were anxious to
reach agreement, and a new treaty was signed on 24 September 1940.
The agreement provided for closing the office of the general receiver of
customs and returning to Dominicans the authority to collect customs
revenues. New arrangements were provided for guaranteeing the servicing of bonds. They included provision for a first lien on total revenues of the Dominican nation in lieu of customs receipts—that is, redemption of the outstanding bonds and payment of the interest charges
were guaranteed without reference to any particular source of revenue.
The United States had the right to select the depository bank for all
revenues of the Dominican government in order to assure service on
bonds held by American citizens.[14]

The U.S. Senate consented to the treaty on 14 February 1941 with a
single dissenting vote; it was proclaimed on 17 March by President Roosevelt. The customs receivership was officially terminated on 2 April
1941, six months after the treaty had been signed. The United States had
earlier suggested that a suitable "neutral agent" would be the First National City Bank of New York (FNCB), as it was the only U.S. bank with
a branch in the Dominican Republic, a fact that might appeal to the
bondholders. The branch was designated the sole depository bank,
undertaking to make no disbursements for the account of the Dominican government until payment of amortization and interest charges on
the bonds had been made. The Dominican Republic later bought the
FNCB branch in Ciudad Trujillo and transformed it into its own National Bank.

Senator Theodore Francis Green (D-R.I.) in support of the treaty said
that the main purpose of the agreement "was not so much in the interest of the bondholders—although we believe it is for their interest—
as to get rid of an irritating feature of the relations between the two
countries." The State Department hailed the treaty as "another step in
the development and coordination of the Good Neighbor Policy based
on mutual respect and confidence among the countries of the hemi-

sphere." A Dominican diplomat said that the new treaty was final proof that the Good Neighbor Policy had completely replaced American "intervention and aggression." The Dominican Congress in 1940 gave Trujillo the title "Restorer of the Financial Independence of the Republic."[15]

Some years later, on 19 July 1947, the Dominican Republic delivered funds to redeem all outstanding bonds, together with all interest due, to a representative of the bondholders. The government also announced that the 1922 and 1926 bonds would be redeemed on 1 September and 1 October 1947, respectively. The convention of 1940 provided that after redemption of the bonds the convention would automatically cease to have effect. Inasmuch as the Dominican Republic had retired the bonds in advance, an exchange of notes was signed with the United States on 9 August 1951, recognizing the termination of the 1940 convention and the fact that the Dominican Republic had redeemed in full its external debts in accordance with the bond contracts.[16]

The Haitian Affair

The concept of peaceful settlement of disputes had been an important principle of the Inter-American System since the Second International Conference of American States in 1902. Closely related to this idea was the procedure of consultation adopted in 1936 regarding problems of mutual concern, especially regarding the peace of the hemisphere. During the Trujillo era until its end in 1961, a number of conflicts involving the dictator's regime were taken up within the multilateral framework of the Inter-American System. The first, in 1937, was a serious dispute between the Dominican Republic and Haiti. In October Dominican military forces attacked and killed large numbers of Haitian peasants near the border between the two countries.

The tragic events are mainly understandable in terms of Trujillo's official policy of "Dominicanization," a euphemism for his personal animosity toward Haitians. Biographers have suggested he felt it more strongly because of having a humble background and himself being mulatto. Dominicanization became a concerted effort to eliminate the perception of "blackness" from Dominican society, reinforced by the fear of "Ethiopianization" of the Dominican Republic by Haitians through racial and cultural mixing. It specifically involved removing Haitians by any means.

A number of economic and political factors contributed to Trujillo's decision to order the killing of Haitians. He was running for reelection in 1938 and economic conditions had resulted in increasing numbers of Haitians crossing the border looking for work. Events in Cuba affected Dominican events. In the early 1930s, when the world depression sank sugar prices and caused great unemployment among sugar workers, Cuban dictator General Gerardo Machado sent many Haitian sugarcane cutters back home. In 1937 his successor, General Fulgencio Batista, decreed the expulsion of almost all the remaining Haitian laborers. The thousands of returning Haitians turned to their Dominican neighbor for employment, but Dominican planters artificially depressed the wages for Dominican workers in order to take advantage of the labor surplus now attributed to the Haitian influx. Those Dominican workers, who believed themselves racially and culturally superior to Haitians, were highly resentful.

In response to the increasing Haitian migration, Trujillo was particularly determined to close the western border and secure Dominican control of it. He had tried for years, with little success, to establish Dominican agricultural colonies in the area by moving in and settling "white" farmers. He pressed Haitian leaders to curb their peasants from moving onto Dominican lands. During the U.S. occupation of the Dominican Republic (1916–24) and Haiti (1915–34), the border area had been surveyed for the first time. The boundary problem had been temporarily solved with the 1929 Dominican-Haitian Boundary Treaty, which gave the Haitians considerable land in the arid southwestern portion of the Dominican Republic. In October 1933 Trujillo met with Haitian President Stenio Vincent to discuss the long-standing border problems. They appointed a joint commission to deal with border issues and subsequently followed up with their own discussions—Trujillo went to Port-au-Prince in November 1934 and Vincent visited Santo

Domingo in February 1935. At the latter meeting the presidents signed a treaty in which the Dominican Republic gave land to Haiti for settlement of its itinerant farmers; in return, Vincent ejected from Haiti Dominican exiles opposing Trujillo (Dominican troops awaited them at the border but they managed to escape to Cuba).[17]

Before the killings began on 2 October 1937, Trujillo visited a central frontier town and gave an inflammatory speech to the farmers, blaming Haitians for goat and cattle rustling. Then the Dominican massacre of Haitian peasants occurred. The number of victims was never firmly established. Some estimates claimed that as many as 25,000 had perished; the Haitian legation in Washington set the number of fatalities at 12,168.[18] Why the massacre took place or what motives lay behind it are unclear, although little doubt exists that Trujillo was responsible for the deed.[19] In any event, the problem was a serious one for the dictator, with external opinion almost totally against him. So certain were his opponents that Trujillo's political end was near that Dominican exiles in Puerto Rico, looking forward to a new regime, pledged their support to follow exile Angel Morales, then living in New York, as the next president.[20] After a series of negotiations, however, Trujillo emerged still in control of the country, although with a reputation even more blemished than before.

The governments of both Haiti and the Dominican Republic exercised strict censorship and succeeded for some time in keeping the news from the rest of the world. In 1936 the problem raised by the long history of border disputes between the two countries had led to an agreement on peacekeeping procedure, and reportedly an investigation was proceeding under the terms of that agreement. On 15 October 1937, the Dominican Republic promised Haiti "speedy action to apprehend and punish the guilty." One week later the Dominican legation in Washington made public a joint Dominican-Haitian statement (with Joaquín Balaguer, acting secretary of foreign relations, representing the Dominican Republic). It was in reality a diplomatic facade, saying that "the cordial relations between Haiti and the Dominican Republic had not been impaired" as a result of "a recent border incident in which several citizens were reportedly injured."[21] Vincent's ambassador in

Washington, Elie Lescot, in a series of confidential letters, later admitted to having depended for personal capital on Trujillo's largesse.[22] Nevertheless, Haiti then decided not to leave the determination of responsibility to the Dominican government; by then the prevailing evaluation was that Haiti had a substantial case against Trujillo. On 12 November 1937, dissatisfied with the "dilatoriness of the Dominican authorities," Haiti asked the governments of Cuba, Mexico, and the United States to mediate the dispute. All three governments readily agreed to tender their good offices.[23]

The United States was concerned over the dispute not only because of its continuing interest in two Caribbean countries in which it had intensely intervened in the past but also because of the existence of inter-American peace treaties. These treaties, eight of which were in effect at the time, exemplified the accelerating stress on nonintervention and the peaceful settlement of disputes. Haiti was to invoke two of the treaties. Minister Norweb later said that Haiti's request for good offices "made the matter squarely a test of that will for peace which found concrete expression at the Buenos Aires Conference." Accordingly, he had "strongly impressed upon President Trujillo the necessity for securing a settlement of the controversy within the spirit of the American peace treaties."[24]

Haiti agreed with the mediators that a commission should be appointed to investigate and fix the terms of a settlement, but the Dominican Republic refused on the grounds that the issues were really domestic ones. The three friendly governments then concluded that the incident fulfilled the conditions described by the Buenos Aires declaration that "every act susceptible of disturbing the peace of any American republic affects each and every one of the republics."[25] Haiti then resorted to other peace treaties to which it and the Dominican government were signatories: the Treaty to Avoid or Prevent Conflicts between the American States (Gondra Treaty) of 1923 and the General Convention of Inter-American Conciliation of 1929. Under the 1923 agreement signatories pledged not to resort to war until a commission of inquiry had made an investigation and submitted a report. The 1929 pact stipulated that the commission was not only to investigate but also to submit a plan of settlement. Trujillo resisted the conciliation procedures and argued they were unnecessary, but on 18 December 1937 he finally yielded and agreed to accept the settlement procedures specified in the treaties.[26] His position had been defended in a full page advertisement in the *New York Times* on 17 December 1937, and he continued to protest even after the matter was settled.

At this time a voice was raised against Trujillo in the U.S. Congress. Representative Hamilton Fish Jr. (R-N.Y.) delivered "a plea; a protest; a remonstrance (against) the most outrageous atrocity that has ever been perpetrated on the American continent." He called for the "withdrawal of recognition" [sic] by the United States "if this matter is not settled after an impartial investigation, and if apologies are not offered, if compensation is not paid, and if guarantees are not given by the Dominican Republic," which was being ruled "by one of the most autocratic and high-handed dictators alive." Representatives James A. Shanley (D-Conn.) and John E. Rankin (D-Miss.) disagreed. Shanley said that Fish's proposal constituted interference with the domestic difficulties of a nation, even if it were ruled by a dictator, and that there should be no interference unless the affair produced some "repercussion" in the United States. Rankin said that Fish's criticism was unfair "since the United States is carrying on the Good Neighbor Policy with Latin America."[27] Unfortunately for the cause of anti-Trujillists, Fish later changed his mind and praised the dictator; in 1942 he was implicated in a twenty-five thousand dollar payoff from Trujillo.[28]

One would have expected that the murder of an American Episcopal priest in Santo Domingo at the orders of Trujillo would have caused a "repercussion" at home. This was not the case, however, because Trujillo successfully arranged a cover-up. After the massacre of Haitian peasants, Trujillo kept tight control over all information and no account of the events was published in the Dominican Republic. The Reverend Charles R. Barnes, a popular clergyman who led a flourishing missionary church and civic center in the capital city, heard rumors about Trujillo's complicity and included the information in a letter intended for his sister in the United States. In late July 1938, after Trujillo's agents intercepted the letter and brought it to Trujillo's attention, he ordered that Barnes be killed. In order to keep the U.S. legation from investigating the murder, Trujillo bribed Barnes's house servant to testify in court that he had killed the priest while defending himself from a homosexual attack, which the court ruled as justifiable homicide.[29]

In the meantime, an inter-American peace commission had gone to work and induced the Dominican and Haitian governments to sign an agreement, on 31 January 1938 at the Pan American Union in Washington. The Dominican Republic agreed to pay an indemnity to Haiti in the amount of $750,000, to fix responsibility for the incidents, and to give the results of its investigation full publicity. Both parties agreed to prevent similar recurrences, and measures were proposed for protecting nationals in the future.[30]

Minister Norweb felt that two pressures had forced the Dominican government into a settlement "against its will." First was the world press, which "gave with considerable accuracy of detail a dramatic picture of the savage murders . . . and enlisted the sympathy of outside nations with the injured party." Second was the "practically unanimous will among the nations of the Western Hemisphere that international disputes should have peaceful settlement." Norweb emphasized that, although the settlement was acclaimed because it utilized the inter-American framework for peaceful settlement, an important aspect had generally been overlooked: "The actual instrument of the settlement was not the Permanent Commission of the Gondra Treaty sitting in Washington nor the American Governments invoking the various instruments for the settlements of international difficulties, but the diplomacy of the Vatican."[31]

Norweb was convinced that the considerable influence of the archbishop of Santo Domingo over Trujillo, and the strong interest in the dispute of the papal nuncio to both countries, allowed the church to offer a common meeting ground. Norweb believed that once Trujillo realized some form of settlement was essential, "he found in the Legation of the Vatican an exit which had been all along the principal object of his government." The role of the nuncio appeared when, on 11 January 1938, he took the Haitian government's demands and proposals to Trujillo. Trujillo was ready then to grant most of Haiti's terms with some modifications, notably a fifty percent reduction of the demand for a cash settlement of $1,500,000. But the convention finally signed was the protocol originally drafted by the papal nuncio. Neither the Dominican government nor press (or any other government or press, for that matter) made reference to the assistance of the nuncio in bringing the parties together. On the contrary, said Norweb, the settlement was "played up as an example of Dominican fidelity to the principles of inter-American solidarity and peace."

The Haitian imbroglio may be closed on the ironic note that in 1939 the Dominican Republic established an annual "Trujillo Peace Prize" of fifty thousand dollars, designed "to rival" the Nobel Prize.[32]

Trujillo's Cultural-Immigration Policies

Trujillo's concern with his reputation, and its potential for undermining his power, led to a paradoxical but enduring aspect of his foreign policies—opening the Dominican Republic to migrating people who were suffering economic deprivation or political repression. But little emigration from the Dominican Republic to the United States occurred during the Trujillo era because of the nature of the police state and strict control over exit visas. The main departures were by Trujillo's opponents, if they were lucky, who went into exile. Juan Bosch, for example, left in 1938, first going to Puerto Rico and then to Cuba, where he lived for nineteen years.

Trujillo's dictatorial control helped perpetuate the mythical cultural and racial image of the Dominican Republic, one he believed was appreciated by and consistent with the views of U.S. civilian and military decision-makers in a racist U.S. society with legal racial segregation. He had experienced firsthand the racial views of U.S. Marines during the military occupation (1916–24) and when he was a cadet at the Haina Military Academy. Trujillo capitalized on the Dominican historical bitterness about the oppressive Haitian occupation (1822–44). He established the official policy that Dominicans had an exclusively Spanish heritage, not only in terms of culture and Roman Catholic religion but racial purity as well.[33] He reinforced this version of the Dominican legacy by stressing fear of the "Ethiopianization" and miscegenation, and seeking "to whiten" (*blanquear*) the population—which included encouraging European, and severely restricting Haitian, immigration.

In pursuit of his policy of *blanquear* and to improve his badly tarnished image in the world after the Haitian massacre, Trujillo in 1938 announced with great fanfare the admission of refugees from Europe—specifically, Jews from Germany and Austria (mostly Viennese) fleeing Nazi oppression and Republican Spaniards escaping from their loss in the Spanish Civil War. The Dominican government provided them with land and subsidies. The north coast town of Sosúa became the site of a well-known Jewish farm community.

In 1939, Trujillo also imposed rigid restrictions on immigrants from Haiti and other "non-white" countries. The Dominican government issued temporary work permits to Haitians and others when their labor was needed on the sugar plantations and in the mills.

Trujillo denied his own Dominican-Haitian mixed mulatto background (a grandparent on each parental side was Haitian). He even recast pictures of his family members and had their racial history officially and falsely authenticated. Trujillo ordered his rubber-stamp legislature to issue a *limpieza de sangre* document certifying that his mother's family was "pure French" and his father's as "pure Spanish."[34]

Notwithstanding the falsity of the racial purity theory and policy denying the majority's African roots, Frank Moya Pons, a leading Dominican historian, has argued that an aspect of Trujillism was the restoration of Dominican confidence in their ability to advance themselves over the Haitians, which resulted in the release of dormant energies causing new increases in the production of wealth that served as the basis for Dominican economic development. Moya also notes how "traumatized" Dominicans were when they visited the United States and were treated not as "white" but as "black"—the same as Haitians.[35]

World War II Cooperation

In the late 1930s, with the principle of nonintervention established as the cornerstone of the Inter-American System, the United States became

increasingly concerned over both the threat of war in Europe and security in the hemisphere. The idea of improving inter-American cooperation for defense purposes thus became the major concern. The question
of military cooperation between the United States and Latin America,
and thus with the Dominican Republic, to promote hemispheric security did not arise until war in Europe appeared likely. Prior to the fall
of France in 1940, the U.S. objective was to maintain American hemispheric neutrality, at the same time developing a defensive system
aimed primarily at protecting the Panama Canal. Other hemispheric
defense concerns were the Natal region of Brazil, which seemed vulner-
able to any attempted German invasion, and submarine attacks in the
shipping lanes of the Caribbean Sea, Gulf of Mexico, and Atlantic
Ocean. After the United States entered the war in December 1941, the
building of a Caribbean defense system became even more important.

During World War II the United States considered the Dominican Republic to be of great strategic importance because of its geographic position as the gateway to the Caribbean and its proximity to the Panama
Canal. The United States felt it could not denounce Trujillo as a dictator
when he was essential to the war effort. Political or ideological principle
was of less consideration than the imperatives of global war. The Dominican Republic was important to the security of the United States and
the hemisphere during World War II if only because of its strategic position on the eastern approaches to the Caribbean Sea and the Panama
Canal, and as part of the island chain leading from the Natal to Florida.
The Dominican Republic was also a source of certain foodstuffs and
materials imported by the United States during the war, such as rice,
sugar, and bauxite.

By the time war broke out in Europe in September 1939, the United
States and the Latin American states, including the Dominican Republic, had issued neutrality proclamations. The First Meeting of Consultation of Ministers of Foreign Affairs of the American states, at Panama
in September and October 1939, decided to establish and patrol a neutrality zone. Since most parties to the declaration were unable to patrol
their own coastal waters, however, the United States was obliged to establish military bases and undertake the operations. The Dominican Re-

public put its facilities at the disposal of the United States in December 1939, signing an agreement that opened its harbors, bays, and territorial waters to U.S. patrol vessels.[36]

In 1939 Trujillo visited Laurence Duggan, chief of the State Department's Latin American Affairs Division, in Washington, D.C. Trujillo made known his desire to obtain four thousand Springfield rifles to replace the Spanish Mausers then in use by his army. He assumed that President Roosevelt could simply order them from surplus stock. Duggan replied that to grant the request would require an act of Congress, since existing legislation for arms shipments to Latin America did not include rifles. He told Trujillo that in the event of a surplus of Springfields, the Department of State would consider a formal request from the Dominican government.[37] This episode is a reminder that a program of military aid and standardization of equipment had not yet been initiated and that the United States had no legal basis on which to supply small arms to Trujillo.

Soon thereafter, however, a variety of military goods was made available to the Dominican Republic. In September 1940 the U.S. Export-Import Bank extended to the Dominican Republic a loan of five million dollars for arms purchases and for the development of Dominican bases and harbors for joint use with the United States.[38] In March 1941, the Lend-Lease Act ended legal restrictions on supplying arms to Latin America by empowering the president to transfer defense articles to those Latin American governments whose defense was deemed vital to that of the United States. On 6 May 1941 the Dominican Republic was declared the first Latin American state eligible for Lend-Lease aid. The purpose of Lend-Lease in Latin America during World War II was ostensibly to help the countries in the region carry out hemispheric defense plans, but an official memorandum in 1940 listed only one reason for supplying arms to the Dominican Republic: "to ensure internal stability."[39] In August 1941, the United States and the Dominican Republic signed two agreements; under their terms the United States agreed to transfer to the Dominican Republic "armaments and munitions of war" up to a total value of about $1,600,000. The Dominican Republic was to pay in advance for the goods received.[40]

The amount of Lend-Lease aid to Latin America during World War II was nearly $459,422,000, of which Brazil, Mexico, Chile, and Peru, in that order, accounted for most of the total. The Dominican Republic's total receipts through 1 September 1945 were $1,590,108. Included in this amount was $521,000 for naval material and $391,000 for aircraft and spare parts.[41]

In 1941 the Dominican government gave the United States permission to build a naval base near Samaná Bay. On 8 December 1941, the day after the attack on Pearl Harbor, the Dominican Republic declared war on Japan, and four days later on Germany and Italy. Shortly thereafter, the United States asked and was granted permission to utilize Dominican airports, to fly over the country and its territorial waters, and to station maintenance personnel in the Dominican Republic. In addition, in January 1943, a four-year naval-mission agreement requested by Trujillo was signed with the United States; at the time of Pearl Harbor the United States had military missions in thirteen Latin American states but the Dominican Republic was not among them— not even a naval attaché was in the country. Also in 1943 the United States supplied three submarine-chasers to the Dominican coast guard and air force for their patrol activities. Later a U.S. Marine Corps air mission arrived and devoted itself to training Dominican pilots, and a number of Dominicans were sent to the United States for flight training.[42]

In 1942 the United States inaugurated a foodstuffs program in the Caribbean. President Roosevelt issued a directive to the Department of Agriculture to establish a revolving fund of $250,000 of Lend-Lease money to finance the stockpiling of food supplies for the Caribbean area. Food was purchased and sold in the Caribbean area, and the proceeds were put back into the fund. The Dominican Republic was included in the program. In 1943 the United States purchased the entire Dominican export production of meat, corn, rice, peanut meal, and sugar. In February 1944 a U.S.-Dominican agreement was concluded whereby the entire exportable surplus of several Dominican food products would be sold to the United States through the Foreign Economics

Administration in order to help meet shortages of food in the Caribbean and other areas.[43]

Technical assistance was made available to the Dominican Republic on a small scale. In 1939 President Roosevelt had established the Inter-departmental Committee on Scientific and Cultural Cooperation to administer operations of various governmental departments and agencies offering their services to other governments. The Dominican Republic was one of fifteen Latin American countries selected for the establishment of agricultural and experiment stations that operated during the war. The wartime agency of the Coordinator of Inter-American Affairs, set up in 1942 as an operating agency in various technical fields and headed by Nelson A. Rockefeller, carried on several projects in health and sanitation in the Dominican Republic. As of 30 September 1946 the United States had contributed $400,000 and the Dominican Republic $175,000 to the cooperative health program. All these programs began theoretically as war measures and were designed to combat Nazi totalitarian influences, among other things. Some of the programs continued to function for a few years after the war; others were taken over by the Dominican Republic.[44]

Attention came to be focused on Trujillo's dictatorial practices and the attitude of the United States toward them. Stirred by the growing totalitarian threat around the world in the late 1930s and during the war itself, Dominican exiles charged that Trujillo was a Nazi, or at least pro-fascist, and was actively aiding the German cause.[45] In the late 1930s, Trujillo admired Hitler and welcomed the establishment of the Nazi-front German-Dominican Institute. He gave serious consideration to substituting German for English as a compulsory language in the schools. Trujillo also respected Franco and welcomed the Spanish Falange to the Dominican Republic.[46] Antidictatorial elements complained that while the United States condemned European dictators, it maintained friendly relations with American dictators like Trujillo. Trujillo himself played the anti-Nazi game, expressing antipathy toward dictators in the name of democracy. For example, ignoring reality for the sake of alliance, President Roosevelt remarked to Trujillo about "the democratic ideals and moral values which we hold dear," and Trujillo replied that "we are at war alongside the United States in defense of democracy and civilization."[47]

U.S.-Dominican cooperation during World War II was clearly based on mutual expediency. Trujillo's collaboration with the United States against Nazi Germany was opportunistic. He probably could not have successfully pursued any other policy, given the wartime importance of the Dominican Republic to the United States. Moreover, cooperation was in Trujillo's best interests and resulted in his receipt of significant (for him) U.S. economic and military aid and technical assistance. For the United States the threat of Nazi Germany was a transcending consideration, even though Trujillo's utterances about freedom and democracy were cynical and facetious. Although U.S. wartime propaganda expressed the goal of destroying dictatorial regimes in the name of democracy, for the United States the defeat of Nazi Germany became an all-important objective and it sought cooperation from all quarters. Its primary objectives in Latin America during the war were political stability and cooperation in preventing Axis influence, and these it got from Trujillo. To secure and maintain these goals, the United States could hardly denounce Trujillo.

Nevertheless, some official coolness toward the Trujillo regime appeared in 1944 after wartime events had turned in favor of the Allies. In that year Ellis O. Briggs was appointed U.S. ambassador to Ciudad Trujillo, and he tried to maintain only circumspect formal contacts with the dictator. He particularly tried to avoid those public appearances that Trujillo manipulated in order to convey the impression that the United States cordially supported his government. A 5 July 1944 dispatch from Briggs to the State Department stated: "Trujillo is a dictator, indifferent to or even hostile to many of the fundamental principles for which our country stands. The fact that Trujillo has declared himself to be 'on our side' in this war, and that he is collaborating with us in certain international matters should not blind us to the realities of his domestic administration nor to the implications within the important area of our general international relations, of our doing business with Trujillo on any except our own carefully considered terms."[48]

Shortly thereafter, in a September 1944 dispatch, Briggs complained that U.S. military attachés and the War Department were not complying with his efforts and those of the State Department to refrain from praising Trujillo and to avoid maintaining close relations with the dictator's government. He recommended guidelines of conduct for U.S. military officials when visiting or assigned to the Dominican Republic and other Caribbean republics.[49]

In 1945 Briggs was succeeded as ambassador by George H. Butler, author of an article appearing in the 15 July 1945 issue of the Department of State *Bulletin* proposing multilateral intervention to enforce democracy in the Western Hemisphere. We have found no evidence of U.S. opposition to Trujillo during Ambassador Butler's tour.

4 The Trujillo Regime and the Cold War

U.S.-Dominican relations from the end of World War II until the assassination of Rafael Trujillo on 30 May 1961 took place in the contexts of: global Cold War, with the Cuban Revolution of 1959 the turning point in the Americas; and intra-Caribbean international conflict, in which the Trujillo regime was intimately involved.[1] Certain themes and issues stood out: the U.S. preoccupation with Soviet communist expansionism, the problem of balancing the inter-American principle of nonintervention with that of promoting democracy and respect for human rights, and the difficulty of military, economic, and cultural relationships with the brutal Dominican dictatorship. Both the Trujillo regime and U.S. policy toward him came under mounting attack, which in the late 1950s in the United States culminated in a general policy debate and the end of U.S. tolerance of the dictator. Trujillo actively promoted his own cause by cooperating with U.S. policies throughout the Cold War. He finally turned against the United States in the late 1950s and early 1960s in retaliation for its hostile attitude toward him.

The U.S. Policy Dilemma

In carrying out its policies toward the Dominican Republic within the Cold War framework of opposition to Soviet expansion and anticommunism the United States experienced a conflict between restrictions imposed by the principle of nonintervention and democratic values that seemed to be ignored or even defied. Washington's policy rationale during most of the postwar period was that opposition to Trujillo would violate the principle of nonintervention; on occasion it would admit that perhaps it had been overly friendly to dictatorial regimes.[2] During the last two years of the Eisenhower administration, this orientation began to change and was reflected in the Dominican case. The major catalyst was Vice President Richard Nixon's hostile reception during his 1958 Latin American "goodwill" tour, especially in Peru and Venezuela. The violence directed at Nixon reflected, among other things, dissatisfaction with U.S. policies toward dictators. Following the Cuban Revolution of 1959, a policy judgment consistent with Cold War concerns became increasingly accepted: dictators bequeathed a political vacuum facilitating the communist alternative, as seemed to be demonstrated by the Cuban experience; the best way to prevent communism was to oppose oppressive regimes. In the case of the Dominican Republic, it was feared that once Trujillo fell from power the United States would be identified with his legacy and held responsible for what might accompany the aftermath of dictatorship, including vulnerability to political chaos and communist subversion.

Trujillo's Tactics

Rafael Trujillo continued to hold absolute power in the Dominican Republic after World War II until his assassination in 1961. In 1947 he was elected in another rigged process for a fourth five-year presidential term; when it expired in 1952, his brother, Héctor B. Trujillo, assumed the presidency. Rafael continued as commander-in-chief of the armed forces and became ambassador-at-large to the United Nations. In 1957 Héctor was again elected president unopposed; when he resigned in 1960, Vice President Joaquín Balaguer became titular head of government, subject to Rafael Trujillo's direction.

Trujillo continued his expediential cooperation with the United States after the conclusion of World War II. Before the Cold War began in 1947, opportunist Trujillo sought to improve his relations with the Soviet Union, the wartime ally of the United States, as well as create the appearance of democracy in the Dominican Republic. To these ends he established diplomatic relations with the Soviet Union and legalized the Popular Socialist party (the Dominican Communist party). He also encouraged the organization of other political parties and the formation of labor unions and then manipulated them for his own purposes. After commencement of the Cold War in 1947, Trujillo suppressed these groups and jailed many of their members. His suppression of Dominican Communists was accompanied by much publicity to demonstrate his anticommunism. By then Trujillo had also realized he ran the risk of losing control of the parties and labor organizations if he tolerated them much longer.

Trujillo purchased a great deal of advertising space in U.S. newspapers to promulgate his message and denounce his critics. In addition, the Dominican Republic became a major foreign-government employer of lawyers, lobbyists, and public relations experts, hired to influence the Dominican sugar quota and promote a favorable image of the Trujillo regime. This hiring was done both in accordance with and contrary to the U.S. Foreign Agents Registration Act (enacted in 1938 and amended in 1939 and 1942). The law called for the registration of nondiplomatic representatives of foreign countries in the United States, including U.S. citizens, and for periodic reports disclosing their activities, income, and expenditures.

An article by Douglas Cater and Walter Pincus published in 1961, citing the Dominican Republic extensively as an example, detailed many of Trujillo's successful efforts to plant stories favorable to him in the U.S. news media. Those stories were often written by public relations people and intended to be printed without indication of their source. Such activity violated the Foreign Agents Registration Act, which specified that any communications intended to influence "any section of the public with reference to the political or public interests, policies, or relations of a government of a foreign country" must be labeled clearly as such.[3]

Trujillo continued to lobby vigorously to the end. On 16 and 17 April 1961, some six weeks before Trujillo was assassinated, Robert D. Murphy, former undersecretary of state, had gone on a confidential mission to the Dominican Republic for President John F. Kennedy. Murphy had been "informally assisted" by Igor Cassini, a New York society columnist who wrote under the name of "Cholly Knickerbocker." Cassini was a friend of prominent figures in the Trujillo regime, including playboy-diplomat Porfirio Rubirosa, who gave Cassini information suggesting a threat of revolution in the Dominican Republic. Cassini informed the President's father, Joseph P. Kennedy, in February 1961, and he passed the information on to the president. Murphy's mission resulted in a "reporting memorandum" that subsequently reached President Kennedy, but no action was recommended and none was taken. Cassini said in a later interview that the talks "dealt with the possibility of leading the Trujillo Government to a liberalization of its policies." At this same time reports from the Dominican consul general in New York indicated that Trujillo was hopeful of arranging a meeting with the president or his father "in an effort to win a reversal of United States diplomatic and economic sanctions from the conference of 1960." [4]

Igor Cassini and his dress-designer brother Oleg were at this time directors of Martial, a New York public relations concern that handled foreign accounts and was registered with the Justice Department. The Dominican Republic was not registered as a Martial account, however. Cassini and R. Paul Englander, who had been associated with Martial, were indicted in February 1963 for failing to register as publicity agents for Trujillo. Cassini was accused of sharing fees of almost two hundred thousand dollars for spreading "political propaganda" to improve the Trujillo government's tarnished image during the period June 1959 to November 1961 in violation of the Foreign Agents Registration Act. On 8 November 1963 Cassini and Englander pleaded *nolo contendere*; they were subsequently fined ten thousand dollars each and placed on six months' probation. [5]

In an exculpatory book published in 1963 after Trujillo's death, Arturo Espaillat, a former Dominican consul general in New York and chief of Trujillo's secret police, declared that at least five million dollars had been paid to certain U.S. congressmen and State Department officials during the last five years of the Trujillo regime. He claimed that hundreds of Americans had shared in money bribes and succumbed to sex lures in both the Dominican Republic and the United States. Espaillat named no recipients but said the complete list of names that had been kept in the Dominican Republic had been removed by the U.S. officials after Trujillo's assassination.[6] The State Department, with good reason, questioned Espaillat's credibility.

Cultural Tactics and Consequences

Trujillo also engaged in a number of cultural policies designed to glorify himself and perpetuate his regime. Yet those tactics had unintended consequences, resulting in enduring social and cultural dynamics.

A major aspect of Trujillo's rule was that all means of communication—radio, press, publishing, and television—were used as instruments of control and to suppress the opposition, glorify Trujillo, and reaffirm the Dominican Spanish heritage. Even U.S. enterprise was involved. A scandal resulted when it was revealed in 1959 that the Mutual Broadcasting System (MBS), a U.S. company, had entered into an agreement with the Dominican government to broadcast in the United States 425 minutes per month for eighteen months of news favorable to the government—meaning Trujillo—for $750,000. The U.S. Justice Department indicted Alexander Guterma, president of MBS, who was fined and sent to prison; MBS filed for bankruptcy.[7]

Television was a particularly notable communications medium. Antonio Menéndez aptly indicates its development: "Dominican television started and was shaped at its beginnings under the dictatorship of Trujillo, adopting a form close to Orwell's *1984*. In its subsequent development, television most closely followed the U.S. model, which bears a closer resemblance to Huxley's *Brave New World*, in which people willingly accept the mechanisms that oppress them."[8]

In 1952 Trujillo established the first television channel, La Voz Dominicana, which was directed by his brother as a means of political control as well as glorification of the dictator. It also stressed the Dominican Spanish legacy and relied heavily on popular entertainment. Another reason for its establishment was that Trujillo wanted to convince the world that his country was one of the most advanced in Latin America. A second channel, Rahintel, was inaugurated in 1959. It was preferred by younger Dominicans because it stressed entertainment, showing mainly U.S. movies; La Voz Dominicana presented Spanish and Mexican films and was heavy on government propaganda.

Trujillo also controlled and determined the nature of the Dominican education system. (Dominicans, notably the clergy, were proud of claiming the oldest university in the Americas—La Universidad de Santo Tomás de Aquino, established by Papal decree in 1538, which evolved into the state-run Universidad Autónoma de Santo Domingo—UASD). Trujillo created a highly centralized system of government control, which was reversed after his departure. He held a highly utilitarian view of education (Germán Ornes titled a chapter in his book on Trujillo "Education for Tyranny").[9] Trujillo used the UASD as academic window dressing to support and embellish his regime with cultural and literary sycophantism. Near the end of his regime Trujillo added the word "Autónoma" to its name, which was meaningless as he exercised complete control. He relocated the institution to University City in 1955, and used it to award degrees to himself, as well as to sympathetic U.S. ambassadors and visiting U.S. senators and representatives.

The dictator also personally regulated migration. In fact, little migration from the Dominican Republic to the United States occurred during the Trujillo era because of the nature of the police state and strict control over exit visas. The number of Dominicans who legally entered the United States from 1953 to 1960 averaged only about nine hundred per year.

Trujillo did make an exception and permitted Dominican baseball players to leave for the United States. Trujillo lacked interest in the game, but one of his brothers and his sister had a strong preoccupation with it. The Liga de Béisbol Profesional Dominicana was formed in 1951 and soon had four teams (a fifth was added in 1984). The Quisqueya

Stadium was built in Ciudad Trujillo in 1955. Beginning in the 1950s, after Jackie Robinson had joined the Brooklyn Dodgers in 1947 and broken the color line, the U.S. major leagues recruited a long line of Dominican players. The first was Osvaldo "Ossie" Virgil, recruited by the New York Giants.

Caribbean Conflict

U.S.-Dominican relations in the post-World War II period took place to a considerable degree within an environment of international Caribbean conflict. While Caribbean strife was nothing new, it became a primary element in intraregional relations during this period, as ideological, boundary, and territorial conflicts ensued and disaffected revolutionary exiles gathered in several nearby countries to plan and execute insurgencies in their national homelands, often in league with rival governments and with the help of mercenaries and adventurers.

The Dominican Republic was directly involved in nine of the twenty Caribbean "situations" that occurred between 1948 and 1959.[10] Inter-American machinery designed for the peaceful settlement of disputes and mutual security was set in motion to deal with chronically bad intra-Caribbean relations. By supporting the use of multilateral procedures, the United States could play the role of impartial good neighbor but not ignore Caribbean international conflict. The problem for both the Inter-American System and the United States was to reconcile the often-conflicting principles of nonintervention and democratic development.[11]

Indeed, the dictatorial nature of the Trujillo regime was a key element in Dominican involvement in Caribbean conflict. Caribbean domestic and international strife were closely linked. In the international sphere, Trujillo accused other governments of designing plots to overthrow him, while those governments directed countercharges at the generalissimo. Trujillo and fellow dictator Anastasio Somoza of Nicaragua were the key targets of revolutionary efforts; they in turn encouraged activities against the struggling democratic governments in Cuba, Guatemala, and Costa Rica; the not easily classifiable government of Haiti was also involved.

Identifying Caribbean conflict only in terms of confrontation between democracy and dictatorship, however, simplifies reality. Personal grudges and adventurism were also among the motivating factors of opposing governments and individuals. In 1950 an investigating team of the Council of the Organization of American States (COAS) reported that many exiles were idealistic individuals who had been deprived of democratic guarantees, but others were "adventurers, professional revolutionaries, and mercenaries whose primary objective appears to be the promotion of illegal traffic in arms and expeditions against the countries with which they have no ties whatsoever."[12] A U.S. Department of State official wrote in the same year that whatever the motivations of the individual revolutionaries might be, their activities had involved territory whose use had violated their governments' international obligations and disrupted relations among Caribbean countries.[13]

The first international conflict involving the Dominican Republic was with Cuba in the summer of 1947. A revolutionary expedition, under the leadership of Dominican exiles General Juan Rodríguez García and the writer (later Dominican president) Juan Bosch, used a key off eastern Cuba (Cayo Confites) as a base of operations against the Trujillo regime. In response to international pressure resulting from widespread publicity, the Cuban government reversed its initial support of the expedition. It arrested the group of more than 1,500 men preparing to leave for the Dominican Republic. Trujillo denounced the attempted invasion as the work "of a Communist International Brigade."[14]

A year later the Dominican Republic and Cuba were again at odds. On 13 August 1948 the Dominican government charged Cuba with organizing revolutionary forces against Trujillo and asked the Inter-American Peace Committee to resolve the dispute. The Peace Committee, composed of representatives of Argentina, Brazil, Cuba, Mexico, and the United States, undertook a thorough investigation and recommended direct negotiations between the disputants. The report was accepted by both parties. The Cuban government, which had been strongly criticized by the Peace Committee's report, arrested the leaders of an expedition that was being organized against Trujillo and seized their ships and aircraft.[15]

Meanwhile, the Trujillo regime and Haiti had become involved in a bizarre episode. On 15 February 1949, Haiti brought before the COAS a charge that the Dominican government was committing "moral acts of aggression." It said that the Haitian minister to Ecuador, Colonel Astrel Roland, in Ciudad Trujillo en route to Haiti to answer charges of plotting revolution against his own government, had used the official Dominican radio to advocate a Haitian uprising against the government of President Dumarsais Estimé. The COAS found no evidence to warrant its serving as the organ of consultation to consider the dispute under the 1947 Inter-American Treaty of Reciprocal Assistance (Rio Treaty). Nevertheless, the Inter-American Peace Committee pursued investigations in Haiti and the Dominican Republic and persuaded the two governments to sign a joint declaration in which they promised not to tolerate activities directed against "other friendly nations."[16]

The Dominican Republic immediately had trouble with other states. On 19 June 1949 an incident occurred at Luperón Bay on the Dominican coast involving two amphibious aircraft and about fifteen men (including three civilian pilots from the United States). It was a fiasco from start to finish, easily suppressed by Trujillo's forces. Trujillo accused Cuba and Guatemala of complicity in the "airborne invasion" and of harboring and encouraging exiles to act against him. He later broadened his charges to include Mexico and Costa Rica and said he would bring the matter before the Inter-American Peace Committee but never did so. Cuba sent a letter to the Peace Committee on 6 December, inviting it to visit Cuba and learn for itself the inaccuracy of Trujillo's claims. The committee replied on 16 December that it saw no reason to conduct an investigation.[17] In December 1949 Trujillo renewed his charges of hostile activity on the part of Cuba and Guatemala. He called the Dominican Congress into special session and had himself empowered to declare war on any country permitting preparations for an invasion of his realm. This move brought a rebuke from Secretary Dean Acheson: "This government deplores the action of the government of the Dominican Republic in having brought up the possibility of the use of armed force for the purpose of 'war.'"[18]

Haiti reentered the scene on 3 January 1950, when it went to the Organization of American States (OAS) with charges of a large-scale Dominican-supported plot to overthrow its government. Haiti invoked the Rio Treaty, asking that a meeting of ministers of foreign affairs be immediately summoned. At a COAS meeting on 6 January, the Haitian ambassador accused the Dominican government of violating the joint declaration of 9 June 1949 and insisted that it had permitted Roland and other Haitian nationals to continue broadcasting and plotting. The Trujillo government went beyond denying the Haitian charges and demanded a hearing on its long-standing contention that Cuba, Guatemala, and other countries were fostering revolution against the Trujillo regime. The COAS invoked the Rio Treaty, agreed to act provisionally as the organ of consultation, and called for a meeting of consultation of ministers of foreign affairs (which was never held).[19]

The COAS, acting as the provisional organ of consultation, appointed a committee to conduct an investigation. The committee, made up of representatives of Bolivia, Colombia, Ecuador, the United States, and Uruguay, devoted ten weeks to its investigation. It held hearings in Washington, D.C., and visited each of the four variously accused countries. It submitted an extensive and plain-spoken report to the COAS published on 19 March 1950 that substantiated numerous charges. It severely criticized three of the parties—the Dominican Republic, Cuba, and Guatemala—and accused them all of plots and conspiracies that had kept the Caribbean in turmoil for the past three years. It found that Haiti alone had not engaged in subversive activities or maneuvers. The committee recommended sanctions if the offending countries failed to keep the peace. The report indicated widespread official irresponsibility in the Caribbean.[20]

The COAS went beyond the immediate cases and weighed the conflicting concepts of nonintervention and promotion of democracy, deciding in favor of the former. On 8 April 1950 the COAS issued a resolution noting that "both the principle of representative democracy and that of non-intervention are established in many inter-American pronouncements," pointing out the existence of "some confusion of ideas as to the means of harmonizing the effective execution and application" of the two principles. It declared that the principles of democracy "do not in any way and under any concept authorize any governments to violate inter-American commitments relative to the principle of non-intervention."[21]

In 1959, after almost nine years of quiescence, Caribbean instability again involved the Trujillo regime. After Fidel Castro overthrew dictator Fulgencio Batista and seized power in Cuba on 1 January 1959, the activities of his revolutionary government contributed to Caribbean turmoil. Castro announced his determination not only to carry out a thoroughgoing social revolution in Cuba but also to work for the speedy elimination of remaining military dictatorships in Latin America, beginning with the Caribbean area. Castro and Trujillo became the principal rivals in Caribbean international politics. When Castro took power, Batista fled to the Dominican Republic. Trujillo and Batista had many differences but, after the United States had ceased its military aid to Cuba, Trujillo had sold him military equipment. Castro intensified his existing hatred for Trujillo when the latter granted Batista asylum.

In mid-June 1959 the Dominican Republic was invaded by groups of various nationalities at Constanza, Maimón, and near Estero Hondo. The intruding forces numbered some 56 men brought in by aircraft and about 140 by yachts, all originating in Cuba. The Dominican government claimed to have annihilated the invaders.[22] On 2 July the Trujillo government appealed to the COAS for action under the Rio Treaty, accusing both Cuba and Venezuela of participating in the preparation of the recent interventions as well as new exile landings and appealed to the OAS to intercede. The Cuban and Venezuelan governments denied the charges, insisting they would not permit an OAS investigation on their territories. After an exchange of threats and counterthreats, on 10 July the Dominican Republic unexpectedly withdrew its charges, apparently recognizing that little support would be forthcoming from other OAS members.[23] By this time Trujillo was isolated from the inter-American community and the United States was becoming increasingly impatient with him.

At the initiative of the United States and several Latin American states, the Fifth Meeting of Consultation of Ministers of Foreign Affairs was held on August 1959 in Santiago, Chile, to discuss the Caribbean situation. Specifically, it sought to reconcile the demand for democratic progress and economic and social change with inter-American principles of peaceful relations and nonintervention in the internal affairs of others. U.S. Secretary of State Christian A. Herter emphasized the inter-American commitment to nonintervention over other principles, a position based on the idea that overthrowing oppressive regimes would produce disorder and tension and give political opportunity to the communists. A few states, including Cuba and Venezuela, favored a compromise of the nonintervention principle in order to oppose dictatorial regimes, promote democracy, and protect human rights. The United States appeared to rebuke Cuba and Venezuela in their dispute with Trujillo. The overwhelming majority of delegates opposed any compromise of nonintervention, although the final act strongly condemned dictatorial governments, without mentioning names.[24]

The Inter-American Peace Committee and a special investigating committee of the COAS played important roles in reporting and publicizing the activities of the Trujillo regime. The United States was represented on both committees. The Peace Committee prepared two major reports in keeping with its mandate at the Fifth Meeting of Foreign Ministers in 1959 to ascertain the contribution to Caribbean tension of the violation of human rights and lack of democratic practices. The first report, published 14 April 1960, stressed that the promotion of democracy and the protection of human rights would be the best means for eliminating political tensions; but it also viewed the principle of nonintervention as transcending any commitment to democracy and human rights. The committee "took a firm position in favor of the peaceful achievement, without foreign intervention, of the political goals" of the American peoples; accordingly, it could "under no circumstances suggest any formula that would violate the nonintervention principle or the solemn inter-American commitments which have as their aim the preservation of the right of each state to work out its own political destiny."[25]

The second report, issued on 5 August 1960, discussed four incidents, two involving the Dominican Republic, that had been investigated by the Peace Committee throughout 1959 and 1960. The first case involving Trujillo began on 19 November 1959, when an aircraft proceeding from the Dominican Republic dropped pamphlets by mistake over the island of Curaçao, a possession of the Netherlands. These pamphlets, destined originally for a Venezuelan city, called for the Venezuelan armed forces to revolt against President Rómulo Betancourt, Trujillo's antagonist and leading member of the Latin American "Democratic Left." On 25 November 1959, the Venezuelan representative to the COAS asked the Inter-American Peace Committee to investigate the incident and at the same time charged the Dominican government with complicity. After completing an investigation the Peace Committee concluded that the flight to drop the pamphlets inciting revolution in Venezuela "could not have been carried out without the connivance of the Dominican authorities."[26]

The second Dominican case resulted from a Venezuelan request on 17 February 1960 that the Peace Committee "investigate the flagrant violations of human rights by the government of the Dominican Republic, which are aggravating tensions in the Caribbean." Trujillo refused to allow the committee to visit the Dominican Republic and conduct a survey. As an alternative the committee requested information from member states, discussed the problem with both Dominican and Venezuelan representatives, and received testimony in Washington. The Peace Committee concluded "that international tensions in the Caribbean region have been aggravated by flagrant and widespread violations of human rights which have been committed and continue to be committed in the Dominican Republic," and that those violations had increased tensions in the Caribbean region that would continue as long as they persisted. The Inter-American Juridical Committee stated in a subsequent report that there was no legal basis in the OAS charter for collective action "in defense of democracy, for its maintenance or for its restoration," the Peace Committee's opinion notwithstanding.[27]

Two subsequent incidents led to another meeting of foreign ministers to consider further acts perpetrated by the Dominican Republic. They reflected an accelerated drive by Trujillo against President Betancourt that culminated in a near-successful attempt to assassinate the Venezuelan chief of state. The first incident involved a military uprising in April 1960 in San Cristóbal, Venezuela, led by former Venezuelan army general Castro León. An investigation disclosed that the Dominican government had issued passports to León and other instigators of the uprising. Far more serious was the attempt to assassinate President Betancourt by detonating a planted bomb near his passing automobile. On 8 July the COAS agreed to the Venezuelan government's request to convoke the Sixth Meeting of Consultation of Ministers of Foreign Affairs. It appointed a committee to investigate and report on the Venezuelan charges.

The five-member investigating committee, composed of representatives from Argentina, Mexico, Panama, Uruguay, and the United States, examined the Venezuelan allegations and heard the Dominican denials and countercharges. It examined many documents, drew on the work and information of the Peace Committee, and visited both Caracas and Ciudad Trujillo. The committee's report, presented to the COAS on 8 August 1960, included detailed discussions of the three acts that comprised the Venezuelan protest against the Trujillo regime: (1) the attempt in November 1959 to drop leaflets on a Venezuelan city inciting revolution against the government, (2) the Venezuelan military uprising in April 1960, and, most important, (3) the assassination attempt against President Betancourt in June 1960. Complicity of the Trujillo government was established in all three instances. With regard to the assassination effort, the report said that the persons implicated in the attempt "received moral support and material assistance from high officials of the Government of the Dominican Republic."[28]

The Sixth Meeting of Consultation met from 16 to 21 August 1960 in San José, Costa Rica.[29] The major objective was to determine what action the OAS should take against the Trujillo government in view of the investigating committee's report that had been presented to the COAS and was now before the ministers of foreign affairs. The Dominican Republic predictably denied the accusations and accused Venezuela, along with the Peace Committee, of intervention.

The discussion during the early stages of the meeting did not embrace the usual preoccupation with nonintervention, although it later surfaced in response to a U.S. proposal. Two reasons explain the initial lack of preoccupation with nonintervention: the Trujillo regime was almost universally detested in Latin America, and the Dominican government itself had violated the nonintervention principle. While the Latin American ministers favored sanctions against the Trujillo government, but with no counterpart desire to intervene to promote democracy, Secretary Herter advocated an unprecedented alternative: that the Dominican Republic agree to receive a special OAS committee to make certain that free elections were held under its supervision. Herter agreed with the indictment against the Dominican government and that its "grave acts against the sovereignty of Venezuela" deserved multilateral condemnation, but he doubted the sanctions would also move the Dominican Republic toward representative democracy.

The U.S. position reflected a shift in policy, attributable to the impact of Castro's rise to power, away from nonintervention as far as dictators were concerned and toward promoting democracy and an attempt to use inter-American sanctions to guide Dominican politics on a democratic—and noncommunist—course.[30] Thus a new means to the end of maintaining stability and preventing communist influence was embraced. The OAS was to be the instrument for bringing about democratic change in the Dominican government and for removing Trujillo from power. Such change would obviate the "political vacuum problem" and the threat of communist inroads following a dictator's overthrow. The U.S. recommendation provoked a typical debate on the principle of nonintervention that indicated rejection by the Latin American ministers. Consequently, the United States abandoned the "free elections" proposal and joined the Latin American consensus.

On 20 August, by a vote of nineteen to zero (under OAS rules neither the Dominican Republic nor Venezuela participated in the voting), the Council passed a resolution in which the Dominican government was "condemned emphatically" and declared guilty of "intervention and aggression" in the attempt on the life of President Betancourt. The "moral and material assistance" from high Dominican officials justified collective action under Article 6 of the Rio Treaty. The ministers agreed to the breaking of diplomatic relations of all member states with the Dominican Republic, and partial interruption of economic relations beginning with the immediate suspension of trade in arms and implements of war of every kind. The COAS was authorized to discontinue the measures by a two-thirds vote of the members "at such time as the Government of the Dominican Republic should cease to constitute a danger to the peace and security of the hemisphere." In the meantime, the COAS could also consider the "feasibility and desirability" of extending the suspension of trade to other articles.[31]

Seven Latin American states had already broken diplomatic relations with the Trujillo regime before the San José meeting; on 26 August 1960 the United States and the remaining Latin American states severed diplomatic ties. The United States had already suspended "trade in arms and implements of war" with the Trujillo government prior to the foreign ministers' decision.[32]

The COAS appointed a special committee to observe the effects of the sanctions with a view to recommending lifting them when it was convinced that the Dominican government was willing to abide by inter-American principles. The committee's first report, on 21 December 1960, concluded that the Dominican government had demonstrated no substantial change in attitude. It recommended not only that sanctions be continued but that they be extended to include petroleum and petroleum products, trucks, and spare parts. On 4 January 1961 the COAS implemented the recommendations by a vote of fourteen to one with six abstentions.[33]

For the first time the OAS had applied sanctions against one of its members, in the process striving not to compromise the principle of nonintervention. The San José meeting demonstrated that nonintervention continued to transcend commitments to democracy and human rights. Thus, the reason that the American community took punitive action against the Dominican Republic was not because that regime had failed to observe democratic principles or had violated human rights, although both these charges could be thoroughly documented. Nor did Latin Americans fear, as did the United States, that communism would find fertile ground in the Dominican Republic as a result of Trujillo's oppressive policies. Instead, the OAS action was prompted by the Dominican attempt to assassinate President Betancourt, which the OAS regarded as both a violation of the nonintervention principle and an act of aggression. Because it had committed this act, the Dominican government could no longer use the nonintervention argument to justify immunity from community action.

U.S. Military Policies

From the end of World War II until 1952, the United States had no organized military assistance program for Latin America, a region peripheral to its security policies. Within this general framework the Dominican Republic was subject to special considerations. Such consideration was indicated in November 1945, when the State Department denied an export license for Trujillo to receive munitions he had arranged to buy in the United States. Spruille Braden, assistant secretary of state for American republic affairs, expressed this pre-Cold War policy in an *aide-memoire*:

> The Government and people of the United States necessarily have a warmer feeling of friendship for and a greater desire to cooperate with those governments which rest upon periodically and freely expressed consent of the governed. This Government has over the past years observed the situation in the Dominican Republic and has been unable to perceive that democratic principles have been observed there in theory or in practice. The foregoing conclusion is based upon the lack of freedom of speech, freedom of the press, and freedom of assembly, as well as upon the suppression of all political opposition and the existence of a one-party system. To furnish large amounts of ammunition in the face of such a system might be held to constitute both intervention in the internal political affairs of the Dominican Republic and support for the practices just mentioned. In the opinion of the United States, the foregoing observations constitute sufficient reason to refuse to furnish the arms and ammunition requested.[34]

The United States continued to supply some military equipment under the Lend-Lease Act, but only that which had been previously committed for delivery as of the end of the war. From September 1945 until April 1949, the United States transferred to the Dominican Republic a total value of $27,258.76 in aircraft and aeronautical material, vessels and other watercraft, and miscellaneous military equipment. In April 1949, the Dominican government paid the $92,691 balance due on its total Lend-Lease obligations assumed in August 1941.

Another basis for the continued supply of military equipment during the immediate postwar period was the Surplus Property Act of 1944, which authorized direct sales of U.S. military surpluses at reduced prices. By May 1949, Trujillo had purchased a number of small arms, vessels, and artillery pieces, paying twenty-three thousand dollars for material that had been initially procured at a cost of five hundred thousand dollars.[35] The Dominican Republic received no military equipment under the U.S. Mutual Defense Assistance Act of 1949, which enabled Latin American countries to purchase arms in the United States.

In the meantime, the Inter-American Treaty of Reciprocal Assistance (Rio Treaty) of 1947 had gone into effect. The United States said its principles of hemispheric defense provided the context for its military cooperation programs in Latin America. Standardization of military organization, training, methods, and equipment, all oriented toward the United States, was considered desirable in order to enhance mutual security and discourage Latin American purchases elsewhere. The United States also wanted to ensure the accessibility of strategic raw materials.[36]

Between 1949 and 1957, the United States and the Dominican Republic negotiated several military-related conventions. In November 1951, the Dominican Republic agreed to permit U.S. missiles to pass over its territory (two years earlier, the United States had established the Atlantic Missile Range for long-range missile testing from the Florida mainland to Ascension Island). Other treaties included an air transport services agreement (19 July 1949), an aviation agreement (11 August 1950), an agreement for a cooperative weather stations program (25 July and 11 August 1956), an agreement concerning atomic energy cooperation for civil uses (15 June 1956), and a navigation agreement establishing a LORAN station at Cape Francis Viejo (19 March 1957).[37]

The most important basis for U.S.-Dominican military relations after 1947 was the U.S. Mutual Security Act of 1951. The Latin American portions of the law were conceived in part by the desire to end Latin American purchases in Europe and to facilitate the standardization of arms in the hemisphere. It made military assistance contingent on the recipient's participation in missions related to hemispheric defense. Under the provisions of the act, Latin American states were able to make cash purchases of weapons and equipment for uses considered important to hemispheric defense, such as antisubmarine patrol and coastal defense. Direct grants of military equipment in addition to purchases were also authorized for selected Latin American countries whose assistance was considered essential to hemispheric defense.

On 6 March 1953, the Dominican Republic was among the first of twelve Latin American governments to sign bilateral mutual defense assistance agreements with the United States, agreeing to maintain a portion of their armed forces exclusively for the inter-American mutual defense mission.[38] (The Dominican Republic's agreement was terminated the month after Trujillo's death in 1961.) From the beginning of the military assistance program in fiscal 1952 through fiscal 1961, the total value of U.S. military deliveries to the Dominican Republic was approximately $6.1 million out of a Latin American total of approximately $336 million.[39] The establishment of military missions was another feature of the mutual security program. In 1956, U.S. Air Force and Navy service training missions were sent to administer the transfer of equipment furnished under the mutual defense agreement.

U.S. military policy toward Trujillo began to change during the latter part of the Eisenhower administration. The change was facilitated by Trujillo's increasing unpopularity in both the United States and Latin America and by the Latin American view that the United States was too kind to dictators. Relations were exacerbated by Trujillo's role in international Caribbean conflict and by U.S.-Dominican disagreement over the facts of the disappearance of Dominican dissident Jesús de Galíndez (discussed below).

The United States began to limit the amount of aid to Trujillo and to impose restrictions on the kinds of armaments and munitions he could buy in the United States. In 1958, shortly after imposing an arms embargo on the Batista government in Cuba, the United States stopped providing Trujillo with arms. Trujillo requested the recall of the U.S. Air Force mission and began to make military equipment available to fellow dictator Batista to aid his struggle against Fidel Castro. In 1960, with the Dominican Republic scheduled to receive $445,000 in aid, the United States announced that it was cutting off military assistance.[40] The cutoff coincided with Trujillo's unsuccessful attempt to kill Venezuelan President Betancourt and subsequent OAS sanctions. The Kennedy administration continued to deny aid to Trujillo.

Trujillo's Military Buildup

Trujillo engaged in an arms buildup in response to the series of incidents beginning in 1947 that exacerbated Dominican relations with neighboring states. Because the United States would not fully respond to his requests for military equipment, from either government stocks or private suppliers with the necessary export licenses, Trujillo went to other external providers as primary sources of arms and equipment. He also developed his own factory to make certain arms and munitions. By drawing on various international sources and developing an internal production capacity, Trujillo developed probably the most powerful military force in the Caribbean. His air force and navy assumed proportions far greater than those of other Caribbean states.

Soon after the end of World War II, Trujillo constructed an arms factory at San Cristóbal. His irritation over the U.S. rejection in 1945 of his effort to buy military munitions in the United States was an important factor in his decision to create his own source.[41] Trujillo accepted the plan of a Hungarian refugee, imported a number of European arms technicians (mainly Hungarian and Italian), and built the San Cristóbal arsenal. The facility soon achieved high standards of workmanship and the capability to produce various types of munitions and weapons and rebuild heavier weapons. It made hand grenades, gunpowder, dynamite, revolvers, automatic rifles, carbines, submachine guns, light machine guns, antitank guns, and munitions. In addition, some quantities of mortars and aerial bombs were produced and light artillery rebuilt.[42] Trujillo not only achieved a certain self-reliance in arms manufacturing, he generated a surplus that he sold to other Latin American governments.

Trujillo also turned to willing European suppliers to get the military equipment he could not buy from the United States or produce at his armory. With the exception of conventional aircraft and small naval vessels, Trujillo had far more success obtaining items in Europe than in the United States, principally from the United Kingdom, France, Spain, and Sweden. U.S. competitors in the arms trade had a different perspective on U.S. motives. The United Kingdom, for example, approaching the arms market as a business matter and seeing no Latin American relevance to its strategic concerns, viewed U.S. avowal of inter-American defense cooperation merely as an excuse to exclude commercial competition.[43] Only about 10 percent of the artillery and mortars for the Dominican army and air force was obtained in the United States, with most of the rest from Brazil, France, Spain, Germany, Sweden, and the United Kingdom. Trujillo obtained rifles from at least a half dozen European countries, machine guns from Italy and Spain, and armored cars from Sweden.

Trujillo greatly increased the magnitude of military expenditures. The percentage of the national budget earmarked for military purposes had been 11.5 percent in 1931; it rose to 25 percent in 1957 and jumped to almost 50 percent in 1959. His army, the largest service, received the most appropriations. Yet it remained inefficient and unprofessional as a result of nepotism and his stress on loyalty over competence. Trujillo insulated the army and the National Police from U.S. influence; he would permit minimal contact with U.S. military advisors, preferring advisors from the Spanish army. He sent very few officers for outside training and then preferably to Spain or another Latin American country. He intentionally kept his army at low levels of training and equipment and made available only light weapons and limited ammunition supplies. While generally distrusting his six-brigade army, he did organize the Fourth Brigade as an autonomous unit, ensuring that it was the best equipped and trained as well as personally loyal to him. Only this unit in the army had heavy artillery; another combat battalion was equipped with armored vehicles, and another with heavy (152 mm) Spanish field artillery but no vehicles.

The Dominican air force, which Trujillo especially favored during his last few years, got its start during World War II with the assistance of the United States, especially the marine corps pilot training mission sent in 1943. By the end of 1952, the air force had 131 aircraft; the number rose to 156 by 1954. Most of them were of U.S. manufacture and World War II vintage, with a few from the 1930s, and about a dozen British Beauforts and Mosquitos. Since the United States made no jet aircraft available, Trujillo bought them from the United Kingdom and Sweden.[44] Inadequate maintenance and spare parts reduced the real strength of the Dominican air force.

Following World War II a German war veteran, Otto Winterer, claiming to be an ex-*Luftwaffe* major, had come to the Dominican Republic and convinced Trujillo of the value of having an elite military organization patterned after Hitler's *Luftwaffe*. Trujillo created such a group in the form of an air force with its own ground combat units, including paratroops, infantry, artillery, and armor (which had the Dominican armed forces' only tanks, mostly from France and Sweden and a few from the United States). The pilots, most of whom had been trained during World War II by the United States, were a professionally competent and highly privileged group. The force soon became a major diversion for Trujillo's oldest son, Ramfis.

Trujillo took particular interest in building a Dominican navy with real operational efficiency, hoping to compete especially with Cuba, Mexico, and Venezuela. As a result, the navy was the one service for which he welcomed U.S. assistance and permitted considerable contact between U.S. and Dominican naval personnel. Contrary to his usual policies of training his officers at home, he would permit certain selected naval officers to go to the United States in order to receive professional and technical instruction. He also sent numbers of his enlisted men and commissioned officers to the Canal Zone and to the United States for professional training. Consequently, the Dominican navy, which had a contingent of marines until 1959 but no air arm, became the most professional of his services. Most of the vessels were acquired from the United States, mostly during World War II and the immediate postwar period, with the remainder from Canada and the United Kingdom. In 1957 Trujillo's navy consisted of thirty-nine combat and auxiliary vessels, including two destroyers, eight frigates, six patrol boats and seven coast guard boats.[45]

Trujillo responded to Fidel Castro's seizure of power in Cuba in 1959 and his subsequent anti-Trujillo activities with a further arms buildup. Since the United States had stopped providing military equipment in 1958, he again turned to European suppliers. In 1959 he created by means of a special tax a fifty-million-dollar National Defense Fund for the purchase of arms. Only an amount somewhat in excess of six million dollars was actually spent for arms; the rest Trujillo appropriated to himself.[46] Part of the six-million-dollar arms-buying spree included the acquisition of a dozen French tanks and a number of British Vampire jets.

Trujillo had been shocked by Castro's success in the face of Batista's apparently overwhelming military strength (to which Trujillo had contributed). He decided to supplement the increase in Dominican arms with organization of a kind of foreign legion for dealing with guerrillas. He planned an elite group of fighting men modeled on French and Spanish foreign legionnaires but was never able to create the force envisioned. Trujillo's recruiters in Europe did attract a number of men, however, primarily from France, Greece, Spain, and Yugoslavia, by promising jobs and high salaries. Some soldiers of fortune in the Caribbean were also enticed to join. Apparently three auxiliary forces were established in the late 1950s involving up to five thousand men.[47]

Economic Relations

The Trujillo government received no direct public economic assistance from the United States during or after World War II. Some Export-Import Bank credits were authorized but none were disbursed. During the war the United States had extended technical assistance to the Dominican Republic on a small scale. Some of the programs continued to function for a few years after the war; others were taken over by the Dominican Republic. The United States revitalized technical assistance with the worldwide Point Four program, later included in the Mutual Security Program, under which a technical assistance agreement was concluded with Trujillo early in 1951. A program in agriculture and natural resources was started in 1952, in industry and mining in 1953, and in transportation in 1955; the education program already in existence was continued, as was a rubber research program that had been carried on by the United States Department of Agriculture since 1942. By 1957 technical assistance was again limited to an education program, which included projects in vocational education, industrial arts, and teacher training for rural schools.[48]

The most important economic relationship was U.S. purchase of Dominican sugar. It continued for a time under the 1944 agreement whereby the United States bought the exportable surplus of several Dominican food products. Under the Sugar Act of 1948, the United States limited the amount of foreign sugar that might be placed on its domestic market. This restriction took the form of quotas on imports and on domestic production as well. The effect was to prevent low-cost foreign sugar from flooding the U.S. market and injuring the domestic industry and to maintain a relatively high U.S. price compared to the world price. The difference of two cents per pound made it highly profitable for foreign states to sell in the United States, if they could obtain quotas.[49]

Trujillo regularly lobbied to get the U.S. government to increase the Dominican sugar import quota. The size of the quota for his major earner of foreign exchange increased over the years, mainly as a result of increased consumption in the United States, although his persistent lobbying played at least a minor role. By 1959 the Dominican quota was almost 81,500 short tons and in 1960 almost 131,000. Additional "nonquota" trade was also available; in 1960 the Dominican Republic had almost 322,000 short tons of such sugar exports to the United States.[50] After mid-1960, when the United States cut and redistributed the Cuban quota, it allotted the Dominican Republic an additional 30,000 short tons. The effect was reduced, however, by imposition of a surtax of two cents per pound on Dominican sugar, in line with the August 1960 OAS sanctions against Trujillo.

In 1960 the U.S. Congress turned its attention to new sugar legislation—the Sugar Act of 1948 was scheduled to expire on 31 December of that year—and faced a number of circumstances that made a simple extension of the act all but impossible. The most important factor was the deterioration of U.S.-Cuban relations after the 1959 Castro revolution. After considerable debate Congress extended the Sugar Act to 31 March 1961. It authorized the president to assign Cuba any reduced allocation he determined was in the national interest and to reallocate the quotas by means of a specified formula and to specific countries to make up the Cuban deficit.

The United States then attempted to align its own unilateral policies with the spirit of the multilateral OAS condemnation of the Dominican Republic. The role of the Dominican Republic in the government-controlled U.S. sugar market was an important issue in the unilateral repudiation of the Trujillo dictatorship. Noting the action taken by the Meeting of Consultation of Ministers of Foreign Affairs in San José, President Eisenhower, in a message to Congress in August 1960, requested discretion in the purchase of Dominican sugar and for authority to take away the reallocated quota for the Dominican Republic. The president pointed out that the Dominican Republic's new allocation represented a sizable increase in its quota, which would give the Dominican Republic "a large sugar bonus embarrassing to the United States in the conduct of our foreign relations throughout the hemisphere." The president asked for legislation that would allow the Dominican share to be purchased instead from any foreign country without regard to allocation.[51]

Congressional hearings were held and the House and Senate passed versions of a resolution to grant the president's request, but these proposals never went to conference and died when Congress adjourned. The effort was blocked by two Trujillo supporters, Senators James Eastland (D-Miss.) and Allen Ellender (D-La.). Lacking authority to reduce the Dominican quota, the president imposed a fee of two cents per pound on sugar purchased from the Dominican Republic, an action the Sugar Act authorized him to take at his own discretion, canceling the amount over the world price that the United States paid for quota sugar.[52]

When President John F. Kennedy was confronted by the question of sugar legislation, he supported the prior appeal of President Eisenhower for authority to decrease the Dominican quota. In February 1961, Representative Harold Cooley (D-N.C.), chairman of the House Agriculture Committee, introduced a bill to extend the Sugar Act without changing the allocation system, a proposal that continued the Dominican Republic's quota share. The Kennedy administration asked that the Dominican Republic be denied any special benefits under the new law. A bill was finally passed and signed by the president on 31 March 1961, extending sugar legislation to 30 June 1962 and specifically denying the Dominican Republic a share of the Cuban cut.[53]

The "Dominican Debate"

A five-year policy debate dating from 1956 went on in the United States over the proper policy posture to assume toward Trujillo, continuing until his death in 1961. It involved a barrage of both criticism and defense of the dictator.

The debate began with the Galíndez-Murphy case of 1956–57. Jesús de Galíndez, a Spanish exile, ex-resident of the Dominican Republic, and lecturer at Columbia University in New York, had just completed his anti-Trujillist doctoral dissertation there.[54] Galíndez disappeared after an evening class in New York on 12 March 1956. Gerald Murphy, a young aviator from Eugene, Oregon, who had been employed for several months as a copilot for the Dominican national airlines, disappeared in Ciudad Trujillo on 3 December 1956. First-year Congressman Charles O. Porter (D-Ore.), whose district included Murphy's hometown, connected and focused attention on these two events. Porter theorized that Galíndez's dissertation had prompted Trujillo to have him kidnapped in New York, flown by Murphy from a Long Island airport to the Dominican Republic, delivered to Trujillo, and murdered. Murphy, Porter said, did not know the nature of his mission at the time but later became suspicious, talked too much, and was also killed on Trujillo's orders.[55] The U.S. State Department was in basic agreement with Porter. The United States informed the Dominican government that it took "a very serious view" of the case and could not accept the Dominican explanation of the disappearances on the basis of available evidence.[56]

The Dominican rebuttal was to dismiss Galíndez as a communist and to label all criticism as a "typical liberal smear job." In reply to U.S. doubts of Dominican explanations, the Trujillo government protested that to accept as conclusive a contrary opinion by the agencies of a foreign power would be equivalent to abdicating its sovereign state rights.[57] The most puzzling defender of Trujillo was the well-known champion of liberal causes, New York attorney Morris L. Ernst. The Dominican government retained Ernst to review the facts and he concluded that no accusation connecting the Dominican Republic with the disappearance of Galíndez or with Murphy's plane was supported by "a scintilla of evidence."[58] Congressman Porter questioned Ernst's objectivity since he had been paid by the accused.[59] The case set off a controversy, carried out largely in the U.S. Congress, over the Dominican policy of the United States and involved an investigation by the State Department in the Dominican Republic.

Congressman Porter had insisted that the United States should "revise the present official policy of toleration, conciliation, and condonation of the Dominican tyranny." He raised his sights from the Galíndez-Murphy case to attack general U.S. relations with Trujillo. In the House of Representatives on 28 February 1957, Porter said that as he delved more deeply into the details surrounding Murphy's disappearance, "it became apparent that we were dealing with the logical result" of U.S. policy toward the Dominican Republic. Porter asked why, if the United States had taken a strong stand against communist tyranny, a "glove-hand approach" should be taken toward the tyranny of Trujillo. Porter recommended that the U.S. Ambassador in Ciudad Trujillo, William T.

Pheiffer, be removed for showing undue cordiality to Trujillo. Perhaps Porter had in mind Ambassador Pheiffer's public characterization of Trujillo as "an authentic genius who thinks and labors, primarily, in terms of the best interests of his people."[60] Porter also felt that the Galíndez-Murphy case should be submitted to the OAS. In addition, he said, the United States should reduce the Dominican sugar quota and terminate Export-Import Bank loans, technical assistance, and military aid. Finally, the United States should insist that Dominican Ambassador de Moya retract a speech delivered in San Francisco in which he insinuated that the Galíndez-Murphy cases were communist plots of which Porter was a dupe; if the ambassador would not make the retraction he should be declared *persona non grata*.[61]

Trujillo had his apologists in the Senate and House. Senator George S. Long (D-La.) actually asserted that the widely held conviction that Trujillo was a dictator was loose talk since the Dominican government, after all, held elections. He said further that even if Trujillo were a dictator, it was no business of the United States "what type of Government is maintained at Ciudad Trujillo, so long as it is not an atheistic Communist government which would endanger our own safety and security." Long also asserted that it was "the Communists who are behind the present smear campaign of the Dominican Republic," but he was making no accusation that Porter "knowingly" served the communist cause. Porter retorted that Long was implying that the Federal Bureau of Investigation and the State Department were also serving the communist cause since their findings supported what Porter said.[62]

Senator Olin D. Johnston (D-S.C.) argued that the Trujillo government was important to the United States for several reasons: it was a staunch friend, had provided a base in the guided missile program, was a foe of communism in the Caribbean, and represented "stability and good government in an area of turmoil." Earlier, on 25 July 1956, Senator Johnston had extolled Trujillo in the U.S. Senate after returning from a trip to the Dominican Republic. A year later Senator Johnston said that "the Dominican Republic has rendered a greater force in deterring the spread of communism in Latin America than any other country in the Caribbean area." Anti-Trujillists said that Senator Long failed to recognize that Trujillo pinned the communist label on all political opposition, perverting the anticommunist drive into a campaign to throttle all opposition, most of it noncommunist.[63]

Porter's main antagonist in the House was Representative B. Carroll Reece (D-Tenn.). He said that the United States could criticize Trujillo through such officials as the secretary of state but that was "a far cry from attempting to undermine or overturn an allied neighbor." Reece noted that the Dominican Republic was "stable" and enjoyed "spiritual and material well-being," supported U.S. policies, had given the United States territory for military bases, and had encouraged U.S. investment. Reece said that "when a member of the Congress of the United States becomes a self-appointed international revolutionary, he necessarily imperils the entire delicate structure of international relations. . . . We are duty bound to observe the sovereign integrity of native government of every complexion no matter how repugnant they may seem to our concept of the body politic."[64]

Part of the U.S. military assistance program involved training Dominican officers in the United States. This training became the focus of a ludicrous controversy in 1958 as a result of the nonmilitary interests of the dictator's officer-son, Rafael Leonidas (Ramfis) Trujillo Jr. Ramfis had been commissioned a colonel at the age of four and promoted to brigadier general at nine; in 1953 the Escuadrón de Caza "Ramfis" was created within the air force under the command of twenty-four-year-old Lieutenant General Ramfis Trujillo; in 1958 he was head of the Dominican air force. Ramfis failed a U.S. Army Command and General Staff college course at Fort Leavenworth, Kansas, because he had not attended classes and, instead, had spent most of his time in Hollywood. While his wife and six children remained at home, Ramfis's lavish and public affairs with movie actresses stirred the U.S. Congress to indignation. Congressmen were disturbed in particular over the relationship between Ramfis's indiscretions and the fact that he was in the United States ostensibly for a program being financed through foreign aid. The Dominican ambassador in Washington protested the attacks in a telegram to Congress explaining that Ramfis was not spending foreign aid money on his spree, that he received a monthly allowance of fifty thousand dollars from his father, and that, anyway, he was buying American. The Trujillos were defended in the House on 18 June 1958, by Representative Overton Brooks (D-La.), who referred to the Dominican Republic as the "bulwark which has protected our southeastern sea frontier from atheistic communism." The Dominican Republic objected specifically, Brooks said, to attacks on Ramfis, "who is the highest military authority in his country and who, in the past few months has shown a propension [*sic*] to carry on a friendship with and associate himself with the highest circles of society existing on our West Coast."[65]

At the time of the "Ramfis imbroglio," another comic-opera incident occurred. A Dominican senator, in a speech to his colleagues, complained about the lack of U.S. appreciation for his country's "fullest cooperation" and "unquestionable friendship." Distressed that the U.S. Congress had been hostile toward the Dominican Republic with respect to the military aid program, the senator said: "In that hundred million dollar project our country is assigned the small amount of $600,000 to be invested in the United States itself for the purchase of equipment that is to be employed solely in the interest of the United States and of its program for collective security." He then presented a draft resolution, unanimously approved by Trujillo's rubber-stamp National Congress on 18 June 1958, terminating the Mutual Defense Agreement, the Atlantic Missile Range Agreement, and several other conventions. A short time later, Senators James Eastland (D-Miss.) and William E. Jenner (R-Ind.) traveled to Ciudad Trujillo and spoke before a joint session of the Dominican Congress in which they fulsomely praised Trujillo. In response, the Dominican Congress rescinded the resolution terminating the agreements.[66]

In 1958 other senators had joined the fray. Wayne Morse (D-Ore.) "deplored a military program of the United States for the benefit of dictators in South America [*sic*] such as Trujillo." William J. Proxmire (D-Wis.) offered an amendment to the Mutual Security Act that would specifically prohibit aid to the Dominican Republic. Referring to the opinion that "if we refuse to give military assistance to the Dominican Republic, we may compromise the long-range missile proving ground," Proxmire said, "I happen to think that would be well worthwhile." Joseph Clark (D-Pa.)

characterized himself as a pragmatist who was unwilling to take the same chances with U.S. security as Proxmire. Theodore Francis Green (D-R.I.) felt that the Proxmire amendment was based on misconceptions: first, that to furnish aid meant that the United States approved of the recipient country's government in power; and second, that if aid were cut off, such action would bring about desirable changes in the country so deprived. Green noted that aid to the Dominican Republic had always been small and that stopping it would probably make little difference but would precipitate a hostile reaction.[67]

The Dominican debate recommenced with the coincidental passage of the Sugar Act Extension of 1961 with its specific denial of benefits to the Dominican Republic and Premier Fidel Castro's 1 May 1961 statement in which he described Cuba as a "Socialist Republic." Concern developed in certain quarters over the possibility that Cuban communism might attempt to gain control in the Dominican Republic. For example, Representative W. R. Poage (D-Tex.) deplored the fact that the Sugar Act was "designed to be used as an instrumentality of power in foreign relations" involving discriminatory treatment of the Dominican Republic. He feared that if the Trujillo government were overthrown it would be succeeded either by "the direct agents of Mr. Castro or a Castro-type communist government." If not overthrown, he argued, Trujillo could not be expected to accept the abuse and continue to maintain his strong anticommunist position.[68] Representative Cooley was quoted as saying that he "hated like hell to see a country trying to be friendly get kicked in the teeth," especially since Trujillo was not the only dictator sharing in the sugar quota.[69] The *New York Times* reported that, in a letter to Trujillo dated 21 April 1960, Senator Johnston of South Carolina suggested that Trujillo enlist the American Legion's support to achieve a better public image for the Dominican Republic in the United States. An improved image, he believed, would help the Dominicans win a larger sugar quota in the United States market. Almost four years later, in December 1963, the *New York Times* reported that Senator Johnston "emphasized his belief that his advice to the Dominican government in 1960 was completely justified." He was quoted as saying:

"Let me tell you one thing. That Government down there was anti-Communist to the core, more so than I've ever seen."[70]

Trujillo's Response

With the August 1960 OAS decision on sanctions and related independent U.S. actions, Trujillo faced the biggest threat of his thirty years as absolute ruler of the Dominican Republic. His problems were compounded by the additional external threats posed by Cuba and Dominican exiles, the internal economic distress caused by three years of drought, low market prices for Dominican exports, and the decreased tourist trade. The series of exile invasions that occurred in 1959 had led Trujillo to increase domestic repression. In addition, his increased military expenditures contributed greatly to a worsening economic crisis. Many Dominicans were consequently disaffected, among them certain government officials, military officers, and members of the Catholic church.

Trujillo announced that he and his entire family were retiring from public life. Brother Héctor Bienvenido Trujillo resigned as president, allegedly because of ill-health. Son Ramfis Trujillo resigned the chairmanship of the combined chiefs of staff and left for Geneva. Vice President Joaquín Balaguer was brought in as president, ostensibly to "democratize" the country, but in reality he ruled as a figurehead for Trujillo. The government "encouraged" the opposition to participate in elections announced for the coming year and promised a general amnesty for political prisoners. Trujillo had resorted to democratic masquerades before, however. Secretary of State Herter understated the generally skeptical view of most observers when he remarked at a press conference that it was not clear whether the new changes were ones of real substance or were simply a reshuffling of the same old regime.[71]

In 1960, in the months before the OAS voted sanctions against his government, Trujillo threatened to align with the Communist world in response to the U.S. and Latin American rejection of his regime. Early that year Trujillo offered détente to Fidel Castro, his previous *bête noire*, with little response from the latter. La Voz Dominicana and Radio Caribe stopped their broadcasts castigating Castro and began attacking the United States in Marxian terms. In June, the same month Trujillo attempted to kill the president of Venezuela, the Dominican Communist party was legalized.

Trujillo also attempted to establish contacts and relations with the Soviet bloc. Sympathetic gestures were made toward Premier Nikita Khrushchev, and Dominican emissaries were sent to Moscow. Trujillo was ignored, however, and in September 1961, four months after he was killed, the Soviet Union initiated a move in the United Nations Security Council to endorse the OAS anti-Trujillo sanctions under Article 53 of the UN Charter. The Soviet resolution was dropped, however, and the Security Council voted instead to "take note" of the OAS measures. The Soviet objective in requesting Security Council approval of the OAS action against the Dominican Republic was to establish the Security Council's competence in regional enforcement actions. Legal and political implications related to the unsuccessful Soviet move were that the Soviet Union would have been able to cast its veto in preventing regional enforcement actions, thus establishing a precedent for Soviet opposition in the eventuality of OAS sanctions against Cuba.[72] In sum, Trujillo's cynical flirtation with communism and the Soviet Union, if designed as a tactic to intimidate the United States and the OAS, failed.[73]

5 The Post-Trujillo Aftermath, 1961–1966

Trujillo's assassination introduced a new element in U.S.-Dominican relations involving problems resulting from the aftermath of dictatorship. The United States and the Organization of American States (OAS) made attempts to influence events in the Dominican Republic from the death of Trujillo in 1961 through the Dominican elections of 1966. They were heavily involved in guiding the political direction of the Dominican Republic through a difficult five-year transition period culminating in civil war and foreign military intervention. Then OAS-sponsored elections ushered in a new era of Dominican politics and U.S. policies based on nascent Dominican democracy.

The End of Rafael Trujillo

On 30 May 1961 Trujillo's thirty-one-year dictatorship came to an end with his assassination. The United States, which by then considered Trujillo a liability and the major impediment to a democratic transition, played a role in the killing. The Dominican conspirators (about thirty in the "action" and "political" groups) were all former Trujillo associates in the armed forces, government, and business. Their motives ranged from patriotism, political ambition, and greed to revenge (Trujillo had ordered the execution of the brother of one of them, and the brother of another had been sentenced to a long prison term).

The roots of the plot dated from Trujillo's murder of Jesús de Galíndez. Trujillo ordered the execution of a "suspect" falsely charged with the crime. This man's brother, Antonio de la Maza, initiated the plan to kill Trujillo. The Central Intelligence Agency (CIA) then encouraged, organized, and planned the assassination, promising to provide automatic rifles. A U.S. citizen living in the country became the leading intermediary, and much of the U.S. business community was supportive. The plan involved three phases. The first was the assassination by an eight-member "action group" led by Antonio Imbert Barrera, former governor of Puerto Plata province. The second was the elimination of the members of Trujillo's family in the Dominican Republic and prevention of those abroad from returning, the responsibility of the "political group" led by Luís Amiama Tió, a businessman and former mayor of Ciudad Trujillo with whom U.S. diplomats had established contact. The third phase would be the formation of a provisional government, which the United States would recognize, and announcement of the holding of elections.

In late 1960 the CIA provided the rifles as promised. Some months later, however, after the disastrous failure in April 1961 of the U.S.-sponsored Cuban-exile invasion of Cuba at the Bay of Pigs, the United States urged that the plan to assassinate Trujillo be postponed. But the Dominican participants refused and proceeded as planned. On the night of 30 May, the action group waylaid Trujillo in his chauffeured car and shot him to death. But the second phase was a botched affair. Trujillo's three sons took immediate action—one took over command of the armed forces and the other two hurriedly returned from Paris—and managed to retain control of the state. They rounded up and killed all of the plotters except Amiama Tió and Imbert.[1]

Policy Problems in the Aftermath of Dictatorship

Trujillism did not end with the demise of Trujillo.[2] The attempt by Dominicans to deal with that continuing phenomenon presented policy dilemmas for the United States and was the major factor contributing to the civil war and intervention of 1965. Dominicans struggled to move from dictatorship to something else. Between 1961 and 1965 they were governed by an interim president who was forced to resign, a council of state, an elected president who was overthrown by the armed forces, and another council of state that evolved into a government whose overthrow precipitated civil war. The United States intervened militarily in April 1965, with a contingent body that was converted into an inter-American peace force. A provisional government subsequently was established, and elections were held in 1966. In that year, a president was inaugurated and foreign troops withdrawn.

After Trujillo's assassination the general U.S. policy was to assist democratic elements in the Dominican Republic and to oppose strongly any attempts to reestablish dictatorship or begin a Cuban-inspired revolution. Trujillo's death occurred shortly after President Kennedy's proposal of the Alliance for Progress, which was subsequently adopted by the Inter-American System. Consistent with the alliance's goals, the United States sought to steer a course between the dictatorial right and the revolutionary left by promoting representative democracy and programs of moderate social reform.[3]

During this period, the United States emphasized economic and military factors over political and social ones in its development policies toward the Dominican Republic. The nature of U.S. assistance indicated an overwhelming economic bias. The United States had made some aid available to Trujillo but had generally been content with the order and stability of his regime and considered the country "safe" in the Cold War. The magnitude of assistance increased once the Kennedy administration decided to use the Dominican Republic to validate the economic, political, and social assumptions of the Alliance for Progress after Trujillo's demise. The total amount of post-Trujillo economic aid through 30 June 1969 was approximately $175 million. The need to change the Dominican milieu as a prerequisite for development of civilian-controlled armed forces was rejected. The United States concluded it was in no position to take on the Dominican army and purge it; the alternative was to seek change through military professional and technical training in the belief or hope that the Dominican military establishment would be part of the transformation of the Dominican political system and the mitigation of its chronic economic and social problems.

The Dominican experience supports the arguments that the United States in the Alliance for Progress confused the relationship between economics and politics in national development and that it naively assumed that it could either export or enforce a U.S. style of liberal democracy. The United States attempted to use economic and technical assistance to fill the vacuum of political underdevelopment attributable to Trujillo; economic improvement was assumed to be the key to democratic political advancement. These programs made a contribution to economic development but they could not compensate for political underdevelopment.

Post-Trujillo Politics

The most urgent political questions in the Dominican Republic following Trujillo's death had to do with problems of succession. Trujillo's heirs said they would try to bring about the gradual development of democracy and respect the civil rights of Dominican citizens. Since they were being pressured by continuing OAS sanctions and a great deal of international attention, they relaxed certain aspects of governmental control and sent a few Trujillo associates into exile, including the dead dictator's brothers, Army Generals Arismendi and Héctor Trujillo. The government promised amnesty for all political prisoners, a safe return for exiles, and free elections in 1962. The relatively efficient police-state apparatus was not dismantled, however. Ramfis Trujillo publicly disavowed any political ambitions but did not give up his control of the armed forces. After a surprisingly calm six-week period following Trujillo's death, violent opposition to the government commenced, triggered primarily by returning exiles and students. Students at the politicized Universidad Autónoma de Santo Domingo, the only public university, opposed Balaguer, the *golpistas* that overthrew Bosch, Reid Cabral, the Loyalists during the civil war, and the U.S. intervention. President Joaquín Balaguer and Ramfis Trujillo encountered increasing demands that the president resign and all members of the Trujillo family leave the country.

A principal issue was whether the sanctions imposed by the OAS against the Trujillo regime in 1960 should be continued. In fact, the successor government's protestations were largely aimed at impressing on OAS members, especially the United States, that the sanctions should be lifted. Prior to the dictator's assassination, in September 1960, the Council of the Organization of American States (COAS) had appointed a special committee to observe the effects of the sanctions and make recommendations concerning their continuation. The special committee met on 2 June 1961, three days after Trujillo's death and decided to send a fact-finding subcommittee to the Dominican Republic. The subcommittee was composed of representatives from Colombia, Panama, the United States, and Uruguay. They visited the Dominican Republic from 7 to 15 June; their subsequent report on 2 July observed the following: (1) no substantial change had taken place in the character and policies of the Dominican government; (2) Dominican officials implicated in the attempt on the life of the president of Venezuela on 24 June 1960 continued to hold positions in the government; (3) Dominican officials who issued the diplomatic passports used by Venezuelans participating in the April 1960 military uprising in San Cristóbal, Venezuela, also remained in the government; (4) the General Amnesty Law was not being applied in an effective way; (5) repressive acts continued against Dominican citizens; and (6) the fate of numerous Dominican citizens was not known. The report noted the Dominican government's declaration of intentions regarding democratic progress but said it was too early "to determine the degree of change that may have occurred in the character and policies of the Dominican Government." The subcommittee recommended continued observation of Dominican activities, and the sanctions remained in effect.[4]

The COAS subcommittee returned to the Dominican Republic in response to President Balaguer's 13 July letter indicating his government's willingness to cooperate "to bring about the discontinuation" of OAS sanctions and welcoming another visit. Riots greeted the subcommittee's arrival on 12 September. The now-active political opposition did not want the sanctions lifted until concessions had been won from the government. They feared their removal would strengthen the government to the point that the opposition would again be throttled. President Balaguer, on the other hand, claimed the sanctions had hurt the nation severely and warned that his government might be replaced by a communist dictatorship if they were continued. He no doubt also wanted to restore Dominican eligibility for U.S. financial aid or expansion of its sugar quota, prohibited while the sanctions remained in force. Balaguer stated his case on 2 October during a visit to the United Nations. In a remarkable speech, he enumerated Trujillo's crimes, including the assassination attempt against President Betancourt of Venezuela in June 1960. "But," he said, "it is not fair that the punishment should continue after the death of the culprit."

The subcommittee departed the Dominican Republic on 1 October and presented its second report to the special committee on 10 November. It again noted the gap between the government's claims of progress and its opponents' charges of continued violations. After acknowledging a limited amount of progress in the "program of democratization" and a degree of change since its last report, the subcommittee concluded that "greater progress than that which has been attained so far should be evidenced before the conclusion can be reached that the Dominican Government has ceased to be a danger to the peace and security of the Continent." They again recommended continued observation.[5]

The Inter-American Commission on Human Rights (IACHR) was also active in the Dominican situation. From its creation in October 1960 through early 1961, the IACHR had received an increasing number of complaints from Dominicans concerning the violation of human rights by the Trujillo government. In April 1961, the month prior to Trujillo's assassination, the commission had begun preparing a document on human rights in the Dominican Republic, which it completed about four months after Trujillo's death (in September 1961).[6] The IACHR visited the Dominican Republic from 22 to 28 October to investigate the continuing complaints of official human rights violations. The Dominican government had agreed to the visit but asked that the study be limited to events occurring after the Trujillo assassination. Based on the fact-finding tour, the commission sent a note to the Balaguer government on 8 November stating that the principal violators of human rights were groups of *paleros* ("stick men") whom Balaguer himself had publicly denounced. The note charged that the police and army had failed to take action against the *paleros* and criticized the public forces for their own excesses during the political disorders and student riots. The note cited the lack of freedom of speech and expression, the denial of freedom for the labor movement, and the mass deportations. It also said that the most flagrant violations of human rights had occurred during the Trujillo regime, that the situation had improved under Balaguer, and that since the start of 1962 the IACHR had received no complaints of human rights violations.[7]

During the post-Trujillo period the United States became increasingly but still cautiously sympathetic toward the Balaguer government. After an initial period of reserve during which the Kennedy administration warned the OAS against haste in lifting the sanctions, it adopted a more conciliatory approach. At a news conference on 22 August 1961, Secretary of State Dean Rusk said that the United States regarded many of the moves toward Dominican democratization as "highly constructive."[8] On 14 November the State Department recommended to the OAS that some of the sanctions be lifted as a "gesture of encouragement" in view of the Dominican government's recent steps toward democracy.[9] The following day the proposal was withdrawn, however, because the two Trujillo brothers had returned to the Dominican Republic.

A brief but dramatic power struggle occurred in November 1961 in which some members of the Trujillo family attempted to regain control of the Dominican Republic. Generals Arismendi and Héctor Trujillo returned to the Dominican Republic from their "vacations" abroad and attempted to reimpose the dictatorship. Their nephew Ramfis Trujillo resigned his military position and fled. At a press conference on 18 November, Secretary Rusk bluntly stated that the United States would not permit the Trujillo family to regain power and was considering "further measures" to safeguard recent Dominican progress toward democracy.[10] The next day a U.S. naval task force of eight vessels with 1,800 marines aboard approached within three miles of the Dominican coast, in view of the capital.[11] The anti-Trujillo opposition mobilized; certain military elements opposed to a Trujillo takeover rallied behind Balaguer. Most important was the air force, led by Major General Pedro Rafael Rodríguez Echavarría. As a result of the combined external and internal pressure, the Trujillo brothers, with twenty-seven other members of the Trujillo family and a number of associates, fled the country. Thus the United States was instrumental in affecting Dominican politics by using the old method of threatening armed intervention.

Balaguer now found himself in a shaky position. The major opposition groups had supported him against the Trujillos but had not intended that he remain in office. Balaguer carried the stigma of being the Trujillo-picked president, and now that the last of the family had left he was politically unacceptable. The opposition parties also disputed the continued presence of General Rodríguez, who had supported Balaguer during the attempted coup and been rewarded with the appointment of secretary of state for the armed forces. Disorders and violence mounted, aimed at dislodging Balaguer, who declared a state of emergency.[12] At this time the removal began of virtually all statues of the slain dictator throughout the country. The capital city was renamed Santo Domingo (its name until 1936). Trujillo's body was removed from Santo Domingo and flown to Ramfis in Paris for burial. Finally, on 17 December 1961, in response to the demands of opposition groups and with U.S. and OAS assistance, a provisional government was established in the form of a seven-member council of state headed by Balaguer. He agreed that when the OAS terminated its sanctions he would resign from the council and that another member, Dr. Rafael Francisco Bonnelly, would become president. General elections were promised by late 1962. President Kennedy commended the "impressive demonstration of statesmanship and responsibility by all concerned" and promised to support the prompt lifting of sanctions.

The day after the last of the Trujillos had departed, the OAS subcommittee returned to the Dominican Republic for a third visit, from 20 to 26 November. Their subsequent report recommended that the sanctions be lifted.[13] On 4 January 1962, seventeen months after they had been imposed and seven months after the dictator's death, the OAS terminated all sanctions. On 6 January the United States resumed bilateral diplomatic relations, and on 11 January the two governments signed an agreement providing for economic aid and a Peace Corps mission.[14] The United States also worked through the OAS in an attempt to reorient certain basic institutions in the Dominican Republic, primarily the military forces, in keeping with the policy goals of the Kennedy administration.

The positive developments were briefly interrupted when a *golpe de estado* was attempted. On the night of 17 January, General Rodríguez Echavarría staged a bloodless coup and led a short-lived military-civilian junta that replaced the council of state. The U.S. government voiced official dismay but this time did not send a fleet to Dominican waters. No OAS action was proposed, although the organization did halt its steps toward renewal of aid and trade. The junta did not survive, however, because the rest of the Dominican armed forces rallied in support of the ruling council.[15] Only forty-eight hours after the coup, the junta fell to the council it had just overthrown. Rodríguez Echavarría and four of his fellow junta members were arrested by air force officers, and the council of state was restored with Rafael Bonnelly as president. Both Rodríguez and Balaguer were sent into exile. On 17 February the United States and the Dominican Republic signed an agreement giving the latter a twenty-year credit of twenty-five million dollars at a rate of three-fourths of one percent. John Bartlow Martin, who had undertaken a special Dominican study mission for President Kennedy in September 1961, was accredited as ambassador in March 1962.

The council of state served as the provisional government until February 1963. During this time the problem of the Dominican sugar quota was resolved. In January 1962, the U.S. Congress had temporarily assigned an additional amount to the basic quota as assistance to the newly established council of state for its "transition to democracy." But under the new Sugar Act of 30 June 1962, the Dominican quota was reduced and no additional "Cuban windfall" was granted. The Dominicans protested that any decrease would interrupt their democratic progress. On 5 July the U.S. Congress approved an amendment to give an extra allotment to several Latin American countries, including an award of considerable tonnage for the Dominican Republic.

The 1962 Elections and the Bosch Presidency

The council of state made preparations for the elections scheduled for December 1962. An extensive campaign instructed Dominican citizens in their voting rights. Eight political parties representing the political spectrum from left to right campaigned for the presidency and seats in the National Assembly. The main contenders were the *Partido Revolucionario Dominicano* (Dominican Revolutionary Party—PRD) to the left of center and the *Unión Cívica Nacional* (National Civic Union—UCN) to the right of center.

Juan Bosch was the PRD's head and presidential candidate. A leading Dominican literary figure and long-time foe of the late Trujillo, Bosch had been in exile for twenty-five years in several Latin American states until his return to the Dominican Republic in October 1961.[16] He had helped form the PRD in 1939 while in exile. Bosch stood for what he referred to as "democratic leftism" and based his campaign on change, promising land reform for *campesinos* and pledging nationalization of foreign property and business. Viriato Alberto Fiallo, a country physician, was the UCN's presidential nominee. He had remained in the Dominican Republic during the Trujillo era and led a clandestine movement against the generalissimo. Fiallo had participated in formation of the UCN, which drew its major support from landowners, shopkeepers, and professional people. Both candidates were friendly to the United States; the Kennedy administration pledged to support whomever won the election.

In late November, the month before the elections, the Dominican representative to the COAS requested that the OAS secretary-general select a group of distinguished American educators, jurists, and publicists to come to the Dominican Republic for the dual purpose of participating in a symposium on democracy and observing the national elections.

The secretary-general selected forty-six persons to be participants and observers, representing all of the American states (except Cuba, Haiti, and Mexico), plus the OAS, the Technical Assistance Mission, and the Inter-American Development Bank. The United States was represented by thirteen individuals.[17]

On 2 December 1962, some nineteen months after Trujillo's assassination, OAS-supervised national elections were held. More than one million Dominicans, almost 70 percent of the electorate, went to the polls. This first free and honest election since 1924 resulted in the choice of Juan Bosch as president by a two-to-one margin over Viriato Fiallo, and a solid majority for the PRD in the national assembly. Bosch was inaugurated on 27 February 1963.

Shortly after the inauguration, another chapter was written in the long record of animosity between the Dominican Republic and Haiti, ruled with an iron hand by François "Papa Doc" Duvalier. In late April 1963, Duvalier's police broke into the Dominican embassy in Port-au-Prince to search for antigovernment Haitians who had been granted asylum after Haiti had refused to grant them safe-conduct passes. This incident was the first time Haitian police had violated the extraterritoriality of a diplomatic mission in order to arrest political refugees. The situation was further complicated by the presence in Haiti of certain members of the Trujillo family and by rumors that they were plotting with Duvalier to assassinate Bosch.[18]

The Dominican Navy put to sea, and tanks and troops moved to the border. Bosch publicly called Duvalier a mad tyrant and on 28 April issued an ultimatum threatening to use force against Haiti if the situation were not "rectified" within twenty-four hours. On the same day, the Dominican representative at the OAS charged Haiti with threatening the peace of the hemisphere. He presented ten specific charges against the Haitian government. The OAS persuaded the Bosch administration to extend its ultimatum for twelve hours until it could investigate; it immediately sent a fact-finding mission.[19]

In the face of the Dominican show of naval and military power, as well as a Venezuelan pledge of military support for the Dominican Republic and the U.S. stationing of naval units offshore ("to evacuate nationals"), the Haitian government announced its compliance with Dominican demands. Duvalier allowed the Haitian political prisoners to leave, thus ending the three-week imbroglio.

Bosch had encountered both internal and international problems almost from the day he took office; the former were largely attributable to the Trujillo legacy. Although a dedicated and honest man, Bosch was a poor organizer and an uncompromising idealist. He offended one group after another. He lost the backing of many supporters because he was unable to fulfill his reform commitments to them. He angered conservative critics because he made only limited efforts to compromise with them, although it must be said that those who opposed him were intransigent and refused to cooperate with him from the very beginning. Bosch's final undoing was alienating the armed forces by permitting extreme leftists to return from exile and failing to take a strong anticommunist stand, used especially as a pretext by his opponents for their actions against him. Unfounded rumors that Bosch was creating his own rival military force increased the military's fear and suspicion.[20]

Finally, at dawn on 25 September 1963, a widely predicted coup overthrew Bosch, after only seven months in office, and dissolved the National Assembly. The coup was led by the army and backed by rightist groups. The prime mover was General Elías Wessin y Wessin, commander of the San Isidro air base garrison, who had helped exile the Trujillo family in late 1961. The rationale for the coup was Bosch's "softness on communism" and his responsibility for "plunging the country into chaos." Two days after the coup the Dominican military chiefs set up a conservative three-member civilian provisional government, although the armed forces had real power. Bosch left the Dominican Republic for exile on 29 September 1963. Thus ended in disappointment and failure the Dominican democratic experiment conducted by the United States and the OAS.

In response to the overthrow of President Bosch, the United States severed diplomatic relations, withheld recognition of the new government, suspended all assistance, and recalled almost all its personnel. The governing junta, after expressing interest in reestablishing relations and the resumption of economic assistance, broadened its political base and scheduled elections for 1965. In mid-December 1963, the new Johnson administration recognized the junta and three months later sent a new ambassador, William Tapley Bennett Jr. In January 1964, the United States resumed its economic and military programs.

Donald Reid Cabral, an automobile dealer who had served in the council of state, emerged as president of the junta and as the dominant figure in government. He pursued an austerity program and attempted to stabilize the regime. The United States supported the Reid government; it was pleased with the Dominican leader's apparent willingness to institute certain reforms in the armed forces.

Military Affairs

A key element during this period was the changing nature of the Dominican armed forces in politics and the U.S. policies aimed at dealing with them. The Kennedy and Johnson administrations both attempted to develop the Dominican National Police as an effective apolitical law-and-order force and simultaneously to "de-Trujillize" the armed forces, particularly the army, and convert them from their traditional role as a political-military force.[21] The United States believed that it could have an impact on the police force, perhaps even remake it, but realized its influence on the army was limited. As part of this plan the National Police was granted autonomy, separated from the Ministry of Defense, and placed in the Ministry of the Interior. The force's size was increased so as better to control the streets and more effectively stabilize emergency situations. (After the rioting in late 1961 and early 1962, during which the National Police had lost control of the streets in downtown Santo Domingo, two Spanish-speaking detectives from the Los Angeles Police Department had been sent to the Dominican Republic to train the police in riot control and investigative and communications procedures.)[22] U.S. military aid programs concentrated on training the police in riot prevention and control. These steps were accompanied by attempts to neutralize the political role of the armed forces by reducing their size (particularly the army), improving their professional competence, and training them in civic action and counterinsurgency.

The United States found it could do little with the armed services, either through de-Trujillization or reduction in size. No meaningful distinction could be drawn between the *trujilloistas* and the non-*trujilloistas*, since the dictator had compromised almost everyone. The council of state already had enough problems to deal with and was unwilling to cut the military budget, a move that it felt could increase the risk of a coup. As a result, the United States attempted to transform the nature of Dominican military services by stressing training and improving professional competence. Its efforts along these lines were not extensive during 1962 and did not assume meaningful proportions until late 1963 and 1964. In March 1962, for example, the U.S. Military Assistance Advisory Group (MAAG), which had been closed in February 1960, was reopened but with only five members. An agreement was signed that same month providing for military assistance "either for the purpose of internal security requirements or for the purpose of defense missions which are important to the maintenance of peace and security in the Western Hemisphere." The agreement did not become effective until June 1964.[23]

President Bosch's inauguration in February 1963 stimulated an acceleration of U.S. military, economic, and technical assistance. The Kennedy administration decided to use the Dominican Republic to prove the methodology of the Alliance for Progress. The Bosch administration represented a constitutional and legitimate government dedicated to change and reform and had come to power soon after the end of an all-pervasive dictatorship. In the military area, the MAAG increased its strength from five members to forty-five and provided for increased equipment, parts, and supplies. More civic action projects were undertaken. Greater numbers of Dominican military personnel were sent to the Canal Zone and the United States for professional and technical training. The United States increased assistance to the National Police, such as sending an AID-sponsored public safety team to provide training.

President Bosch had his own ideas, however. He distrusted the National Police and feared its growing power and effectiveness, sharing the general populace's view of the police as Trujillo's gestapo. Shortly after coming to office, Bosch cut off National Police funds, a move that the United States saw as undermining its training program.[24] Bosch was cautious toward the armed forces, however, not willing to reduce their budget and size or retire some of the old-line Trujillo holdovers as the United States wished, although he was able to reduce some graft and corruption at the upper echelons. Bosch supported civic action efforts but saw little need for counterinsurgency programs.

Donald Reid Cabral's efforts to reform the armed forces involved limiting their exorbitant fringe benefits and smuggling monopoly, forcing out certain old-line officers, and cutting the military budget. The military assistance agreement that had been signed in 1962 became effective in June 1964 and the MAAG was reopened. The civic action program that had been initiated in October 1964 was resumed. Reid cooperated with the United States by stressing counterinsurgency training and sending an increasing number of Dominicans to receive training in the United States, and Mobile Training Teams from Fort Bragg supervised related programs in the Dominican Republic.[25]

The military reforms, modest as they were from the U.S. point of view, caused increasing dissension in the armed forces. Senior old-guard army officers, the "San Cristóbal group" who bore the brunt of reform, wanted to oust Reid and recall Balaguer from exile. An opposing group of young officers interested in some reform and their own advancement complained that the retirement of old-line Trujillist officers was not proceeding rapidly enough. The younger contingent also favored removing Reid but desired the return of Bosch and the PRD. The stage was set for violent conflict.

The 1965 Civil War and U.S. Intervention

On 24 April 1965 the pro-Bosch army faction staged a coup that turned into civil war.[26] This group referred to itself as "Constitutionalist" because it favored Bosch's return to complete his term of office as president; its opponents called it the "Rebel" faction. Supported by a few defecting military units, mainly from the army, and by thousands of civilians in Santo Domingo, it removed Reid from office. The Constitutionalists were first headed by José Rafael Molina of the PRD, who had been Bosch's vice president and next in line of succession; he was replaced within a few days by Colonel Francisco Caamaño Deñó, after U.S. Ambassador Bennett refused the Constitutionalists' request to mediate a cease-fire. The opposing faction preferred the designation "Loyalist" on account of its allegiance to the deposed government, although, in fact, it did not support Reid but advocated Balaguer's reinstatement; its primary goal was preventing Bosch's return.[27] Its opponents referred to it as the "Military" group because it had the backing of most of the armed forces and the National Police. General Antonio Imbert, who had participated in the assassination of Trujillo (by which he had acquired his military rank), emerged as head of the Loyalists.

The alignments in the civil war reflected the economic, political, and social divisions in Dominican society, which explain attitudes toward the U.S. intervention. The Constitutionalists included members of Bosch's PRD and had the support of other leftist parties, students, urban workers, labor unions, small farmers, the poor, and some members of the middle class. The Loyalists included the majority of the regular and traditional military with the backing and sympathy of the elite, the wealthy, the business community, large farmers, and many members of the middle class. The Constitutionalists and their supporters opposed U.S. intervention, which they viewed as preventing the success of their revolution. The Loyalists strongly favored U.S. intervention—in fact, they requested it to assure their control. While not all of their economic and social backers preferred such U.S. action, they agreed that under the circumstances it was a short-run necessity.

The days following the coup and before the landing of U.S. troops were full of turmoil and uncertainty, with both sides in the conflict appealing to the U.S. government and Ambassador Bennett for support. First the Reid government, and then the Loyalist leadership, requested U.S. intervention in order to forestall what they called a communist plot. The United States helped to set up a three-member military junta as the "legal" body representing the Loyalists. Mr. Molina and Colonel Caamaño, representing the Constitutionalists, asked Ambassador Bennett to mediate, a task that he refused to undertake. The military junta lodged another request for U.S. intervention. During this time civilians supporting the Constitutionalists acquired arms that they captured from the National Police arsenal. This incident was the first time since the military occupation of 1916–24 that a sizeable number of civilians were armed, an unthinkable situation during the Trujillo era. The populace turned on the National Police, symbol of the Trujillo legacy, and vented their hatred by beating and killing many police. Dominican Air Force planes from the San Isidro air base strafed the National Palace, which had been taken over by the Constitutionalists during negotiations between the opposing factions, galvanizing the Constitutionalists to action and resulting in a rapid polarization of the opponents. Military advantage fluctuated between the two sides, as first one and then the other seemed to gain the upper hand in the streets.[28] The United States then decided to intervene militarily when it appeared that the Constitutionalists would win. Intervention began on the evening of 28 April 1965, with the landing of 405 Marines. Two days later, army troops began arriving and the complement of personnel ultimately reached a high of about twenty-three thousand ashore. General Bruce Palmer Jr. was placed in command of the operation.

The U.S. intervention consisted of two phases, each having its own justification. The first phase was the landing of marines justified as protection of U.S. nationals; the second phase was the increasing complement of troops explained as prevention of a communist takeover. The first rationale was soon transcended by the second. President Johnson's press release on 28 April stated that Dominican authorities had requested military assistance since they could not guarantee the safety of U.S. citizens. Two days later he noted a changing situation; in a national broadcast he referred to "signs that people trained outside the Dominican Republic are seeking to gain control." Then on 2 May, in another address to the nation, he declared that communist leaders, many of them trained in Cuba, had joined the revolution and were taking more and more control. He lamented that "what began as a popular democratic revolution" had been "seized and placed into the hands of a band of Communist conspirators." Now the U.S. goal was "to help prevent another Communist state in this hemisphere."[29] General Palmer later said that the decision to intervene was "the president's personal decision" because all civilian advisers and his only military adviser "had recommended against immediate intervention." As U.S. commander, Palmer said, "My stated mission was to protect American lives and property; my unstated mission was to prevent another Cuba and, at the same time, to avoid another situation like that in Vietnam."[30]

Although President Johnson's public rationale for intervening was associated with the Cuban threat, domestic political concerns were also evident, linked to his own reelection and the Democratic Party's continuing control of Congress. It was also related to demonstrating U.S. resolve against North Vietnam.[31] Efforts by Ambassador Bennett and his staff to document the number of Communists among the Constitutionalists failed to yield convincing support for the U.S. claim. A number of analysts found little credible evidence supporting the fear of "a second Cuba" resulting from victory by the Constitutionalists and other supporters of Juan Bosch.[32] Some of them said that the United States was caught up in its decision-makers' paranoia about communism and Cuba. This statement applied especially to Ambassador Bennett and certain of his advisors in the Dominican Republic, including the U.S. military attachés who were influenced by their Dominican counterparts.[33] The majority of Dominicans were antagonized by the intervention and felt it prevented the democratic revolution and maintained the political status quo. They viewed the action as a clear-cut violation of international law: a violation of Dominican sovereignty and of the principle of nonintervention emphasized in the OAS charter and other treaties in the Inter-American System. The significant minority included the traditional military, the elite, and much of the business community.

The response to the intervention in the United States was a general endorsement of President Johnson's policies by public opinion, most members of Congress, and conservative correspondents and periodicals. In opposition were a few Congressmen, most academic specialists on Latin America, a few prominent international lawyers, and correspondents and periodicals of a liberal orientation. Among the latter, a group of 103 "Latin American Specialists" sent a letter to President

Johnson opposing the intervention on the grounds that it violated the non-intervention principle in articles 15 and 17 of the OAS charter, contradicted the traditions of President Roosevelt's Good Neighbor Policy and President Kennedy's Alliance for Progress, and antagonized Latin America's "democratic forces."[34]

While most members of Congress supported the second phase of the intervention without OAS approval, three senators did not, including most significantly Senator William Fulbright (D-Ark.), chair of the Senate Foreign Relations Committee; the other two were Senators Ernest Gruening (D-Alaska) and Wayne Morse (D-Ore.). In July, Fulbright's committee began an investigation of the Dominican intervention that resulted in so much disagreement among the committee members that they decided not to issue a report; only a few committee members supported the chair's views. Senator Fulbright presented his critical analysis of the intervention in a speech on the floor of the Senate on 15 September; his strong indictment provoked anew the Dominican controversy.[35] Years later General Palmer wrote that he thought Senator Fulbright had been "particularly hard" on Ambassador Bennett, whom Palmer defended. General Palmer justified the intervention but agreed that it had a "devastating effect" on U.S.–Latin American relations; he joined the critics over the U.S. failure to consult with the OAS.[36] On 20 September the House of Representatives passed House Resolution 560 by a vote of 312 to 52 endorsing the unilateral U.S. use of force as President Johnson had explained in his 2 May speech.

The Latin American reaction to the Dominican intervention was particularly adverse. Protest was manifested in many countries through demonstrations, legislative resolutions, official statements, and critical resolutions in both the OAS and UN. The 20 September House resolution was widely criticized.

After the initial landing of marines, the United States directed its efforts toward securing the multilateral endorsement of the OAS for its unilateral action, as well as an inter-American involvement and presence in the Dominican Republic. The United States concentrated on the creation of an inter-American peace force as the instrument for these purposes. These efforts provoked great controversy since certain Latin

American states believed that the United States was manipulating the OAS and using it as a tool of U.S. policy. This belief was in keeping with the view that the United States was continuing to use the OAS as "an anti-communists alliance" as it had against Guatemala in 1954 and Cuba in the 1960s.[37] Nevertheless, an inter-American meeting was called at which the United States prevailed.

In response to the request of the Chilean ambassador to the OAS to convoke the organ of consultation of the OAS, the Tenth Meeting of Foreign Ministers began discussion of the Dominican situation on 1 May 1965. After considerable debate and U.S. diplomatic arm-twisting, on 6 May the Foreign Ministers passed a resolution creating the Inter-American Peace Force (IAPF) by the bare minimum of fourteen required votes (including that of the representative of the overthrown Dominican government). The U.S. intervention was criticized especially by Chile, Mexico, Uruguay, and Venezuela. Two other resolutions were also passed by the bare two-thirds majority: on 10 May the creation of a unified command for the IAPF and on 22 May the authorization that Brazil and the United States function as IAPF commander and deputy commander, respectively. On the basis of these resolutions, the U.S. military command was transformed into an OAS force; General Hugo Panasco Alvim of Brazil was named commanding general and General Palmer, the former U.S. commander, his deputy. With the arrival of contingents from Latin America, the United States began withdrawing some of its troops. The Latin American presence in the peace force during the summer of 1965 was essentially a token one, however; the portion of Latin American troops was small. As of 3 July they comprised the addition of 1,735 military personnel plus some policemen from six Latin American states: from Brazil, 1,115 officers and troops; from Costa Rica, 20 policemen; from El Salvador, 3 officers; from Honduras, 250 troops; from Nicaragua, 164 troops; and from Paraguay, 183 troops.[38]

Two features of the IAPF especially were subjected to criticism. First, the major Latin American contributors were military regimes (Brazil and Honduras) or personalist dictatorships (Nicaragua and Paraguay). No democratic governments made contributions except Costa Rica, which sent policemen. Second, the Latin American portion of the IAPF, of which that of Brazil constituted a large majority, constituted a small percentage of the total. On 3 July, when the Latin American complement was at a peak and the U.S. portion reduced to 10,900, the Latin American percentage was only about 14 percent. A year later, after the formation of a provisional government in the Dominican Republic, the relative Latin American proportion increased to about 30 percent as the United States reduced its contingent.

In the meantime, while the OAS was debating the creation of the IAPF, the UN Security Council, at the request of the Soviet Union, also discussed the U.S. intervention. This development of UN involvement made the U.S. strategy of working through the Inter-American System as an "anticommunist alliance" less successful than it had been in past regional situations. The United States was unable to keep the Dominican issue out of the UN and thus maintain a regional OAS *de facto* authority monopoly over inter-American crises with the UN doing little more than accepting OAS reports on them. In addition to the UN Security Council members, representatives of Cuba and the Constitutionalist and Loyalist sides from the Dominican Republic were permitted to participate. A compromise resolution was passed in mid-May authorizing the secretary-general to send a personal representative to Santo Domingo and call upon the parties there to cooperate with him. Secretary-General U Thant chose as his representative José Antonio Mayobre, executive secretary of the United Nations Economic Commission for Latin America; he also sent a party headed by his military advisor, General Indar Jit Rikhye. Thereafter Mr. Mayobre began playing a controversial role, both in competition and cooperation with the OAS and often critical of the United States, with occasional contributions from General Rikhye.[39]

Negotiations within the Dominican Republic for a settlement remained stalemated. In an attempt to break the impasse, in mid-May President Johnson sent a high-level, four-man mission composed of four officials from his administration: National Security Advisor McGeorge Bundy, Deputy Secretary of Defense Cyrus R. Vance, Assistant Secretary of State for Inter-American Affairs Thomas C. Mann, and Peace

Corps Director Jack Hood Vaughan. They proposed an interim coalition government under Bosch's former minister of agriculture, Antonio Guzmán. The proposal suited Colonel Caamaño but was opposed by General Imbert, who believed that victory was imminent and he had no need to compromise. The United States then applied economic pressure to Imbert, threatening to suspend the salary payments it had assumed for Dominican civil servants and military personnel. The pressure was ineffective, however, and General Imbert remained intractable throughout the negotiations. This aspect of the process was ironic, since the United States clearly preferred General Imbert's faction, but because of its uncompromising position, it received the brunt of U.S. pressure for a settlement.[40] General Palmer later wrote that "a major U.S. policy shift" occurred on 15 May, one of "strict neutrality" between the warring factions. He said that an aspect of the implementation of the policy, decided by Secretary Vance, was the replacement of the U.S. military attachés because they were too close to their Loyalist military counterparts.[41]

In early June the OAS sent a three-member ad hoc committee to Santo Domingo, composed of representatives from Brazil, El Salvador, and the United States (Ellsworth Bunker). The committee presented a "Declaration to the Dominican People," providing for termination of the armed struggle, formation of a provisional government, and the holding of general elections.[42] Although neither faction accepted the declaration, it served as a basis for later discussions that led to an agreement. Negotiations for a settlement continued throughout July and August; they revolved around the composition of the provisional government, particularly the nomination of a provisional president. It became clear that the only person acceptable to both sides would have to be a respected "moderate." He turned out to be Dr. Héctor García-Godoy, a businessman and diplomat who had served as Bosch's foreign minister. Once again the United States had to pressure the Loyalists to accept.

Then ensued the far more difficult task of negotiating the terms of the final acts. In early August the ad hoc committee presented a new proposal for a settlement, called the Act of Dominican Reconciliation, which provided the basis for a final accord. Several of its provisions posed problems of persisting difficulty for both the provisional president and the IAPF: those calling for the immediate "demilitarization and disarmament" of civilians in the Constitutionalist zone; ordering the armed forces to return to their barracks; specifying the reincorporation of Constitutionalist units "in the armed forces without discrimination or reprisal"; and insisting that "no officer or enlisted man of the armed forces will be submitted to court martial or subject to punishment of any kind for acts, except common crimes, committed since 23 April 1965."[43] Finally, in late August, the Act of Dominican Reconciliation was signed. In early September, somewhat more than four months after the Dominican crisis had begun and U.S. troops landed, the provisional government and President García-Godoy assumed control in preparation for holding elections in spring 1966.[44]

The final agreements leading to creation of the provisional government, its head, and the *modus operandi* were primarily attributable to the integrity, diplomatic, and negotiating skills of, and freedom of action accorded to, Ambassador Bunker. Prior to his appointment in 1951 as U.S. ambassador to Argentina, Bunker had been president of the National Sugar Refining Corporation, a leading East Coast sugar refiner. He later served as ambassador to Italy and India, and in 1964 became the U.S. ambassador to the OAS. Bunker was in his seventies when he became involved in the Dominican situation after the U.S. troops had landed. His remarkable success in negotiating the political reconciliation and provisional government was due to his extensive diplomatic experience, reputation for fairness and personal integrity, and the wide authority and discretion President Johnson gave him (Bunker reported directly to the president).[45]

During this difficult period García-Godoy's government achieved reasonable stability and survived only because of the peace force, which, among other things, served as a buffer between opposing political groups on the left and the right. For example, the IAPF stopped a major battle between the two factions in Santiago in December 1965; this last battle was the only one to occur outside of Santo Domingo. The peace force also pressured into exile some of the leading protagonists, especially General Wessin y Wessin, commander of the elite

Armed Forces Training Center, who left in September 1965; and Colonel Caamaño, who left in January 1966. One major objective of the Act of Dominican Reconciliation was not realized—the disarming of civilians and the collection of arms. Despite the assistance of the peace force, this problem was passed on to the future government. Under the circumstances the general maintenance of conditions permitting a political campaign was in itself an important achievement and a credit to the provisional government of García-Godoy.

The 1966 Campaign and Election

The backgrounds of the two major presidential nominees and the nature of their campaigns provided some interesting features. Former President Bosch was again the PRD nominee, but this time the United States was unfavorably disposed toward him, in contrast to the attitude of the Kennedy administration in the election of December 1962. U.S. officials had become increasingly critical of Bosch during the civil war because of his role outside the country and his refusal to return in order to help end the hostilities. The United States therefore preferred the election of his chief opponent. In the face of a number of threatening campaign incidents, Bosch decided to conduct his campaign from the confines and safety of his home, by way of interviews, press releases, and radio. This refusal to campaign in person throughout the country weakened his cause; he was unable to demonstrate his considerable talents as a debater and campaigner. Furthermore, his opponents accused him, apparently with effect, of cowardice in refusing to campaign in person. As the election neared, Bosch believed that the hostility against him would preclude a free election and that, if elected, he would not be permitted to assume office.

Dr. Balaguer, the nominee of the Reformist Party, had been the titular president of the country when General Trujillo was assassinated in May 1961, after which he had attempted to stabilize the situation and cooperate with the OAS in order to have its sanctions lifted. In early 1962, he had been exiled as a result of U.S. policy and pressure, for he was viewed as a part of the Trujillo legacy and an impediment to change in the Dominican Republic. Some three years later when Bosch was overthrown, senior Dominican military officers preferred Balaguer's return but the United States supported Reid Cabral. After the civil war, the United States clearly preferred the election of Balaguer. Balaguer and the Reformist Party conducted an excellent campaign throughout the country. The party was well-organized, and the candidate had a shrewd sense for the crucial issues. One successful strategy on his part was an appeal to the women's vote; he won an argument with the Election Board that women be permitted to vote even if they did not have their registration cards. He also promised to appoint a woman to be governor of each of the thirty provinces.

On 1 June 1966 the Dominican electorate went to the polls in what were generally considered to be fair and free elections observed by the OAS and the private Committee on Free Elections in the Dominican Republic. Significant irregularities and fraud did occur, although probably not enough to change the outcome. Balaguer defeated Bosch, receiving more than 56 percent of the votes cast. Bosch won only 39 percent while Rafael Bonnelly, candidate of the National Integration Movement (MIN), realized about 3 percent; the pro-Castro Fourteenth of June Movement (1J4) received less than 1 percent. Bosch carried Santo Domingo, the capital and largest city, but lost the rest of the country to Balaguer. The winner obtained the support of not only status quo groups (such as most of the business community), but a majority of the peasant vote, which had been Bosch's mainstay in 1962. Bosch again enjoyed the support of youth and students and of most urban workers, especially in Santo Domingo and on the sugar estates.[46]

In his inaugural address on 1 July 1966, President Balaguer stressed the need for national cooperation and unity in solving the country's serious problems; he announced an austerity program as one means. He discussed Dominican-U.S. relations and emphasized the need for continued U.S. economic assistance; and he requested that the Dominican sugar quota be doubled. President Balaguer announced that the national industries, particularly sugar, would be taken out of politics, and that public service employees would be prohibited from striking.

He also accented the need to eliminate corruption and graft in the bureaucracy and military services. He concluded his address by explicitly recognizing the importance of women and peasants in Dominican society.[47]

In the weeks that followed, President Balaguer began to implement his campaign promises and the policies announced in his inaugural address. His cabinet appointees, in keeping with the concept of national unity, reflected a balancing of the various positions on the Dominican political spectrum, with the exception of the far left. He kept his campaign promise and appointed women to head all the provincial governments, and a woman became secretary of labor in his cabinet. He also worked out an agreement with Bosch and the PRD about their cooperation on military reform. President Balaguer honored the agreement by replacing the head of the National Police and sending a number of officers from various military branches abroad to serve as military attachés or to pursue professional education. These measures, especially the transfer of military personnel, were made possible by the presence of the IAPF, which was recognized as a backstop to the president. Finally, in late September, the peace force, by then reduced to a strength of less than five thousand, was withdrawn at the request of Balaguer. Thus ended the sixteen-month role of the peace force, which had assured the mandate of the provisional government and the initial policies of President Balaguer.

The Political Role of UASD

At the time of the death of Trujillo, the public Universidad Autónoma de Santo Domingo (UASD) was the only university in the country. Most of the post-Trujillo political leaders had graduated from UASD during the Trujillo era (among them were Rafael Francisco Bonnelly, Donald Reid Cabral, Salvador Jorge Blanco, Jacobo Majluta, and others). UASD became politically important as the place where opinion was organized and action mobilized against the continuation of Trujillismo, and later its reestablishment. UASD was largely responsible for the departure of

Balaguer, who, as Trujillo's longtime vice president, had replaced Héctor Trujillo as president in 1960. A few months after Trujillo's assassination, UASD students rebelled, destroyed statues and other symbols of Trujillo's megalomania, and demanded the formation of a faculty-student body to govern the university. Soon after, the government approved the University Autonomy Law, giving administrative authority to the rector in consultation with the University Council, which was composed of the elected representatives of the faculty and student bodies. The smaller *Claustro* was made up of representatives of both bodies, elected to handle daily administration. After continuing agitation and the closing and reopening of the university in early 1962, the new administrative system was implemented. UASD became, through its politicized students, an important force galvanizing opposition to Balaguer. As a result of this mounting opposition, in early 1962 Balaguer took refuge in the legation of the Holy See and then went into exile in New York City. Thereafter the students functioned as "phalanxes" (*falanges*), especially leftist, of the political parties. According to Frank Moya Pons, the students enjoyed "a capacity for national mobilization" that at times threatened the government's stability. Further, he says, the impact of new ideas and ideology caused by the revolutionary turmoil in Latin America and the example of the Cuban Revolution generated "intellectual and political ferment" at UASD, which soon extended to the high schools and even to the lower grades. The student body thus became "an important variable in the Dominican political system."[48]

Most of the students at UASD were politically activist members or supporters of Bosch's PRD, and they campaigned and mobilized support for him in the December 1962 election. While Bosch was in office, they supported his policies against his many critics. When the armed forces overthrew Bosch in September 1963, the students opposed the military junta and favored the Kennedy administration's policy of nonrecognition, suspension of aid, and recall of military personnel. They insisted that the military and police respect the university's autonomy and not enter the campus. They opposed the council of state headed by Reid Cabral and the Johnson administration's recognition of him as "president." The students welcomed the pro-Bosch faction in the army that initiated a coup in April which removed Reid Cabral, and when the civil war broke out, they supported the Constitutionalist side. At the same time at UASD, a group of pro-Bosch professors and students approved a new set of bylaws governing the university, which amounted to their control of both the Council and the *Claustro*. During the civil war many students, as members of the leftist Fourteenth of June Movement and the Revolutionary Social Democratic Party in addition to the PRD, were combatants against the Loyalists and some were casualties in the fighting. They strongly opposed the U.S. intervention, which they believed prevented a Constitutionalist victory and Bosch's return. They viewed the IAPF as no more than a U.S. front. During the 1966 presidential campaign the students actively supported Bosch and strongly opposed Balaguer.

In the meantime, in 1962, the private Universidad Católica Madre y Maestra opened in Santiago de los Caballeros, intended to be an apolitical counterpoise to UASD. It had the advantage of being located almost one hundred miles northwest of Santo Domingo and removed from the site of the civil war (with the exception of a single battle). Its enrollment expanded during the civil war.

Conclusion

Let us consider the various costs of the instability and turmoil caused by the coups removing Bosch in 1963 and Reid Cabral in 1965, and by the subsequent civil war and external military intervention. The U.S. estimate of the number of those killed or missing on the Loyalist side was 825, about 500 from the armed forces and 325 from the police. Losses for the Constitutionalist military forces were around 600. The Dominican Red Cross estimated that 2,000 people were killed and 3,000 wounded, figures that included civilians and the Constitutionalist military but not the Loyalist military. Total Dominican civilian and military casualties were about 6,000. Among the U.S. forces, there were 44 deaths (27 killed in action) and 172 wounded. Among the IAPF, 6 Brazilians and 5 Paraguayans were wounded.[49]

Another dimension of the human cost were the increasing numbers of Dominicans, particularly professionals, leaving their country on account of the turmoil, coups, and war. Following Bosch's removal in 1963, the United States admitted almost eleven thousand Dominicans, a multiple increase. One study showed that during the years 1961–65, which included the civil war and U.S. intervention, hundreds of Dominicans departed. The loss of physicians, engineers, and accountants constituted a Dominican "brain drain" amounting to more than 10 percent of the total number of graduates in those fields.[50]

The politicization of UASD was another consequence of the tumultuous Dominican situation. Although the university came alive in terms of independence from the government and academic freedom, and was no longer an appendage of the political regime as during the era of Trujillo, student political activism resulted in UASD's role mainly as part of the political system, with the sacrifice of academic freedom and the educational mission. UASD largely became an institution for political mobilization, with professors rarely providing academic and professional class instruction and students infrequently attending classes or seminars. Once in office with the external military force withdrawn, President Balaguer retaliated against UASD and further impaired its educational functions.

Political consequences and costs were significant. U.S. actions were generally popular with the public in the United States and in the Congress, with some members of the press and Congress and certain academics the principal exceptions. In the Dominican Republic and Latin America, however, the United States paid a high political price for the intervention.

In the Dominican Republic, U.S. actions further exacerbated economic, political, and social divisions by bringing about a reestablishment of the status quo—the one that Bosch had been overthrown for trying to change. The United States intervened in the Dominican civil war in order to prevent the victory of the Constitutionalists and the return to power of former President Bosch, consequently maintaining the status quo of the military junta, justified primarily in order to avoid "a second Cuba." The majority of Dominicans, especially the younger generation, urban workers, and many in the middle class, were antagonized by the intervention; this antagonism eventually also included many of the elite and business people, who had favored the U.S. action only as a short-run necessity. The political reaction against the United States laid the basis for a continuing negative view of the U.S. government and its policies in certain Dominican cultural, economic, and political circles. Opponents saw the intervention as the latest in a series of denials of the Dominican Republic's historic quest for autonomy, freedom, and independence from foreign control. Many of them held the United States responsible for Trujillo's long and oppressive rule; they saw the election of Juan Bosch as president in 1962 as the rejection of the Trujillo legacy and the initiation of Dominican democracy. Cultural and literary criticism of the United States was extended to the succeeding Balaguer government, which proponents saw as being tied to the United States.

The Inter-American System was severely weakened with regard to its conflict resolution and mutual security functions. President Johnson was so concerned about "a second Cuba" that he was willing to violate inter-American law, to throw around U.S. diplomatic weight in the OAS, and to antagonize Latin American governments. After the military intervention and the troop buildup, the U.S. strategy was to get *post hoc* OAS approval and legitimization with the creation of the IAPF. Despite great criticism, the United States was successful in arranging the endorsement of the OAS but only by the bare fourteen votes required. Thereafter, the U.S. worked through the IAPF, which, except for Brazil, had only token Latin American contingents, to end the fighting, create a provisional government, provide for an electoral campaign, and hold national elections. The intervention and the related inter-American diplomacy impaired U.S. relations with Latin America and weakened the OAS. Never again would the OAS members consider the creation of a peace force, not even when a good case could be made for its initial positive involvement as in dealing with Somoza and the insurrection in Nicaragua in 1979. This action became known as the Johnson Doctrine and was viewed by some as his corollary to the Monroe Doctrine.

Notwithstanding the negative effects of the illegal intervention and the political costs to the United States, a case can be made that the price of the civil war—human, political, and economic—would have been much higher had the United States not intervened. A reasonable assumption is that the Loyalists would have prevailed and defeated the Constitutionalists, which would have resulted in far greater casualties during a protracted struggle and continuing afterward when the victors engaged in reprisals against their opponents.

The most important question to be considered, however, deals with the intervention and the IAPF, principally the role of the United States, in laying the basis for the transition to democracy under Balaguer. By considering this question and the U.S. goal of achieving stability by establishing democracy under Balaguer, one is able to evaluate the 1965 intervention, whatever the U.S. motivations were. The basic reality of the Dominican situation was the legacy of personalist authoritarian government over a long period of time and the consequent lack of political institutions and democratic experience as an alternative to personalist politics. The real problem of the Dominican Republic was not to keep all political parties and factions satisfied but to persuade them to settle their disagreements by peaceful means and to refrain from branding all political opponents as communist. The necessary bridge between opposing groups was the province of political development and Dominican leadership; it could not be constructed through U.S. efforts, whether through large amounts of economic assistance or forceful tutelage, unilateral or multilateral. This is not to say that U.S. and OAS policies had no impact; it is to say that outsiders may help or hurt democratic development, but they cannot determine it.

6   The Balaguer Regime, 1966–1978

President Joaquín Balaguer was successful in establishing and consolidating a personalist regime during three presidential terms over a twelve-year period from 1966 to 1978. He paralleled his political control with dependence on U.S. public economic assistance, which he later shifted to reliance on foreign private investment, mostly from U.S.-based sources. During this period emerged the notable cultural trend of what Frank Moya Pons calls the *norteamericanización* of the Dominican Republic.[1] The phenomenon of Northamericanization had begun earlier but accelerated after the late 1960s. Balaguer attempted to counteract the process by stressing the Spanish cultural and historical legacy, at the same time resisting the rising popular *cultura criollo* movement that emphasized the country's black African roots. Elements of Northamericanization and national identity include the role of communications and entertainment media, the consequences of Dominican migration to the United States, the competing views of race and society, the interaction of U.S. and Dominican educational systems, and the special position of baseball.

The Balaguer Regime and the U.S. Presence

President Balaguer's primary concern during his first elected term (1966–70) was to establish and consolidate his political control. He constructed a personalist regime with authoritarian elements within a democratic facade. By employing a number of carrot-and-stick measures, he instituted and assured his authority. Strongly supported by the armed forces and conservative political sectors, Balaguer was easily returned to office in 1970 and 1974 in less-than-free elections. His rule would have been unbroken by the election of 1978, when the armed forces attempted to interrupt the counting of ballots that clearly favored the Dominican Revolutionary Party (PRD) candidate, if the Carter administration, in concert with the Venezuelan government and a strongly negative reaction by the Dominican electorate, had not forced resumption of the process. In any event, from 1966 to 1978, Balaguer was the single most important actor in the Dominican political system.

Balaguer also sought the Dominican Republic's economic recovery and development, which he saw as a key element of political control. He turned to the United States, which was willing to provide considerable assistance since it was also interested in the country's stability (an important U.S. Cold War consideration in the Caribbean) in the wake of the Dominican civil war and the U.S. military intervention. The United States greatly augmented its economic and military aid during Balaguer's first term and continued the large Dominican share of the sugar quota. As a result, the Dominican Republic increased its economic dependence on the United States. Once Balaguer had consolidated his control, however, the United States cut back its public assistance. Balaguer consequently sought to attract foreign private investment, especially from the United States, by providing numerous economic and tax incentives and creating Industrial Free Zones (IFZs). Balaguer came to rely heavily on this investment.

The Dominican-U.S. economic relationships were symbiotic (perhaps codependent). This aspect was reflected in the large number of U.S. officials in the country and the important level of U.S. assistance provided. At the time of Balaguer's inauguration, some four hundred U.S. advisors and officials were scattered throughout the Dominican government—in the Ministry of Agriculture, Office of Community Development, and Dominican Agrarian Institute, as well as a U.S. Military Training Mission and a Public Security group working with the National Police.[2] The size of the U.S. embassy in Santo Domingo was exceptionally large in proportion to the size of the Dominican Republic. At this time the Dominican government could do little in the way of economic policy without consulting with, and often gaining the approval of, the U.S. embassy or the Agency for International Development (USAID).

The extent of U.S. assistance also made clear Balaguer's dependence.

The amount of military aid from 1967 to 1978 was $22.1 million.[3] U.S. public assistance during Balaguer's first term constituted 32 percent of Dominican national income; the United States also covered the balance of payments deficit. In addition, USAID determined the government's priorities for public investment by directing it toward agricultural development.[4] Balaguer was later more interested in the political impact of such investment and thus favored projects related to economic and social development. The Dominican Republic built a police academy with U.S. funds, which opened in 1968 for the training of recruits; Dominican officers attended the International Police Academy in Washington, D.C. Dominicans derived a crucial source of income from their sugar quota, the largest single share of the U.S. international market and the major earner of Dominican foreign exchange. The U.S. price was above the world price, which at less than ten cents a pound was low in the 1960s and early 1970s—but it rose dramatically to seventy-six cents in 1975. The United States ended the quota system in 1974 but resumed it in 1977.

Balaguer was interested in attracting foreign investment. He changed the laws on foreign ownership of land and offered financial incentives to attract external capital. Many foreign companies, mostly from the United States, consequently invested in the Dominican Republic and began operations there. The first and largest was the multinational Gulf + Western, which became a major producer of Dominican sugar for the U.S. market. It was involved in numerous other activities—such as cattle raising, food processing, real estate, and tourism—and soon had an investment in at least ninety businesses worth more than two hundred million dollars. In 1969, under a 1955 Dominican law, Gulf + Western organized and operated the first IFZ in its La Romana complex. By 1971 six companies were operating there; before the end of Balaguer's tenure in 1978, three additional IFZs with more than forty mainly export assembly plants were in operation. (By August 1988 the number of IFZs had risen to eighteen, most of which were capitalizing on the low wage rates and assembling goods for export to the United States.)[5]

In the early 1970s, Falconbridge Nickel Mines commenced a ferronickel operation. Although a Canadian firm, much of its capital was U.S.-based and its investment guaranteed by a U.S. government agency, the Overseas Private Investment Corporation. In 1975 the Rosario Dominicana Mining Company began a major gold-mining operation, with 80 percent of its capital from the United States. A number of other U.S. firms followed: American Can, Arco, Atlantic Richfield, Beatrice Foods, Carnation, Colgate-Palmolive, Citibank, Exxon, Nabisco, Philip Morris, Texaco, Tenneco, Wometco, and American, Eastern, and Pan American airlines, among others.[6]

The American Institute for Free Labor Development (AIFLD) constituted an instrument of U.S. organized labor influence. The AFL-CIO had organized the AIFLD in the early 1960s to combat communist-infiltrated unions in certain parts of the world; it received some public funds. During Bosch's presidency the AIFLD trained Dominican labor leaders in both the Dominican Republic and the United States and organized the Dominican National Confederation of Free Laborers (CONATRAL). During the period 1962–88, 164 Dominicans were trained in the United States in one of three AIFLD programs.[7] CONATRAL favored collective bargaining and resisted Juan Bosch's efforts to bring all labor unions together into a federation affiliated with the PRD.[8] CONATRAL backed Balaguer in the 1966 election while other unions supported Bosch. Following the election, the Balaguer-affiliated Autonomous Confederation of Christian Unions (CASC) became the most powerful labor group. The government repressed the pro-Bosch labor organizations and they disintegrated. A new pro-Balaguer labor organization emerged, the Confederation of Organized Labor (COSTO), which in effect succeeded CONATRAL. Despite AIFLD's purpose and Balaguer's alliance, labor unions were suppressed and banned in the IFZs.

The Balaguer Regime and Continuismo

Balaguer incorporated his personal monopoly of power and assured his reelections in 1970 and 1974 with a number of measures. U.S. support, with economic and military aid and political backing, was important. The United States had favored Balaguer's election in 1966 and his subsequent reelections because of its interest in Dominican political and economic stability. It also saw no viable alternative to Balaguer and accepted his heavy hand as necessary to maintain order and economic development. The United States had written off Bosch after he was overthrown in 1963, and its critical view of him had been reinforced by his 1968 advocacy of a popular dictatorship, his unrelenting criticism of the United States and its policies, and his creation of the Dominican Liberation Party (PLD) in 1973. The U.S. business community welcomed Balaguer's pro-business stance in contrast to the PRD's and PLD's attacks on foreign companies.

Also beneficial to his position was the economic improvement that took place, even though its benefits were malapportioned. From 1970 until 1977, the Dominican annual economic growth rate rose from 5 to 12 percent, and per capita income increased substantially (although the privileged classes primarily benefitted). During this period Balaguer spent hundreds of millions of dollars on improving the country's infrastructure and on the expanding tourist industry.[9] The high price of sugar was a key element in the prosperity and Balaguer's popularity.

Through his Reformist Party (PR), which Balaguer entirely dominated, he rewarded friends and co-opted foes with jobs and sinecures and an expanding government bureaucracy. He kept the armed forces loyal and hesitant with transfers, promotions and demotions, retirements, and, especially, playing ambitious general officers against each other—as well as overwhelming them intellectually.[10] Balaguer promoted and established control over officers loyal to him and opposed to Colonel Francisco Caamaño Deñó and General Elías Wessin y Wessin and their respective backers. Colonel Caamaño had led the Constitutionalist forces during the civil war, and General Wessin had commanded the Loyalist forces. Shortly after his inauguration, Balaguer confirmed the foreign assignments of these two exiled and troublesome military officers. The general was permitted to return in January 1969 to head an opposition political party.[11]

Balaguer intimidated his opponents—especially labor leaders, students, and politicians, and in particular members of Juan Bosch's PRD, the leading opposition party. If playing one political group off against another did not succeed, he permitted the suppression of dissident leaders and groups with harassment and violence, including assassination. Government forces physically attacked critics and opponents. In April 1971 the armed forces and police helped to create and then sponsored a right-wing terrorist group of young men known as *La Banda* (its euphemistic full name was Anti-Terrorist and Anti-Communist Democratic Front of Reformist Youth) for the purpose of silencing the opposition. *La Banda* dealt violently with activist government opponents; it was responsible for thousands of often indiscriminate attacks upon individuals, about three hundred of whom were killed. Five months after the formation of *La Banda*, apparently in response to international criticism, Balaguer announced that he had ordered its dissolution—it had in fact served its purpose and become a liability.[12]

Balaguer benefitted as the PRD became fragmented, partly as a result of government co-optation and suppression as well as internal leadership problems and dissension. The problems within the PRD began when Bosch, after his electoral defeat in 1966, went into exile in Spain and left the younger and more radical General Secretary José Francisco Peña Gómez in charge. A division developed between Peña Gómez's faction and the "moderates." Further debate was provoked between the two groups when in 1968 Bosch abandoned social democracy and advocated "dictatorship with popular support." As the May 1970 election neared, police violence mounted against the opposition parties, violence that accelerated in April when Bosch returned. Balaguer's reelection was assured with the violence committed against the opposition, the division of the vote among several opposition parties, the PRD's boycott of the election, and electoral fraud. Bosch, anticipating the 1974 elections, strongly opposed a united front of the opposition parties, which contributed to the PRD's continued fragmentation.

In the meantime, in June 1971, General Wessin y Wessin attempted a coup that was completely suppressed. Balaguer turned it into a public relations victory by accusing the general in person on national television, an event that strengthened Balaguer's popularity. Wessin y Wessin was deported in July.

In February 1973, Colonel Caamaño landed with a small invasion force, one he hoped would precipitate Balaguer's overthrow. Balaguer declared a state of emergency and mobilized the army, which quickly defeated the insurgency (Caamaño was killed). Balaguer used the episode to suppress further the opposition. He claimed Bosch and Peña Gómez were implicated in the insurgency and ordered their arrest, but they went into hiding. In late 1973, Bosch formed the Dominican Liberation Party (PLD), and Peña Gómez became head of the PRD.

In the 1974 elections the opposition parties formed a coalition slate of candidates. Antonio Guzmán, moderate PRD member, was the presidential nominee, and Wessin y Wessin, leader of his personalist Quisqueyan Dominican Party (PQD), was the vice presidential nominee. On account of governmental suppression of the opposition, Guzmán advised abstention. Most opposition leaders agreed, and they withdrew a few days before the election. Balaguer, who warned of chaos and economic collapse if not reelected, easily won.

The election and subsequent events, such as a major shake-up of the armed forces in May 1975 and the army's easy elimination of a small guerrilla force the next month, indicated that Balaguer was firmly in control. His position was strengthened by continued economic improvement, which was facilitated by generous U.S. assistance, the flow of foreign private investment, and the high price of sugar in the regulated U.S. market (although in 1977 the price of sugar fell significantly as another election approached).

Northamericanization and Dominican Identity

Frank Moya Pons equates the Northamericanization of the Dominican Republic with its modernization. He argues that the former was inevitable because of the proximity of the two states and the consequent migration, commerce, and cultural contact and "penetration."[13] The process had begun in the late 1880s; after 1930 Trujillo had laid its economic bases when he created a capitalist state (which he later took over as a family fiefdom).

Northamericanization coalesced and increased its pace after the end of the era of Trujillo and the phenomenon "took off" after 1966. Northamericanization alludes to the impact of not only U.S. goods but also cultural values by way of radio, television, and motion pictures, as well as the influence of U.S. culture on the increasing number of Dominicans living in the United States as exiles, students, and immigrants.

Northamericanization has complicated and made more difficult the development of a Dominican identity. The country's economic dependence, whether on public aid or private capital, illustrated what Howard Wiarda and Michael Kryzanek call the Dominican Republic's "dual identity."[14] Dominicans slowly accepted but resented this situation, realizing they could not advance without help but indignant about taking it.[15] The political left, notably Bosch, Peña Gómez, and the PRD, was especially critical of Dominican economic dependence, which it viewed as a form of U.S. intervention designed to keep Balaguer in office. This criticism was also directed toward U.S. companies and investors.

The process of Northamericanization resulted in something of a Dominican sense of inferiority (with the important exception of baseball) and ambivalence about the United States. On the one hand, many Dominicans, especially in the middle and lower classes, developed a preference for U.S. products and lifestyle. At the same time, they displayed resentment of U.S. cultural influence on the Dominican Republic, which was especially strong among the elite and with Balaguer himself. They particularly objected to U.S. popular culture and materialist and secular values and to hearing exaggerated claims of the quality of U.S. goods and life and denigration of Dominican culture.

President Balaguer reinforced, probably unintentionally, the trend toward Northamericanization with his reliance on U.S. values of materialism. Yet he took exception to U.S. cultural influence and, soon after assuming power in 1966, championed the point of view called *hispanidad*—a sharp focus on the Spanish legacy in Dominican culture, especially the religious element of conservative Roman Catholicism and the racial element of white superiority and purity. In fact, Balaguer was returning to Trujillo's stress on *hispanidad*; thus, even in the cultural arena, "Trujillism without Trujillo" remained. (In the mid-1930s Bala-guer had been a diplomat in Spain). In the 1970s, Balaguer's enthusiasm for *hispanidad* was reflected in his commitment to an extensive program to restore much of colonial Santo Domingo and to construct galleries, museums of high culture, and La Plaza de la Cultura (Trujillo had initiated the restoration process in the early 1950s).[16] Balaguer not only glorified the Spanish colonial heritage but refused to recognize the emergent Dominican populist African heritage movement of *la cultura criollo*. (Balaguer continued to stress *hispanidad* after his return to the presidency in 1986.)

The end of the Trujillo dictatorship in 1961 had removed some barriers to change. New nationalist thought emerged, opposed to both Northamericanization and to the *hispanidad* alternative. The new freedom of expression following Trujillo's death allowed black and mulatto Dominican writers and artists to explore African-Dominican themes. A group of activists at the Museo del Hombre Dominicano revived interest in the recognition of African contributions to Dominican society. A similar group became active at the Universidad Autónoma de Santo Domingo (UASD). President Bosch had extended recognition and support to *la cultura criollo*. While in exile, Bosch had presented new images of blacks and of Haiti in some of his novels and short stories. During his presidency and the council of state headed by Reid Cabral, the Dominican African roots were made respectable, a different (more positive) view of Haiti was offered, and a new form of social criticism emerged, themes that the government presented on radio and television.[17] The Dominican revolution of 1965 had stimulated an upsurge of nationalism and pride. The events galvanized a sense of being Dominican, particularly on the part of younger people in the middle and lower classes, and produced a new body of thought expressed in art and literature. One group of writers, provoked by the U.S. intervention, formed to develop an anti-U.S. revolutionary literature; its members were also revisionist in terms of Dominican-African roots and views of Haiti. The group, who called themselves El Puño, met weekly in Santo Domingo on Sunday mornings. (One of its members, Marcio Veloz Maggiolo, became minister of education in 1978 under PRD President

Guzmán.) Another emerging movement was a broader and younger one called *la nueva ola*. It was strongly anti-Trujillist and antiforeign and particularly opposed to Northamericanization. The members were highly nationalist and concerned about Dominican cultural identity, seeking to develop strictly Dominican forms of expression in art and culture—in sculpture, literature, dance, music, and painting.[18] They, too, rejected *hispanidad* in favor of *la cultura criollo*.

Balaguer resisted and even suppressed the demand for official recognition of the movement to legitimate the Afro-Dominican heritage, which he viewed as an antiwhite campaign. In fact, Balaguer reversed the recognition and support that President Bosch in 1963 had extended to *cultura criollo* and that the PRD continued to support. With the passage of time and for political reasons, however, Balaguer found that he could not completely suppress the popular African heritage movement and deny the reality of or refuse to tolerate sympathetic outlooks about the African roots of most Dominicans. During Balaguer's third term (1974–78), he found it politically expedient to relax opposition to Afro-Dominicanism and at least tolerate it.

Northamericanization, Television, and Movies

The role of motion pictures and, especially, television in the Northamericanization process deserves further commentary. For many years from its earliest days, the U.S. motion picture industry had sent its products to the Dominican Republic. Although the first television channel began operating in 1952, the strong acculturating effect was a post-Trujillo-era dimension of Northamericanization and became increasingly influential. In 1952 Trujillo had established the first television channel, La Voz Dominicana, and a second one, Rahintel, in 1959. Trujillo's death paved the way for privately owned television and much greater U.S. influence, particularly evident during the Balaguer regime. The other channels or networks that followed were Colorvisión in 1969, Teleinde in 1973, and Telesistema Dominicano in 1978. Television was first used politically in the 1974 election. Television relied on U.S. commercials promoting U.S. products, and it and the movies (which were also transmitted over television) portrayed the lifestyles, values, and material goods of the highly developed, prosperous, and secularized U.S. society. Among other things, these elements contributed to English becoming the Dominican Republic's second language.

Antonio Menéndez, in a scholarly work, argues that the governments' various efforts to reduce the consumption of luxury goods and to create savings for investment had been regularly undercut by television's stress on stimulating consumption and emulating lifestyles in the developed countries, especially the United States. The major sponsors of programs were the producers of spirits (sixteen brands of Dominican rum and two of beer), the tobacco industry (Philip Morris), and soft drink producers (Coca-Cola and Pepsi Cola). All programming involved imported shows, mainly serials and movies from the United States. The U.S. serials were especially popular among viewers with low education levels; Hollywood movies continued to be popular since they provided "an escapist and fantasy type of entertainment" preferred by Dominican audiences.[19]

Dominican writer José Cabrera was highly critical of Northamericanization by way of U.S. advertising, products, and films—a process he referred to as *dominación cultural*. He listed the many U.S. products Dominicans were familiar with, examined Philip Morris's investments, noted the influence of the *Mundo Marlboro*, and strongly objected to how John Travolta had been converted into a hero along with Superman, Batman, and *La Mujer Maravilla*. He made a case for protecting the *patrimonio cultural*, which, he said, included the Spanish language.[20]

Migration and National Identity

The role of Dominican migration to the United States in relationship to Northamericanization and the reaction against it was also a matter of special consideration. U.S. popular culture, styles, tastes, and values especially influenced Dominicans who emigrated from home to the United States, either legally or illegally, to live and work. The magnitude of this influence is made clear by the fact that about 10 percent of the population of the Dominican Republic migrated to the United States from the mid-1960s to 1990. During Balaguer's presidency the yearly numbers of legal immigrants alone varied from more than sixteen thousand in 1966 to a high of more than nineteen thousand in 1978.[21] Many other Dominicans went to the United States without the required documents; the majority of illegal immigrants were black and mulatto coming from urban areas, primarily Santo Domingo. Most of them crossed the Mona Channel in small boats to Puerto Rico, which became the main transit point to the mainland. A significant number remained in Puerto Rico to live and work. Attracted by opportunities for a better life in the United States and often joining relatives and friends who had moved there, the largest number of Dominicans went to New York City. Large groups of Dominicans were also found in Boston, Providence, Hartford, and Miami. The Dominican community in New York City especially developed rapidly and became important to the Dominican Republic both economically and politically.[22] Both Balaguer and Bosch had gone into exile in New York City, in 1961 and 1963, respectively. As a magnet for immigrants, New York City was not limited to Dominicans; it became a Caribbean cultural microcosm.

Many Dominicans intended to work in the United States, save their money, and then invest in a business or retire in the Dominican Republic. Large numbers of both legal and illegal immigrants returned home for the Christmas and Easter holidays. Some Dominicans maintained two households, one in each country, in order to assure permanent legal residency in the Dominican Republic. Although U.S. life was often difficult because of competition for jobs and discrimination against those who were black or mulatto, Dominicans earned more money than was possible in the homeland. Life was even more difficult for those male heads of household who attempted to maintain the traditional Dominican patriarchal family system, which resulted in frustration and the alienation of some family members. Dominicans also recognized the benefits of the U.S. public education system as well as of the medical care and public welfare systems. The number of Dominicans in the United States, their ambivalence about loyalty to two countries, and their movement back and forth illustrates Kryzanek and Wiarda's idea of the "dual nation": "they end up half here and half there, feeling that they really don't belong in either place."[23]

Dominicans participating in the U.S. popular culture had an impact on their friends and associates when they returned to Dominican society. They were often admired or envied for their dress, styles, and relative wealth. Since most of these individuals came from New York City, the term "Domyork" was created to refer to them. It was sometimes used pejoratively, as when applied to those who had become wealthy in the illicit drug trade.

An important benefit for the Dominican economy, and a form of dependency, was the millions of dollars in remittances (*remesas*) that Dominican nationals in the United States sent to their families at home. The importance and the increasing magnitude of the remittances in the 1970s was illustrated by their increase from $8.5 million in 1970 to $33.3 in 1975, and then to $123 million in 1976 and $146 million in 1978.[24] The amount continued to increase thereafter.

In the 1960s, when the Dominican community in the United States began to expand rapidly with exiles, intellectuals, and professionals, it came to reflect the cultural, political, racial, and social profile of those emigrés and exiles. In this earlier period the clubs and organizations reflected the elite and upper class, mainly white and politically conservative, who held traditional values and were sympathetic to *hispanidad*. Some forty societies developed, whose regular activities involved devoting attention to prominent Dominican figures, organizing Dominican concerts and programs (including in Lincoln Center), and always celebrating Dominican Independence Day on 27 February in a luxury hotel in the center of the city. This community broadened and became more active with additional centers and associations, such as the Dominican Civic and Cultural Center and the New York Association of Dominican Professionals.[25]

In the 1970s a new phase occurred in the development of the New York Dominican community as it expanded in size and more organizations, particularly political, began functioning. The organizations developed like those in the popular barrios at home and became affiliated with their Dominican counterpart political parties, many to the left of the spectrum. The Dominican candidates campaigned and raised funds among these community groups. In the elections of 1970, 1974, 1978, and 1982, Balaguer, Bosch, Guzmán, Jorge, and others came to New York. The Committee for the Defense of Human Rights was an important political entity created in opposition to Balaguer. Another important new organization was the Center for Dominican Assistance, supported by the U.S. Episcopal Church and partially financed with U.S. government funds. The center expanded its services in the 1970s to help Dominicans with immigration documentation, offer English classes and high school instruction, and promote cultural activities.[26]

The activities and role of the Dominican community through its organizations, in New York in particular but in other cities as well, indicated two reciprocal trends: the Caribbeanization of the United States and the Northamericanization of the Dominican Republic. The former was demonstrated by the impact of Dominican fashion designers like Oscar de la Renta; Dominican dances like the merengue, bachata, and salsa; and Dominican musicians like Angela Carrasco, Juan Luis Guerra, Wilfrido Vargas, Johnny Ventura, the group La Patrulla 15, and others.[27] Northamericanization was indicated by a preference for U.S. consumer goods and the materialist, secular lifestyle as presented in U.S. commercials, serials, and movies on Dominican television. It also included a passion for baseball and increasing interest in basketball, and borrowing the U.S. educational model.

Many Dominicans learned the importance of political activism at the local level, particularly affecting school boards. Interestingly, while they participated in the "formal North American system" they did not really become assimilated.[28] Dominicans knew how to use the U.S. system to benefit themselves but they were more interested in political events in the Dominican Republic. Many of them learned U.S. techniques, procedures, and styles and applied them to Dominican politics. In the 1974 elections, for example, television was used for the first time as an important campaign instrument. The activities and role of Dominicans in New York became an important adjunct to the Dominican political process. The Dominican political parties established highly active branches in New York, where they developed issues, campaigned for the candidates, and raised money. This political activity is why Dominican presidential candidates found it necessary to visit New York. They urged Dominicans to return home to vote (there was no provision for absentee ballots). The candidates also went to Washington, D.C., to visit key senators and representatives, congressional committees, foundations and think tanks, and universities, in order to make themselves and their views known and to discuss specific issues such as U.S. foreign aid.[29]

Race and Society

Dominican ambivalence about race and society was an important and highly sensitive aspect of Northamericanization and Dominican identity. The problems of race posed a major obstacle to establishing a national cultural identity. Dominican views about race were paradoxical, stemming from Trujillo's overt effort to deny Dominican blackness, mixed and changing racial attitudes in the United States, and the difficulties faced by the African roots movement to gain legitimization. Dominicans had long observed U.S. attitudes about race, and many who visited or lived in the United States had firsthand experience with those ambivalent outlooks. Trujillo's long dictatorial control had perpetuated the false cultural and racial image of the Dominican Republic as a white rather than black or mulatto society. During the Trujillo era, Balaguer, who served as diplomat and government official and became a popular intellectual and literary figure, helped maintain the legacy and stressed the white-black dichotomy.[30] Many mixed-race Dominicans who considered themselves to be white as a result of the conditioning process during the Trujillo era were shocked to discover that in the United States they were seen as black (the same as Haitians) and were treated as second-class citizens.[31]

While prejudiced U.S. racial attitudes had a negative impact on certain Dominicans' racial views, the civil rights movement in the United

States had a positive one. In the 1960s into the 1970s, most Dominicans followed the civil rights movement with interest and sympathy; blacks and mulattos witnessed the way it revised U.S. racial relations. They tended to be affected positively by the movement and the slogan that "black is beautiful," which reinforced the *cultura criollo* movement in the Dominican Republic. Thus the traditional Dominican stress on the Spanish heritage came into conflict with the new emphasis on African-ness. Interestingly, this aspect of Northamericanization contributed to the furtherance of the *cultura criollo* movement as a critical element of national identity within the Dominican Republic, inasmuch as the U.S. civil rights movement especially influenced a large number of young Dominicans studying and working in the United States. The Black Power movement in the Commonwealth Caribbean had a similar impact. Young Dominicans began to copy the style of dress and music of the U.S. blacks with whom they were associated (although they did not copy speech patterns, since Spanish remained their first language). Thus many Dominicans actually discovered their Dominican negritude in the United States. When they returned for visits to the Dominican Republic, their shocked families initially greeted them negatively.[32] These attitudes began to change, however, and the "new negritude" became more acceptable. Frank Moya Pons observed that the Dominican emigrants who returned became agents of social change, not only of modernity and capitalism but also of "racial emancipation."[33] This discovery had a corollary at home with radical professional groups and university intellectuals who called attention to the "cultural and racial alienation of the Dominican people," a claim that was increasingly popular.[34]

Education and National Development

Another important aspect of Northamericanization was found in the great influence of the U.S. educational system, which was also an important aspect of Dominican migration. For decades thousands of Dominicans had earned their graduate and professional degrees in the United States, and they continued to do so during the Balaguer regime. The students were sent by their families and were later also sponsored by USAID. The U.S. government and private foundations provided funds to institutes and programs in the Dominican Republic. A result was that the U.S. model was emulated in the Dominican Republic by returning students who sought to improve Dominican educational institutions in order to contribute to the country's modernization.

The Universidad Autónoma de Santo Domingo (UASD), the only public and the oldest university in the country, employed a highly traditional curriculum and pedagogy. Degrees were offered in architecture, dentistry, medicine, engineering, finance, accounting, law, and philosophy; most degrees awarded were in law, medicine, and philosophy. Mainly part-time faculty provided the instruction with formal lectures in large halls without discussion, and examinations stressed memorization at the expense of analysis.

Within the Dominican Republic, the UASD in the 1960s was a center of pro-Bosch and anti-Balaguer (and thus anti-United States) activity. This activity prompted a number of conservative professors and students to leave and establish in 1967 a new private institution, La Universidad Nacional de Pedro Henríquez Ureña (UNPHU) in Santo Domingo. The same year a group of business people in Santo Domingo founded the Instituto de Estudios Superiores, a Dominican version of a U.S. community college. These two institutions and the Universidad Católica Madre y Maestra (UCMM) together presented new educational opportunities for Dominicans.

UCMM had a special position in the matter of Northamericanization. It had been founded in 1962 far from the capital in the northern city of Santiago de los Caballeros, the result of an initiative by progressive business people who had studied in the United States and the leadership of two Roman Catholic bishops, who served as dynamic rectors of the university.[35] The university, however, was not controlled by the church and was not a religious institution. The same business people in 1962 created the Development Association (Asociación para el Desarrollo), and establishment of the university was one of its first projects. The Ford Foundation funded one position in the Development Association.

The university paradoxically contributed significantly to both establishing and reducing educational Northamericanization. While it was formed on and then emulated the U.S. model of higher education, it served as an important catalyst for reducing the educational dependency of the Dominican Republic. It also provided leadership in the development of a Dominican identity that included the country's African roots. Put another way, although the UCMM was significantly formed by U.S. influences, it was also a uniquely Dominican institution.

The UCMM was patterned after the U.S. style of administration, curriculum, and pedagogy and was to be insulated from partisan politics. Part of the reason for following the U.S. educational model was that a number of the founding members of UCMM had been among the many Dominicans who had undertaken graduate and professional studies in U.S. universities.[36] UCMM continued to participate in beneficial Dominican-U.S. exchange programs—Dominicans continued to study in the United States under special programs and UCMM to receive grants from USAID and private U.S. foundations.[37] At the same time, the curriculum emphasized education and training in disciplines and programs that were directly relevant to the needs of a developing and modernizing country. The university was committed to developing national cultural values and identity, to serving the country's development needs, and to improving the quality of life for all Dominicans. It undertook a social mission to break down class and social barriers, to provide educational opportunity for as many qualified Dominicans as possible, to provide the advanced study and training that Dominicans were seeking in the United States and elsewhere, and generally to reduce and even reverse the Dominican "brain drain." One of UCMM's objectives was to address the ambivalence of Dominican views toward Northamericanization and to contribute to the development of a balanced Dominican cultural identity.

After Balaguer became president in 1966, he retaliated against the

UASD for the student body's political opposition to him by temporarily cutting off the government's budgetary support. He then greatly reduced public payments for the operation of the university, on which it was completely dependent, and at times closed down the campus. It did not matter that he had been secretary of education and fine arts in the early 1950s, was a graduate in law from UASD, and had been dean of the law school and later rector of the university.

In 1968 USAID tried to arrange with Balaguer's government an Education Sector Loan Program, but it was reluctant to approve the plan because of the latter's insistence on certain conditions. At the same time, the "diversified schools" feature of the proposal was "criticized by the political left as an attempt to impose an American type education system."[38] Nevertheless, USAID signed contracts with U.S. universities to provide technical aid, including pairing agreements between St. Louis University and UASD and between the American Institute for Research and both UASD and UNPHU. UASD continued to receive grants from the Ford Foundation, the United Nations, and the governments of France and Mexico. The Ford Foundation also financed a number of visiting U.S. professors to help develop certain fields at UCMM in Santiago.

Balaguer's denial of funds to UASD led its rector, Hugo Tolentino Dipp, to protest publicly in 1975, but the government did not respond. Instead, Balaguer continued to favor the private universities with grant funds. For example, in 1975, he contributed $1.2 million to UNPHU and $2 million to UCMM (both of which charged tuition), and only $8.4 million went to the UASD, which depended entirely on government funds and enrolled more than half of all the university students.[39] At the end of Balaguer's third term, UCMM enrollment was approaching five thousand, with the government paying 50 percent of its budget and contributing forty million dollars for the construction of a regional university hospital as part of the faculty of medicine. USAID continued to help, mainly in faculty training. For example, in 1979, thirty-six UCMM faculty members were teaching and specializing in the United States. In addition, the Inter-American Development Bank and the

United Nations Development Fund provided grants. The United Kingdom contributed toward a department of mining.[40]

Baseball and National Pride

The importance of baseball as an element of Dominican national pride also requires special examination. Sports in general were important in the Dominican Republic, but U.S. baseball was paramount, with U.S. professional basketball also widely followed. In 1974 the Central American Olympic Games were for the first time held in the Dominican Republic, which built a new stadium and track and field complex for the events.

Baseball provided an important example of both Northamericanization and Dominican self-esteem during the period under examination, and perhaps reverse Northamericanization as well, since Dominican teams have at times literally beat the United States at its own game. In the 1890s U.S. seamen had introduced baseball to Cubans, who in turn took it to the Dominican Republic. Dominicans organized baseball teams before the U.S. occupation beginning in 1916, and during the occupation U.S. marines reinforced the sport by playing baseball as members of civilian Dominican teams. In the 1930s the U.S. Negro Leagues played throughout the Caribbean, where they were very popular; they played Dominican teams and recruited the best Dominican players. The phenomenon fully bloomed as important in the U.S.-Dominican relationship after World War II. In the 1950s the U.S. major leagues had begun to recruit Dominican players. By the 1970s and continuing thereafter, between forty-five and sixty Dominicans played in the United States in the major leagues in any year, and three hundred to four hundred in the minor leagues.[41] Both the Atlanta Braves and the Los Angeles Dodgers established training camps in the Dominican Republic, outside Campo Las Palmas near the city of San Pedro de Macorís, the site of the Tetelo Vargas Stadium.

Manual (Manny) Mota, former outfielder for the Los Angeles Dodgers, described Dominican pride in baseball: "If you ask any Dominican what he is proudest of, he will read you a list of ballplayers. This country doesn't have much, but we know we are the best in the world at one thing [baseball]. That's not bragging, because it's true. And we plan to continue being the best in the world at it."[42]

Baseball is not only a sport in which Dominicans have excelled but one in which they have competed well with the United States. Dominicans were proud that more Dominicans per capita had been recruited for the U.S. major leagues than from any other country outside the United States. Alan Klein argues, however, that in the process Dominican players were "becoming less Dominican and more American," while in the past baseball had been a form and symbol of Dominican resistance to U.S. hegemony.[43]

Baseball was the national sport in the Dominican Republic (a Baseball Academy was formed in mid-1970s) probably even more than in the United States, where football and basketball offered strong competition. Extensive press and television coverage is given to baseball in general and to Dominican players in particular. Many Dominican boys see the game as their chance to escape poverty, first by making a Dominican league team, second by playing in the Caribbean series or the World Series of Latin American Baseball, and then by being recruited by a major league team in the United States. They know that success will bring them wealth and wide acclaim at home.

7   Dominican Democratization, 1978–1986

Dominican-U.S. relations in the eight-year period from 1978 to 1986 were marked by the rule of two presidents from the Dominican Revolutionary Party (PRD), and Dominican domestic events had foreign policy implications for both states. The era was an interregnum between two long periods dominated by President Joaquín Balaguer (1966–78 and 1986–96). During this intervening period, the Dominican Republic struggled to institutionalize a democratic political system. Events at this time significantly affected Dominican political development and were influenced by important decisions and actions on the part of the United States.

The dramatic Dominican election in 1978 involved foreign factors, especially the crucial U.S. "electoral intervention," and had implications for the campaign and election of 1982, including economic, political, and military problems and policies. The Dominican Republic continued to be concerned with Haiti and Cuba, and the U.S. was preoccupied with the Central American conflict. Transnational economic and social linkages, in which Dominican migration to the United States loomed large, continued; added to the mix was the new problem of drug trafficking as part of the Dominican-U.S. relationship.

Dominican Elections and the U.S. Role

As the 1978 election in the Dominican Republic approached, President Joaquín Balaguer seemed to have advantages that the PRD could not overcome.[1] But a number of internal economic and political developments undermined his reelection prospects, leading the PRD to decide against abstention and to mount a major electoral challenge to Balaguer's continued rule. Thus Balaguer faced a serious confrontation that had not been present in the 1970 and 1974 contests. This time the opposition, particularly the PRD, decided to take him on vigorously. The Carter administration, like the Johnson and Nixon-Ford administrations before it, was interested in the stability of the Dominican Republic, but President Jimmy Carter emphasized the importance of establishing in that country a functioning representative democratic system that protected human rights. He had been critical of Balaguer's authoritarian government and concerned about the approaching 1978 elections, when Balaguer would have been in office for twelve consecutive years.

Incumbent Balaguer enjoyed a number of political advantages: he was popular in the countryside, especially in the heavily populated Cibao Valley around Santiago; he was the candidate of the armed forces; he had control of the government resources from the presidential office for patronage and public relations; and the opposition groups were splintered. On the other hand, a major factor working against Balaguer was the beginning of an economic decline. The significant decrease in the price of sugar in late 1976 and early 1977 depressed the economy, resulting in increased unemployment and reduced government expenditures. Even when the economy had been growing, the poorer classes had complained that they did not share in the benefits, yet they suffered from the increased cost of living. The poor sometimes manifested their discontent in public demonstrations and strikes. A growing and more prosperous middle class became more active and turned against Balaguer's government, criticizing its corruption (including in the armed forces). Many Dominicans, in the middle class and particularly in the lower class, believed that Balaguer's policies inordinately favored Dominican and foreign business communities. Some members of the commercial elite began to question Balaguer's ability to manage the economy, control corruption, prevent disorder, and protect their interests. These problems and concerns had been accumulating for several years and began to impact negatively on the economic, political, and social atmosphere as the election neared. It became clear that Balaguer's well-funded but ill-organized campaign was not going well, perhaps due to overconfidence.

As Antonio Guzmán, the PRD's presidential nominee, continued to gain strength in the 1978 campaign, the possibility of victory united the opposition. The PRD pursued a well-organized strategy of mass mobilization throughout the country. It had strong support among the urban poor and lower middle class in Santo Domingo and took advantage of rural dissatisfaction over Balaguer's economic performance and faltering land reform with organizations in the countryside.

José Francisco Peña Gómez, the PRD's secretary-general and leader of the party's left wing, became an issue in the campaign even though he was not a candidate for any office. Conservative Dominicans and military leaders still regarded him as a "communist rabble-rouser," dating from April 1965 when he had led the urban masses during the civil war.[2] A continuing rumor from the past circulated that the dark-skinned Peña was Haitian. Balaguer and other *reformistas* tried to capitalize on such talk by branding Peña a dangerous "anti-nationalist" (meaning pro-Haitian) demagogue. They portrayed Guzmán as a weak leader unable to control his party's secretary-general, suggesting that Peña would be the real power and policy maker in a Guzmán government. They also claimed that Peña was "pro-Cuba," again trying to raise the specter of the 1965 civil war. This rhetoric was aimed at the traditional Dominican upper class, the new-rich sector, and the growing middle class, all of whom otherwise had little to fear from Guzmán.

Peña Gómez responded to these charges by downplaying his past attacks on the United States, foreign investors, and multinational corporations, and on the Dominican upper class for exploiting the poor. He used the term *modificación* to describe his revised political position. He rarely mentioned the United States, was only mildly critical of Gulf + Western, Falconbridge, and other foreign companies, and appealed to all Dominicans to vote for the PRD as the party of change for the benefit of all. He emphasized his absolute Dominican loyalty and promised to resign his party post and leave the country for a period of time if the PRD won.

A number of external factors affected the campaign in important ways, including the roles of the U.S. government and U.S.-based companies and the candidates' and parties' relations with them. Balaguer, interested in maintaining U.S. economic assistance and private investment, portrayed his close friendship with the United States as a major economic asset—at the same time he indicated his independence in the relationship. The PRD, as noted, moderated its attitude toward the United States and U.S. investors, while trying to use the Carter administration's commitment to free elections and human rights to restrain and criticize the Balaguer regime. The two parties' actions and attitudes toward the United States, and the ways they used the U.S. factor against each other, fluctuated during the campaign. At the September signing of the Panama Canal treaties in Washington, President Carter had singled out Balaguer among the other American presidents present for special applause (which was surprising in view of his prior criticism of the Dominican president). Carter extolled Balaguer as the man who had restored democracy and "transformed his own country" and promised to restore human rights. (Another strong exponent of human rights, Congressman Donald Fraser [D-Minn.], chair of the House Foreign Affairs Subcommittee on International Organizations, strongly protested this "unwitting" violation of non-partisanship in the Dominican elections.) Balaguer used Carter's statement in the campaign to associate himself with the U.S. president; the PRD leadership resented both Carter's praise and Balaguer's exploitation of it. The PRD also criticized Balaguer for his close ties with U.S. Ambassador Robert Hurwitch, who had been ambassador for more than four years and who had developed a close personal relationship with and, apparently, sympathy for Balaguer. In October seven key PRD officials—among others, Guzmán, Jacobo Majluta, Salvador Jorge Blanco (he had been defeated by Guzmán as the PRD nominee), and Peña—at their request met with visiting Assistant Secretary of State for Inter-American Affairs Terence Todman at the U.S. embassy in Santo Domingo. They complained about Balaguer's violation of the constitution with repressive actions against the PRD. Later in the campaign Guzmán appealed to the U.S. military advisors to exert pressure on their Dominican counterparts to abstain from partisan political activity. Balaguer responded negatively to a statement made in November by Ben Stephansky, former U.S. ambassador to Bolivia, who criticized the nature of Dominican democracy and warned that certain private U.S. groups would be watching the election in order to assure its fairness. Balaguer reacted by defending the "right of the Dominican people to live free of foreign interference" and emphasized that the elections would be free "because that is the way that the government and the Dominican people want them and not because a foreign power wants or is trying to impose this."[3]

In fact, the PRD and other opposition parties suffered some violence at the hands of the armed forces, police, and a group of young toughs called *la banda colorado*. This violence increased sharply during April as election day approached. At the same time, senior military officers publicly praised Balaguer, while more junior ones, joined by some police counterparts, openly campaigned for him. They destroyed PRD literature and provoked disorder at its rallies. (Members of Congressman Fraser's staff had observed and reported on some earlier similar actions during a late October–early November 1977 visit.)[4] Balaguer made a number of direct overtures for the support of the armed forces beyond the top officer echelon, playing on their fears about the PRD and Peña. He also promised to increase retired officers' retirement pay and benefits if reelected.

In preparation for the 16 May election, the Dominican government opened the electoral process and invited foreign observers so as to avoid charges of fraud. The Organization of American States (OAS) sent an election-monitoring mission, composed of three former Latin American presidents: Galo Plaza Lasso of Ecuador (also a former OAS secretary-general and the group's leader), Julio César Méndez Montenegro of Guatemala, and Misael Pastrana Borrero of Colombia. Congressman Fraser and the Democratic Conference sent as their representative Gregory Wolfe, dean of the School of International Service of the American University in Washington, D.C., and former director of the State Department's Latin American Office in the Bureau of Intelligence and Research. The Dominican government also granted official observer status to the Spanish member of the Socialist International (of which the PRD was a member; PRD Secretary-General Peña Gómez was vice president for the Latin American regional affiliate).

The Central Electoral Commission (JCE) in Santo Domingo, headed by a Balaguer appointee, was in charge of preparations for the balloting. In keeping with the electoral law, the armed forces retired to their barracks on 13 May, and the JCE was assigned seven thousand security personnel. The day before the election Balaguer said that he would accept the choice of the voters and he expected the armed forces to do the same. On election day the entire country was peaceful and a large number of voters turned out, giving the PRD cause for optimism about the outcome. The early returns indicated that Guzmán had a substantial lead over Balaguer in the crucial capital city.

The hopes of the PRD suddenly seemed dashed in the early morning on 17 May, when elements of the Dominican armed forces took over the JCE headquarters and ordered that the counting of votes be stopped. Dominican troops occupied the JCE headquarters as well as most polling places around the country, and shut down radio and television stations that were reporting the vote count. At the time about 25 percent of the votes had been counted, with Guzmán leading Balaguer three to two. The head of the JCE and his staff disappeared. Throughout the country most business and educational activities came to a halt. Troops patrolled the streets. Every fifteen minutes a general's recorded message interrupted radio and television transmissions, insisting that no coup had occurred, that the military would respect the returns, and that the electoral situation was "normal." Evidence strongly suggested that a *golpe* was initiated by a few senior military officers who desired Balaguer's continuation in office so strongly that they forcibly interrupted the election in order to prevent a victory by the PRD and Guzmán. Within a short time, however, the attempt to steal the election had little credibility or support. In time the counting was resumed and Guzmán was duly elected.

Three factors contributed to preserving the election: the Dominican electorate's strong opposition to a coup; external pressures, especially by the United States and Venezuela, partly in concert; and significant resistance to the plotters from most of their military colleagues. The domestic reaction and the division in the armed forces were crucial elements. Without them the U.S. and other external constraints would not have sufficed to restore the electoral process; in combination they were a potent political mix.

President Carter threatened to cut off aid if the counting was not resumed. If the Carter administration had not pressured and threatened the Balaguer government to resume the counting of ballots, democracy would probably have been aborted and authoritarianism continued and strengthened. The OAS and other governments in Latin America and Europe were also involved.[5] This U.S. action indicated a new rationale for intervention, one involving the promotion of democracy and human rights, as contrasted with the 1965 military intervention designed to prevent a "second Cuba."

The PRD responded in a low-key manner but it was determined not to be denied victory by fraud. This approach reflected PRD anticipation that there would be mounting internal and external influences on Balaguer and certain general officers. Guzmán referred to the PRD's ability to call a general strike but emphasized that the JCE had the responsibility to declare him winner of the elections. He noted that Presidents Carter and Balaguer had "committed themselves before world opinion to free elections that would be clear and respected," and added: "We are convinced Balaguer will abide by that promise."[6] Peña Gómez talked of Balaguer's accomplishments and expressed confidence that the president would oversee a peaceful transfer of power by curtailing the armed forces. Juan Bosch called for unity among the opposition. PRD and other opposition leaders stressed the general public belief that the PRD had won an overwhelming victory. Indeed, a remarkable general public outcry against military intervention issued from virtually all economic, political, and social sectors. Prominent ads appeared in the newspapers expressing dismay and shame. Leading church, civic, educational, and professional groups purchased space with statements urging Balaguer to resume the vote counting. Santiago community leaders, mainly from the conservative upper class, joined the flood of public declarations in the press.

The idea of a *golpe* was generally unpopular within the armed forces.

Some military men believed that Balaguer would not condone one since he wanted history to credit him with establishing democracy in the Dominican Republic. Others anticipated the adverse world reaction; they were concerned mostly with that from the United States. Few of them, however, foresaw the intense internal reaction. Many officers felt that a coup would lead to another civil war and a cliché became popular: "no one wants another 1963 because no one wants another 1965." (Perhaps some officers remembered a similar explanation of why the armed forces supported García-Godoy's provisional government following the civil war: "It is no longer the masses who fear the military here but the military who fear the masses.") Most were suspicious of the PRD and feared economic instability under Guzmán; some officers worried about an alliance with Cuba. Under the circumstances, however, they were willing to give Guzmán a chance, perhaps for a given period, during which they would monitor and then judge his performance.

An important military association that had formed a year before the elections strongly opposed the military intervention. Dissatisfied with the corruption at high military levels, the "Colonels' Group" (as it became known) had initially focused on the depoliticization and professionalization of the armed forces. U.S. armed forces attachés and advisors had for years stressed professionalization and may have had an important influence on this group of military counterparts. Galvanized by the seizure of the JCE, the colonels came together in opposition to it. They met on 19 May, the day after ballot counting had resumed, to organize and take a stand against their superiors—they thus became known as the "Nineteenth of May Group."

The United States responded rapidly and clearly against the military intervention. The Department of State and the U.S. embassy in Santo Domingo prepared a coordinated statement to be delivered to the Dominican presidential office and the armed forces secretariat. A few hours after the counting was stopped, the U.S. defense attaché arrived at the armed forces secretary's office. Although he was not permitted to see the commanding general until the next morning, he delivered a firm message to the staff about the great concern the United States had over the events and the bad effect they could have on U.S.-Dominican relations. The U.S. military opposition came as a great shock to Dominican officers; since the 1965 civil war, they had felt they could rely upon their U.S. counterparts for sympathy regarding their policy positions and roles.

U.S. Ambassador Robert Yost (who had recently assumed his post) attempted to deliver a message from President Carter to President Balaguer, in which Carter expressed his disappointment and recalled the promises Balaguer had made at the Panama Canal treaties signing ceremonies. Unable to see Balaguer, Ambassador Yost presented the foreign minister with a similar message from Secretary of State Cyrus Vance. Balaguer later sent a reply to Vance's message, saying that the situation was "normal," accusing the opposition of spreading rumors, and promising a "clean process" of elections.

On 19 May in Washington President Carter, Secretary Vance, and a number of legislators made strong statements about the situation. Carter warned that future U.S. cooperation with the Dominican Republic would depend upon the integrity of the elections and the results being honored by the armed forces. He mentioned that he had consulted with the presidents of Costa Rica, Colombia, Panama, and Venezuela, all of whom were in agreement. Secretary Vance warned that "subversion of the presidential elections" would have a serious effect on U.S.-Dominican relations. Six U.S. legislators—Congressmen Fraser, Thomas Harkin (D-Iowa), Dante Fascell (D-Fla.), and Millicent Fenwick (R-N.J.), and Senators George McGovern (D-S.D.) and Theodore Sarbanes (D-Md.)—issued a declaration deploring the military interruption of the election.[7] Shortly after the armed forces took over the JCE, well-known Dominican academic Frank Moya Pons gave a private briefing to election observer Gregory Wolfe, after which Wolfe called and discussed the situation with Stephansky and Congressman Dante Fascell (D-Fla.), chair of the House Foreign Affairs Subcommittee on the Western Hemisphere. They in turn contacted Secretary Vance, who soon issued the first U.S. statement of concern.[8] Congressman Fraser announced the scheduling of hearings before his subcommittee, which were held on 23 May.

The United States had good company in its actions. On the morning of 17 May, Galo Plaza Lasso, head of the OAS observer team, met with Balaguer. At a press conference after the meeting, Plaza said that he viewed the situation as "grave and abnormal." He related that he had praised Balaguer for saving his country from chaos and told him that accepting the results would assure his place in history, but that permitting a "shady ending" would be "to commit political and historical suicide." More international pressures followed. The Socialist International issued a statement condemning the military intervention, urging respect for the people's will, and expressing its solidarity with the people, the PRD, and Peña Gómez. It orchestrated protests from other European social democratic presidents or prime ministers in Austria, England, France, the German Federal Republic, and Portugal. President Carlos Andrés Pérez of Venezuela organized a joint protest with the presidents of Colombia, Costa Rica, and Panama, all threatening to break diplomatic relations. Dominican dependence on Venezuelan oil was prominently noted by the press.

Balaguer had met regularly with high-ranking military officers after the takeover of the JCE. They were indecisive in the face of the intense internal and external pressures, including pressure from so many other military officers. They soon gave in to the pressure, thus assuring Guzmán's election. In the late morning of 18 May, Balaguer went on national television, announced the resumption of the vote counting, and promised to honor the outcome. He did not concede defeat and charged the PRD with electoral fraud. He also denounced "interference from friendly countries in our America" who threatened to suspend their "supposed aid." Balaguer called for an end to the protests and acceptance of the results; he promised to maintain Dominican democracy and support the constitution.

When the JCE began releasing incomplete election results on 18 May, it was clear that Guzmán would win. Not until seven weeks later, however, on 8 July, were the official returns made public. The JCE declared Guzmán the winner with 856,084 votes to Balaguer's 698,273, a margin of 50 percent to 41 percent (70 percent of the electorate had voted). Balaguer then conceded. Because of a JCE ruling about contested seats in the Senate the Reformist Party (PR) ended up with a sixteen to eleven majority, while the PRD had a forty-eight to forty-three majority in the Chamber of Deputies.

A period of bargaining and maneuvering ensued prior to Guzmán's inauguration on 16 August; Atkins calls it the "second campaign" between the defeated PR and the victorious PRD, and a period of "political-military tension."[9] Spokesmen for the disorganized and weakened PR, who were strongly anticommunist, charged that the PRD government would pose a subversive threat and that it would "Cubanize" the country under Peña Gómez.

In response, president-elect Guzmán reiterated his earlier promises that he would respect private enterprise and human rights, and that his government would continue Balaguer's Cuban policy of nonrecognition but friendly relations through cultural and sports exchanges. He also said that his administration would be a representative democracy and would pursue friendly relations with the United States. Guzmán promised to respect existing contracts with multinational corporations (MNCs) but future ones would have to involve more Dominican participation. Peña Gómez continued to be an issue, particularly his socialist views as presented in an interview published in the *New York Times* on 21 May. He claimed that socialism would be achieved by democratic processes and that relations with Cuba would be restored. Guzmán deflated the resulting controversy by declaring that he himself would be the only official spokesperson for his government's policies. He further announced that Peña would have no governmental position and would leave the country for at least a year following the inauguration. Peña later affirmed the arrangement.

Another PR charge was that the PRD had encouraged foreign intervention in the election by the United States and Venezuela. Juan Bosch rejoined the fray and denounced U.S. intervention and the PRD's "total dependence" on the United States.

A part of the "second campaign" was directed by the PRD toward the armed forces in an effort to gain their confidence. Guzmán repeated previous statements that his government would respect the institution of the armed forces and that he would not dismiss any members except if a law had been violated. He attempted to reassure conservative officers of his moderate policies and views. Nevertheless, Balaguer, before he left office, created new military positions, promoted certain officers, and transferred personnel. At his initiative the legislature enacted laws pertaining to the control and organization of the armed forces that were intended to create a new military balance favorable to Balaguer by freezing PRD enemies into top command positions. On the other hand, Guzmán had the full support of the Nineteenth of May Group of colonels.

The strengthening and functioning of Dominican democracy depended to an important degree on the health of the Dominican economy. This health of the economy in turn was related to important external factors, including, in a major and inextricable way, Dominican relations with the United States. Such dependence included U.S. public assistance, private investment, and the size of the U.S. sugar quota and the market's price level. The reality of the link between democracy and the economy was noted by President Guzmán's ambassador to the United States, Francisco Augusto Lora, when he presented his credentials to President Carter in January 1979: "In order to establish democracy permanently in our country—a democracy with the orderly transition of public office . . . —we urgently need the prices of our export commodities on the international markets, especially the United States market, to be higher than those which now prevail."[10]

President Guzmán, 1978–1982

Silvestre Antonio Guzmán, sixty-seven at the time of his inauguration, was a party rather than personalist politician. A wealthy *hacendado* businessman-rancher from Santiago, he enjoyed a reputation for honesty and strong character.[11] A longtime member of the PRD, he represented the moderate political center of his party. He had been Bosch's secretary of agriculture in 1963, active on the Constitutionalist side during the 1965 civil war, Bosch's vice presidential running mate in the 1966 election, and the 1974 presidential candidate of a coalition ticket led by the PRD (which withdrew from the election).

Guzmán was sworn in as president on 16 August 1978, the 113th anniversary of the Restoration of the Republic from Spanish rule. Great
public optimism was manifested at the time. A U.S. delegation attended
the inauguration, headed by Secretary of State Cyrus Vance and including United Nations Ambassador Andrew Young, Assistant Secretary of
State for Inter-American Affairs Viron Vaky, and commander-in-chief
of the U.S. Southern Command General Dennis McAuliffe. Also present
were Alejandro Orfila, secretary-general of the OAS, Galo Plaza Lasso,
and former president José Figueres of Costa Rica.

In his inaugural address, Guzmán denounced retiring President
Balaguer for his system of political and military corruption and announced an immediate and general program for the "depoliticization,
institutionalization, and professionalization" of the armed forces. Guzmán promised to bring a "true institutionality" to Dominican democracy in a "climate of national unity."

Guzmán was the beneficiary of a new Dominican pride. A military
golpe had been prevented and the electorate had achieved the first constitutional transfer of power from one leader to an elected opposition
president in the country's history. A few months later, in February 1979,
Dominicans were also gratified with the visit of Pope John Paul II to
Santo Domingo. Ironically, the Balaguer legacy was also part of Dominican good feeling. Although by the end of Balaguer's presidency he
had lost considerable popularity and the corruption in his administration was deplored, Dominicans continued to appreciate his high intellectual standing, especially on Dominican history and literature, and
pointed to his visible monuments such as colonial restoration, la Plaza
de la Cultura, and public housing projects.

Military Policy

During his first six months in office Guzmán gave primacy to military
over economic matters. Interestingly, while he was stressing the professionalization of the armed forces, the Carter administration was cutting
U.S. military assistance and shifting its support to democracy and human rights—and once again attempting to make the Dominican Repub-

lic a "showcase." Even though a professional military establishment was related to democracy and human rights, U.S. military training funds (IMET) were cut by more than half for fiscal 1980. At the time of Guzmán's inauguration, the size of the U.S. Military Assistance Advisory Group (MAAG), long the primary vehicle of U.S. military influence, consisted of three officer-advisers and two sergeants. It was true that many Dominican officers in important positions under Guzmán as under Balaguer had received training, either in the United States or in Panama.

Guzmán was politically astute in his handling of military affairs and he soon solved problems related to the role of the armed forces. He was successful in gaining military acquiescence to his policies. His approach was not to balance power, which had been Balaguer's method, but to segregate and fragment it. He isolated individual officers by means of transfers, promotions, and retirements, and appealed to a new generation of officers who shared his reform policies. He also formed a commission of high-ranking officers from all the services that visited military bases throughout the country and talked to military people about their duties toward the new government, in particular the requirement that they stay out of politics.

Six months after the inauguration, in late February 1979, on the same day the nation celebrated the 135th anniversary of independence from Haiti, Guzmán delivered his state-of-the-nation address to the National Assembly, accounting for his first six months in office. He stressed the democratic nature of his government and the positive changes that had taken place in the military establishment. But he admitted the existence of serious economic problems that required his undivided attention.

Economic Policy

Guzmán had a different approach to the economy than had Balaguer. He favored the agricultural sector over the industrial, while Balaguer had preferred industrialization as the means to modernization. Balaguer had endorsed government subsidization of both private sector and foreign investments. Although the left wing in the Dominican Republic and of the PRD were openly critical of foreign investment and favored nationalization, Guzmán believed more in government regulation of foreign investment and announced that all existing contracts with foreign firms would be honored while new rules would apply to new contracts. In fact, as the economic problems deepened, he turned toward foreign investment as a matter of necessity. His policies led to problems with the Santiago industrialists, who favored Balaguer's approach and regional development over Guzmán's national development plan. His policies resulted first in a confrontation with the *santiagueros*, followed by their victory.[12] This victory was politically costly—and ironic, since Santiago was the president's home and power base, and he was a part of the Santiago economic elite (his wife and daughter had been professors at the Universidad Católica Madre y Maestra [UCMM]). The *santiagueros'* success was facilitated by the high educational level and training of most of the businessmen. Many of them had been educated in the United States and they had a network of contacts throughout the government bureaucracy.[13]

Economic Problems

Shortly after Guzmán's inauguration, the Dominican Republic was devastated by Hurricane David, with thousands of deaths and more than one billion dollars in damage. Guzmán's economic program and reform policies were frustrated and undermined, despite his dedicated efforts, by the declining economy and increasing political problems, including the growing division in the PRD and opposition of the Santiago business community. Guzmán attempted to cope with the internal economic situation by doubling the minimum wage, which Balaguer had frozen for twelve years, and imposing price controls. While labor complained that the raises were insufficient, business considered them inflationary. Tensions increased between labor and business over the government's inability to mediate, and disputes developed between the government and business over economic and social reforms. Labor unions strongly objected to the more than 100 percent increase in the price of gasoline; from 1979 to 1981 there was more than a three-fold increase in the number of strikes, work stoppages, and other demonstrations.[14] These actions resulted in thousands of detentions and hundreds of injuries. In the rural areas peasants also increased their demonstrations and the occupation and seizure of land.[15] Guzmán was forced to institute an austerity program.

The agricultural sector, the major earner of foreign exchange, was subject to depressed world prices for the major exports of sugar and coffee. The price the United States paid for sugar recovered from its low between 1976 and 1977 when it temporarily discontinued the quota program; however, when the program resumed, prices slowly rose and then rapidly increased to forty cents a pound in 1980, only to drop to fifteen cents in 1981 and 1982. The Dominican Republic had the largest quota in the U.S. program, with 17.6 percent of the total, followed by Brazil with a quota of 14.5 percent.[16] Another important export, ferronickel, was beset by a world glut of the product. In addition, the great increase in the price of imported oil dealt a major blow to the Dominican economy. During the Guzmán administration, the 30 percent decline in the price of sugar and agricultural exports was accompanied by a four-fold increase in the cost of oil.[17] This oil-sugar disparity was mitigated somewhat by the concessional financing provided by Mexico and Venezuela in their joint sale of oil to the Dominican Republic.

The United States, the primary source of foreign assistance, did not provide aid in sufficient amounts to alleviate the economic situation. The Carter administration, which was sympathetic to the Guzmán government, provided aid that was more politically symbolic rather than economically beneficial. Despite Guzmán's economic problems, particularly after Hurricane David, he refused to accept emergency aid from Cuba when it arrived—aid that had been arranged by Peña Gómez and Senator Salvador Jorge Blanco (president of the PRD) without Guzmán's consent. He did accept emergency hurricane assistance from the Carter administration, which was considerable and was accompanied by two hundred U.S. military personnel.

Political Problems

Guzmán's increasing political difficulties further impaired his ability to carry out economic reform and undermined his credibility.[18] The

PRD lacked full control of the government. As noted above, it held a majority of seats in the Chamber of Deputies but was in the minority in the Senate. Furthermore, the PRD was internally divided. A few months into his presidency Guzmán faced a major schism in his party. Many PRD members were unhappy with his cabinet and other high-level appointments, charging favoritism for the business elite, a shortage of PRD member appointments, and nepotism. Senator Jorge Blanco was the most important dissenter. Other party members were critical of the ties with the Dominican "oligarchy" and foreign business interests, and felt that Guzmán was too close to the United States. The most strongly criticized person was Central Bank president Eduardo Fernández, former vice president of Gulf + Western, the largest U.S. multinational in the country. It was true that Guzmán demonstrated a bias in favor of *santiagueros* affiliated with UCMM.

In addition, nepotism appeared to influence Guzmán's political appointments. Critics charged that Balaguer's "personal government" had been replaced by Guzmán's "family government"—he appointed at least thirty-seven members of his family to government positions. The most visible and influential was his daughter, Sonia Guzmán de Hernández, who was appointed private secretary to her father and deputy to her husband, who was the president's administrative secretary.

Finally, one of Guzmán's most difficult and delicate tasks was dealing with Peña Gómez. Despite Peña's promise to leave the country he later announced that he would not do so. Although on the defensive, Peña could not be ignored because of his leadership, mass urban following, energy, and organizing skills. He did travel widely outside the country and made an extended visit to the United States, but his "moderated" statements did little to alter the belief of conservatives that he was an opportunist biding his time.

Relations with the United States

The Dominican left—particularly Bosch's Dominican Liberation Party (PLD) and Peña Gómez's wing of the PRD—widely criticized investments from U.S. private sources in general and Gulf + Western in particular, which they viewed as evidence of Dominican dependency on and subjugation to the United States. Less was said about the reality of the bulk of Dominican exports, including most of its sugar and those of the IFZs, going to the United States. Anti-U.S. feeling was provoked and Guzmán's economic difficulties were increased when the U.S. Congress passed protectionist legislation and the Reagan administration refused to grant special status to Dominican sugar. Howard Wiarda and Michael Kryzanek call these economic realities in the U.S. relationship with the Dominican Republic a matter of "suprasovereignty."[19] Although Guzmán was far less favorably disposed toward foreign investment than Balaguer had been, he realized its importance and was forced to turn to such investment as a matter of necessity.

The Carter administration had decreased both military and economic assistance but had been generous in 1979 with emergency hurricane aid. The Reagan administration, however, in 1982 increased economic aid to the Guzmán government to $82 million from $38.5 million in 1981. U.S. military assistance was also increased more than $1 million for the same period, from $4 million to $5.5 million, with $1 million for the training of the Dominican armed forces and police.[20]

Relations with Cuba

The Dominican Republic had maintained cool relations with the Castro government since it had broken diplomatic relations in 1962. Guzmán legalized the Dominican Communist party (Partido Dominicano Comunista—PDC) and moderated relations between the two countries but did not establish formal diplomatic relations even though Jorge Blanco urged him to do so. When Cuba sent aid relief following Hurricane David that had been arranged by Jorge and Peña Gómez, Guzmán refused to accept it. He did permit unofficial ties in sports and cultural exchanges, as had Balaguer, as well as a modicum of official contacts. In the 1970s Dominicans had begun going to Cuba for medical treatment at the suggestion of their physicians, travel that continued during Guzmán's presidency. This care was one-fourth to one-third the cost of medical care in the United States, where most Dominicans had traditionally gone. The number of people traveling to Cuba for care greatly increased in the late 1980s. These mainly informal relations with Cuba served the double purpose of minimizing the Dominican left's criticism and providing some leverage to bargain with the United States.[21]

Central American Policy

In 1978, when it appeared likely that the Sandinista-led popular insurrection against general-dictator Anastasio Somoza in Nicaragua would win, President Carter organized the International Commission of Friendly Cooperation and Conciliation. Headed by the United States and including the ambassadors of the Dominican Republic and Guatemala, it attempted to mediate a settlement. Guzmán's ambassador was active in this unsuccessful effort, which Somoza rejected. The Dominican left, including members within the PRD, criticized Guzmán for pandering to the United States. Guzmán recognized the Sandinista government, which came to power after Somoza was overthrown in July 1979, after the United States had done so. He and his party praised the Sandinista victory and the goals of its revolution.

Relations with Haiti

Guzmán improved relations with Haiti in two fields: the particular problem of the treatment of Haitian workers in the Dominican Republic and general political relations. The predicament of Haitian laborers, employed primarily to cut sugarcane during the season in the Dominican Republic, whether entering illegally or by agreement between the two governments, was a long-standing one. This problem was largely a function of Dominican cultural and racial views of Haitians, reinforced by the economic gap between the two countries that resulted in low wages and miserable working conditions for Haitians. Most Dominicans believed that the arduous task of cutting sugarcane was fit only for Haitians, an attitude that reinforced their dependence on Haitian labor.[22] Guzmán took far more seriously than had Balaguer the treatment of Haitian workers and tried to reduce Dominican antipathies.

On the broader political level, Guzmán normalized relations with Haiti. In 1979 he met with President Jean-Claude "Baby Doc" Duvalier to sign a cooperation agreement; on a later occasion they opened a joint irrigation project. In another accord the two presidents created a one-million-dollar fund for trade promotion.[23] An old problem between the two countries had been the use of Dominican territory by anti-Duvalier exiles trying to organize a *coup* in Haiti, including the transmission of critical radio broadcasts. Trujillo had encouraged such activities and later governments had tolerated them. Guzmán, however, suppressed these activities and arrested some of the Haitian exiles. In 1982 he ordered the deportation of one exile, Louis Roche, whose subsequent imprisonment in Haiti provoked a public controversy in the Dominican Republic.

The Campaign and Election of 1982

Guzmán had been expected to seek a second term in 1982, but his surprising announcement in June 1981 that he would not left open the PRD nomination. He chose his vice president, Jacobo Majluta, as his successor but was defied by his party at its November 1981 nominating convention. The PRD was divided because Peña Gómez, the secretary-general, wanted the nomination and led a separatist movement. Another issue was that the left wing members of the party wanted the new government to address the reform issues, especially the social ones, that Guzmán had neglected. After a nomination struggle, Jorge Blanco became the party's candidate.

Balaguer was the nominee of his personalist PR, his effort to return to power notwithstanding physical problems (especially hearing and vision difficulties) at the age of 75. Although the major political struggle was between Jorge Blanco and Balaguer, another grand old man of the political system—Juan Bosch of the PLD—was a candidate. He returned to the political fray after an absence of many years. In addition,

General Elías Wessin y Wessin, vintage 1965 and candidate of the Quisqueyan Dominican Party (PQD) in 1970, joined the political battle.

The 1982 Campaign and Election

During the campaign, Jorge Blanco announced that he would base
his government on Guzmán's "political democracy" but would have
as his specific goal the achievement of "economic democracy." This
announcement worried some members of the business class, who considered his purpose to be shorthand for more government control.
Jorge seemed to have in mind solving the economic and social problems of education, land distribution, and unemployment. Balaguer
campaigned on the basis of the sorry state of the economy and the resultant instability, reminding the electorate of the relative economic
prosperity and stability during his government in the 1970s. While
Jorge appealed to the urban masses and the lower middle class, particularly in Santo Domingo, Balaguer appealed to the middle class and
business community.

In mid-May 1982 some 74 percent of the electorate went to the polls.
Jorge Blanco was elected president, and the PRD gained a majority in
both the Senate and Chamber of Deputies. Jorge received 46.7 percent
of the vote to Balaguer's 39.2 percent. In the Senate, the PRD had seventeen seats to the PR's ten; in the Chamber of Deputies, the number of
seats was sixty-two to fifty. Majluta was elected to the Senate and, as
president, soon sharply criticized Jorge just as the latter, in the same
position, had opposed Guzmán. Peña Gómez won the mayorship of
Santo Domingo. In 1983 he gave up his post as PRD secretary in order
to concentrate on his own campaign to secure the presidential nomination for 1986.[24]

In early July, six weeks before Jorge's inauguration in mid-August,
Guzmán killed himself. The official explanation was an accidental
death. Vice President Majluta took over as acting president until inauguration day. Although there is agreement that Guzmán was personally
honest, credible support exists for the theory that his daughter Sonia
was corrupt and an influence peddler and that some close aides were

skimming government contracts. Her activities and others had become known and Jorge Blanco informed Guzmán that her acts would have to be investigated in order to head off an exposé. Guzmán's fear of a family scandal and its impact on his government led to his self-destruction.[25]

The Jorge Government, 1982–1986

Salvador Jorge Blanco, fifty-seven years of age at the time of his August 1982 inauguration, was a progressive urban lawyer from the left wing of the PRD with a strong reputation for honesty. After the U.S. intervention in 1965 he had represented many of the Constitutionalist combatants in negotiations with the Nationalist side and the United States.[26] His political power base was among the urban masses, centered in Santo Domingo. During Guzmán's presidency he had been the head of the PRD minority in the Senate, where he criticized Guzmán's appointments and ties with business and often opposed his policies. In his inaugural address he announced that the Dominican Republic was "financially bankrupt" and that it was the "victim" of external forces such as European and U.S. "protectionism." Despite blaming many of the economic problems on the United States, he declared his intention "to maintain excellent relations" with it, saying that those relations "may become a priceless instrument of dignified and fruitful co-existence."[27] He announced an austerity program as an absolute necessity.

Economic Policy and Problems

Jorge, like Guzmán before him, took certain actions to assure that the armed forces took no hostile action against him. He retired and transferred those high-ranking officers about whom he was doubtful and promoted and appointed to important positions those he trusted. Whereas Guzmán had favored the agricultural and rural sector, Jorge's economic problems required him to turn to the cities and urban centers, although he also tried to expand agricultural production. His efforts focused on Santo Domingo, the capital and largest city, which was bearing the brunt of his austerity program and manifesting increased opposition. Jorge also tried to modernize industry and engaged in public works to reduce unemployment, but the Senate blocked his legislative proposals for stimulating the economy, including obtaining international loans. Senator Jacobo Majluta, Guzmán's former vice president, was a prime mover in the opposition in the PRD-controlled body.

Jorge soon faced an economic crisis far worse than Guzmán had confronted, which vitiated his economic program. The prices for the Dominican Republic's main exports were declining and the balance-of-payments deficit mounting—the Reagan administration had recently cut the Dominican sugar quota by 32 percent (from 780,000 to 528,000 metric tons). To deal with the situation, Jorge first banned the import of certain luxury goods and then raised taxes on other luxury imports as well as on capital gains and real estate. These measures antagonized the business community with which he formerly had good relations. The worsening economic situation forced Jorge to turn to the International Monetary Fund (IMF) for credits and loans; the IMF conditioned its assistance on increased austerity. By taking such measures Jorge lost the support of his natural constituency among urban workers and the lower and middle classes.

In the fall of 1982, Jorge signed a three-year standby agreement with the IMF providing for a total credit of $467 million. The IMF requirements were the following: ending most import restrictions, including those on luxury goods; moderating export restrictions; and devaluing the Dominican peso.[28] Jorge found it necessary to engage in what he had criticized Guzmán for—seeking foreign investment with few restrictions. In 1983, out of the total of $248 million foreign investment in the Dominican Republic, the United States provided $148 million. In January 1984 Jorge wrote to President Reagan about the potentially dangerous social impact of the IMF's conditions on stability and democracy, but to no avail.

Jorge's concern was prescient: riots broke out in April 1984 when he began implementing the series of restrictions. Two phases were involved in carrying out the IMF's conditions that culminated in the riots. The first included a new series of price increases resulting from imports being subject to the new exchange rates: the prices of imported goods increased 200 percent. The second involved the government ending subsidies on many basic foodstuffs, such as bread, cooking oil, and flour. In response, business and labor unions jointly announced a twenty-four-hour strike. Barricades went up, the police were challenged and resisted, and riots broke out accompanied by looting and arson. The violence began in Santo Domingo and spread to other cities. Jorge ordered in the police, who dealt with the problem with the use of tear gas and occupation of the unions' headquarters. Police forces were not willing to take lethal measures, however, and a special military unit, the Cazadores de la Montaña (which the United States had trained), was ordered in. Using deadly force, this unit soon ended the rioting. The result was some one hundred deaths among the rioters, several hundred more casualties, and more than four thousand arrests.[29] Soon after these events the IMF relaxed some of its conditions and the Reagan administration provided a fifty-million-dollar loan so that the Jorge government would not default on certain loans.

Another worry for Jorge was caused by the June announcement of the new president of Gulf + Western (the former president had tried to change the company's image) that the company was for sale and was disposing of its sugar properties because of the continually declining price of sugar. This announcement was gratifying to many leftists, who over the years had criticized the company's influence and receipt of special treatment. Jorge had been among the critics (as had Peña Gómez) but now President Jorge was afraid that the company's sale would discourage the foreign investment that he desperately sought. (In 1985 the Fanjul brothers, U.S. citizens of Cuban extraction in Miami who had sugar interests in Florida, bought the company. The group of Florida investors backing them also included a group of Dominicans. Carlos Morales Troncoso, a Dominican businessman, became titular head of the umbrella company; in 1986 Morales became Balaguer's vice-president).[30]

Political Problems

The violence referred to above, the worst since the 1965 civil war, and the great human and economic cost, had a strong impact on the political system and set the stage for the 1986 elections. The Jorge government lost much of its popular support because of economic policy reversals and failed social reforms, even though these problems were largely attributable to a combination of the worsening global economy and the opposition of Senator Majluta. Jorge's willingness to permit the use of force in dealing with the rioting alienated many of his supporters, who thought him as oppressive as Balaguer had been.

In early 1985 the Dominican government signed a new accord with the IMF. Its implementation required new government-mandated increases in the prices of food and gasoline, which were accompanied by public demonstrations and several hundred arrests in numerous cities. Leading business, labor, professional, and political organizations jointly supported a general strike, which shut down the capital and some other cities. The Jorge government had lost its legitimacy among most groups, including its base constituency.

Relations with the United States

Despite Jorge's criticisms of the Guzmán administration while he was PRD president and a senator, particularly for not regulating foreign investment and for catering to the United States, he felt compelled to maintain good relations with the United States as he had promised in his inaugural address. Early in Jorge's term, in October 1982, the United States had strongly supported the Dominican Republic to occupy one of the two Latin American non-permanent seats on the United Nations Security Council, which was being actively sought by Nicaragua. In the ensuing controversy, most of the Third World and the Soviet bloc states supported Nicaragua, which won out over the Dominican Republic. The contest was widely viewed as a U.S. defeat.

Although the Jorge government became active in the Nonaligned Movement (NAM), it remained silent about the October 1983 U.S. intervention in Grenada. Peña Gómez and other PRD members were highly critical. In the same year Jorge actively lobbied for President Reagan's proposed Caribbean Basin Initiative (CBI), which provided for low tariffs or duty-free access of most Caribbean countries' exports to the

United States, as well as subsidies for industry. (Nicaragua was expressly excluded; the Cuban embargo continued.) The CBI went into effect in 1984, and the Dominican Republic became one of the leading beneficiaries. Although the Reagan administration cut the Dominican sugar quota in January 1984, it lifted the 2.8 cents per pound tariff on Dominican sugar. That same year the Jorge government sold 135,000 metric tons of sugar to the Soviet Union. The United States and the IMF had been pleased with Jorge's ready acceptance of IMF conditions for credits and loans and its compliance with them. This acceptance assured the continued disbursement of IMF funds and renewal of the agreement in 1985. Following the April 1984 violence and its suppression, Jorge sought additional military aid, especially for police training. The United States increased its military assistance in fiscal year 1985 to almost $6 million with the addition of $750,000 for police training. In 1984 Jorge visited Washington, D.C., and made the rounds of various U.S. agencies and the Congress, requesting additional economic assistance. The Reagan administration agreed to provide one hundred million dollars in fiscal 1985, less than Jorge had sought.

Drug Trafficking

A new problem, drug trafficking, emerged in the mid-1980s as part of the U.S.-Dominican relationship, as the Dominican Republic became a major transit and transshipment point for the Cali drug cartel in Colombia. The drugs from Cali went to San Francisco de Macorís and Santiago de los Caballeros in the Dominican Republic, and then to Puerto Rico and on to New York City. A criminal link developed between Santo Domingo and New York, and Dominicans in New York (both legal and illegal residents) became the dominant street-level distributors. In 1984 the United States arrested a Dominican who was in the Cali cartel. The Jorge government cooperated with the United States in forming a Joint Information and Coordination Center, which began operating in late 1985 (administered on the U.S. side by the Department of Justice's Drug Enforcement Agency [DEA]). Although the Dominican Republic was a party to only a few of the treaties dealing with drug trafficking,[31] its constitution prohibits the extradition of Dominicans.

Migrants to the United States

The increasing economic problems in the Dominican Republic during the Guzmán government, and particularly the economic crises and riots during Jorge's presidency, stimulated a growing exodus of Dominicans to the United States, primarily to New York City. This increasing "Dominican diaspora" reinforced and expanded the Dominican community in New York. This time more blue-collar workers migrated as well as more people with higher educational levels. The flow of remittances (*remesas*) during the Jorge government became especially important to the Dominican economy. This wave of Dominicans became a part of a developing "transnational identity," using the characterization of Eugenia Georges, one that transcended both countries as Dominicans circulated between the two.[32] Fully 20 percent of all outside travelers to the Dominican Republic came from the United States, a large number of whom were Dominicans. Many migrants saved sufficient money in the United States to be able to return home for long periods of time. Others had enough to open businesses or retire in the Dominican Republic. The returnees stimulated a new housing industry in which 60 percent of new units were owned by them. Money earned by the survivors of drug distribution in New York also helped the Dominican economy. The Dominicans returning for visits, or to start a business or retire, were stigmatized as "Dominicanyork" ("Domyork" for short). Those associated with the drug trade, who often wore neck chains, were referred to as "cadenú."[33]

Another dimension of migration related to Dominicans recruited by U.S. baseball scouts. To deal with abuses, President Jorge in 1984 issued a decree for the purpose of preventing baseball scouts from exploiting Dominican youngsters. It provided for the registration of all scouts, government approval of all minor league contracts signed in the country, prohibiting the signing of anyone under seventeen years of age, and compulsory English classes for all players in the Dominican Republic.[34]

Circum-Caribbean Relations

In 1983 the Jorge government sought full observer status in the Caribbean Community (CARICOM). It was rejected on account of the strong opposition of prime ministers Maurice Bishop of Grenada and Forbes Burnham of Guyana, who argued that the Dominican Republic was too dependent on the United States. Prime Minister Edward Seaga of Jamaica strongly backed the Dominican application. Jorge was silent about the Reagan administration's intervention in Grenada in September 1983 (after Bishop's execution), and he did not attend the 1985 inauguration of Daniel Ortega in Nicaragua. He did, however, support the Contadora Group's proposals for Central American peace that directly challenged the Reagan administration's actions. The summer 1985 Central American and Caribbean Games, which included Cuban participation, were held in Santiago in the Dominican Republic.

Relations with Haiti

In 1983 the International Labor Organization (ILO), a specialized agency of the United Nations, released a critical report about the treatment of Haitian sugarcane cutters in the Dominican Republic, how they were contracted for, exploited, and treated as slave labor. The same year Jorge ratified a United Nations convention on discrimination.[35] The ILO report was the latest exposé of a long-standing scandal of Dominican maltreatment of Haitians in general and in particular those contracted to cut sugarcane each fall during the sugar harvest. The system of exploitation had been reinforced by the fact that Haiti had been so poverty-stricken in comparison with the Dominican Republic. Shortly after the release of the ILO report, the Dominican Roman Catholic Church, which had become socially active in the 1980s and concerned about Haitian workers, issued a message on the subject. It was widely circulated and led to demonstrations outside the Dominican embassy in Port-au-Prince. President Jorge sent a personal letter to the church hierarchy in which he rejected the Church's position but promised to investigate.[36]

A new concern among Dominicans that reinforced their negative views of Haitians was the emergence in the mid-1980s of AIDS (Acquired Immune Deficiency Syndrome, SIDA in Spanish), which appeared to justify the isolation and expulsion of Haitians. Dominicans had long blamed them as the purveyors of venereal disease in the Dominican Republic; even Balaguer, in his 1983 edition of *La isla al revés: Haití y el destino dominicano*, had commented on such a Haitian impact on Dominican health.

Conclusion

The two PRD presidents had ideological and operational differences, characterized as conservative Guzmán's *democracia política* and liberal Jorge's *democracia económica*. They were especially notable in terms of the serious economic situation and U.S. relations. Nevertheless, in sum, each of their moderate and progressive policies and efforts to strengthen democracy and stabilize the economy were frustrated and undermined by the worsening conditions in each arena—and set the stage for the 1986 elections and the beginning of the second Balaguer era.

8 The Second Balaguer Regime, 1986–1996, and the Election of Fernández

Joaquín Balaguer, president of the Dominican Republic from his first electoral victory in 1966 until voted out in 1978, in 1986 established a second regime that again directed the Dominican Republic's domestic and foreign policy. He was reelected in 1986, 1992, and, for the sixth (and final) time, in 1994 (a post-election agreement limited his tenure to two years). During this time, the United States, as a world superpower and key regional actor, shifted to and pursued foreign policies strongly influenced by changing global and inter-American conditions. With the end of East-West conflict, and the neoliberal political and economic transformations around Latin America, the United States sought to reformulate policies in terms of post-Cold War considerations.

Elements of the continuing Dominican-U.S. relationship influenced the nature of the Dominican political system and the extent to which foreign policy calculations were revised on the part of U.S. decision makers. Some specific elements include various cultural, economic, human, political, and social dimensions. The extent of the "dual" interdependent and symbiotic relationship in the new era often transcended official government-to-government relations. The election of 1996 marked the end of the Balaguer era and began the presidency of a newcomer to the political scene, Leonel Fernández.

The Campaign and Election of 1986

Former President Balaguer, already a leading political and intellectual figure at the time of his first election in 1966, which marked the

beginning of a presidency that lasted for twelve years until 1978, returned to the presidential electoral fray in 1986 after an eight-year absence from the office.[1] Although seventy-nine years old, virtually blind,
and in declining health, he decided to be a contender—and won the
elections. In 1984 Balaguer had amalgamated his Reformist Party (PR)
with the Christian Social Revolutionary Party (PRSC) to form the Christian Social Reformist Party (also abbreviated PRSC). It was a symbiotic
merger: the PRSC joined Balaguer's well-organized personalist organization, while the PR benefitted from the multiclass and programmatic
nature—and financial help—of the PRSC. Balaguer's running mate,
Carlos Morales Troncoso, had several attractions: he was a young candidate at age forty-five; he was well known as a successful executive,
past president of the country's largest sugar company (Central Romana), and former head of Gulf + Western; and he was not a politician.

The Dominican Revolutionary Party (PRD) suffered from seriously
eroded public credibility after eight years in power under presidents
Antonio Guzmán and Salvador Jorge Blanco. According to Rosario Espinal, the "disastrous performance" of the eight years of PRD rule was
due to "adverse economic conditions, business opposition, . . . international pressures to impose austerity measures, and a highly ineffective
political leadership."[2] Add to this evaluation the fragmentation of the
PRD and the stage was set for the campaign and election—and the return of Balaguer.

The PRD entered the 1986 electoral period on the heels of a divisive nomination contest stemming from long-standing animosities and
competition among the three major competing personalities: outgoing
President Salvador Jorge Blanco, Senator Jacobo Majluta, and Santo Domingo Mayor José Francisco Peña Gómez. The national party convention in November 1985 had deteriorated into violence. While Peña Gómez thought he had won the nomination (and evidence suggests that
he had), Majluta and his supporters charged fraud and claimed that
Majluta actually had a majority of the primary votes. Jorge had backed
Peña Gómez, but his support vacillated. Majluta had out-organized
and out-maneuvered the competition. The two rivals subsequently
launched separate campaigns supported by their respective personal
intra-party *tendencias*: Majluta with *La Estructura* (LE) and Peña Gó-

mez and his *Bloque Institucional*. Jorge organized his element without a designation. After months of public squabbling, a "unity pact" was worked out in January 1986 that gave the presidential nomination to Majluta and that of vice president to Peña Gómez. The latter soon withdrew his name, however, charging that the primary election had been stolen from him. He later said that the 1990 nomination should be his and warned those who would try to prevent it. Since Majluta was from Santo Domingo, a wealthy businessman from Santiago was selected as his running mate to balance the ticket.

Juan Bosch, a long-established major figure of the political scene, again ran for president. At age seventy-eight, he was the nominee of his Dominican Liberation Party (PLD).

The major issue in the campaign was the economy. The PRD was on the defensive after eight years of rule. Its claims of making social reforms, reducing corruption in government, professionalizing the military, and blaming the dependent economy for many of its problems, rang hollow. Balaguer faulted the PRD for mismanaging the economy, reminded voters of the economic prosperity during his presidency, and promised to restore the economy with a major public works program. He also emphasized the importance of Dominican sovereignty and resisting foreign pressure, especially from the international financial community (that is, the United States and the International Monetary Fund [IMF]). Bosch stressed the same theme. Some violent incidents occurred and the usual charges of fraud were made.

At the request of the opposition and to make the process legitimate, the government appointed a *Comité de Notables*, headed by the archbishop of Santo Domingo, to supervise the election. When most of the returns showed a narrow margin favoring Balaguer, Majluta stopped the counting by means of a legal challenge and called for a recount, which tied up the process for weeks. The final outcome of the election was determined by negotiations between the Central Electoral Commission (JCE), the *Comité*, and representatives of the three leading candidates agreeing on Balaguer's narrow victory margin.[3] The announced final results were the following: Balaguer, 41.6 percent; Majluta, 39.5 percent; and Bosch, 18.3 percent.[4] Balaguer's PRSC won a majority in the Senate, twenty-one seats to the PRD's seven and the PLD's two; and also in the Chamber of Deputies, with fifty-six PRSC members to forty-eight for the PRD and sixteen for the PLD.[5]

The New Balaguer Regime

President Balaguer was interested, first, in establishing his control over the armed forces and the government bureaucracy, and, second, in trying to improve the economic situation that continued to worsen. He made the armed forces commanders subordinate and loyal to him with key appointments, transfers, and retirements. Balaguer then undertook to transform the PRD carryover bureaucracy into his own, using his appointive powers to reorganize and expand it. He enjoyed a rubber-stamp majority in the Senate, and the opposition PRD and PLD in the Chamber of Deputies were unable to overcome their partisan rivalry to offer a united opposition.

Economic Policy and Problems

Although Balaguer blamed the declining Dominican economy on his predecessor's policies, mismanagement, and corruption, he soon found it necessary to pursue much the same course that President Jorge Blanco had followed. Economic problems stemmed primarily from a combination of deficit-financing in the face of declining world prices for Dominican exports (especially sugar) and the high cost of imported petroleum and petroleum products (the Dominican Republic imported virtually all of its oil, mostly from Venezuela). By this time the major foreign exchange earnings came from a combination of tourism and foreign private investment (mainly U.S.-based and in the expanding Industrial Free Zones [IFZs]). By late 1988, seventeen IFZs comprising 220 companies had been established, with four more underway. Foreign remittances from Dominicans resident in the United States were increasingly important. Despite the declining importance of sugar, the United States delivered a major blow to the Dominican economy when it cut the Dominican sugar quota for 1987 by 48 percent.

Balaguer sought to revive the economy by keeping wages low, engaging in extensive construction and public works projects, increasing the money supply, and attracting foreign investment. These efforts resulted in a rapid 50 percent increase in the inflation rate. The combination of the rising cost of living and low wages in early 1988 led to mounting protests. Strikes and violence spread throughout the country. In March Balaguer ordered that a major general strike be suppressed, which resulted in ten deaths, many injuries, and thousands of arrests. But he also responded by granting large wage increases to public employees and freezing food prices. Nevertheless, the protests continued, as did riot police actions and more casualties.[6]

The church entered the tense scene and the archbishop of Santo Domingo brought together representatives of the government, business, and labor for negotiations in a "Tripartite Dialogue." Shortly thereafter the archbishop announced an eight-point program that included changes in the Labor Code and an increase in the minimum wage. A few weeks later, however, the labor confederations withdrew from the agreement, charging violations by the business community.[7] Relations between labor and the government returned to confrontational. Relations between business and the government steadily deteriorated—mainly due to the latter's strict control of exchange rates, restrictions on imports, and stabilization programs.

Relations with Cuba and the Soviet Union

The Dominican Republic had never established diplomatic relations with Castro's Cuba or with the members of the Soviet bloc. On occasion Balaguer threatened to do so with Cuba, mainly as a ploy to bargain with the United States. However, cultural and sporting contacts had been made with Cuba, and Dominicans went to Cuba for medical care.[8] For economic reasons and as an expression of anger over the U.S. reduction of the Dominican sugar quota, in 1987 Balaguer negotiated with the Soviet Union for the sale of 150,000 tons of sugar at very favorable terms for the Dominican Republic.[9] The United States expressed displeasure with the arrangement.

Relations with Haiti

Haitian dictator Jean-Claude "Baby Doc" Duvalier's involuntary departure from power in February 1986 was followed by months of political instability in Haiti. In 1966 Balaguer and Baby Doc's dictator-father had signed an agreement regarding Haitian sugarcane cutters working in the Dominican Republic, but it had not been renewed when it expired. (While the accord was in effect the number of Haitians per year varied from ten thousand to sixteen thousand, but usually amounted to about twelve thousand). The expiration of the agreement led to a great labor shortage on the Dominican State Sugar Council (CEA) plantations. In response, the Dominican armed forces rounded up Haitians in the country and forcibly took them to the CEA estates. The Dominican army set up roadblocks, raided certain Haitian communities, arrested Haitians, and took them involuntarily to the sugar estates. Even "dark" Dominicans were forced to cut sugarcane. In 1989 Americas Watch issued a hard-hitting critical report of these activities, bringing international attention to the human rights abuses. Dominican government officials denounced the report as a false attack on the Dominican Republic.[10] Balaguer delayed further action until after the 1990 elections.

The 1990 Campaign and Election

Balaguer and Juan Bosch were again candidates for the presidency in the 1990 election. Bosch hoped to expand on the 19 percent of the vote he had received in 1986 and return to office twenty-seven years after his overthrow in 1963. He and his PLD party were optimistic, as they moved from the left more to the center and were even conservative on some issues. In the PRD Peña Gómez continued to lead the "leftist" wing while Majluta headed the "moderate" wing. The chronic PRD divisiveness further encouraged Bosch. Peña proposed in late 1989 that, in the name of party unity, he and Majluta present a joint-presidency ticket in which each would serve as president for two years. After weeks of discussion and squabbling, however, Peña Gómez became the

PRD nominee and Majluta that of his own independent party. Following his long practice of announcing his candidacy at the last minute, Balaguer preempted the announced candidacy of another member of the PRSC who had raised the issue of Balaguer's age and competence with the slogan "time for a new generation" (referring to both Balaguer and Bosch).[11]

Campaign issues focused on Balaguer's economic policies. Balaguer stressed that he had increased the number of IFZs and foreign companies operating in the country, and augmented private investment, particularly in the IFZs. By 1990 the number of IFZs had increased to thirty and also included what were called the Section 936 funds from Puerto Rico.[12] Balaguer also noted the important increase in tourism. The PRD stressed the economic diversification it had achieved while in office from 1978 to 1986. Both parties had come to accept and adopt economic austerity measures.[13] Rumors again circulated that Peña Gómez was Haitian and not a loyal Dominican.

The election was held in May but the results were not announced until mid-July. Balaguer was reelected with 35.1 percent of the vote, Bosch was a close second with 33.8 percent, and Majluta received only 7 percent. The PRSC won sixteen Senate seats, the PLD twelve, and the PRD two. In the Chamber of Deputies the PRSC won forty-two seats, but the PLD had a plurality with forty-four, and the PRD held thirty-two.[14]

Balaguer began his 1990 term with continuing economic problems and the opposition of both labor and business. Even before his August inauguration Balaguer sought to improve relations with the latter by proposing a Pact of Economic Solidarity and granting some of the business community's requests. In 1990 Balaguer implemented an economic stabilization plan. In 1991 he signed the long-postponed agreement with the IMF under which the IMF agreed to provide $113 million. The agreement resulted in a renegotiation of $926 million in debt with the Paris Club, an intergovernmental group that dealt with government-to-government loans during the "debt crisis" after 1982. The required liberalization program, which ended price controls and subsidies to state agencies, had the effect of beginning a "turnaround" in the economic situation. This improvement greatly benefitted Balaguer in the 1994 election.[15]

Until the economic improvement became apparent in late 1992, however, labor agitation and strikes continued in protest of the austerity program. In an attempt to placate the strikers, Balaguer promised to hold early national elections in 1992 and to have the constitution amended to limit presidents to a single term. This promise, however, turned out to be another shrewd tactic to buy time and undermine the opposition. A long strike by doctors and medical workers was finally settled in 1991 by a government promise to increase their salaries by 50 percent.

The V Centenario

Balaguer had long anticipated and prepared to celebrate the five-hundredth anniversary of Columbus's discovery of America. It was to culminate on Columbus Day, 12 October 1992, with the official inauguration of the Columbus Lighthouse (*El Faro á Colón*). In the 1970s Balaguer had overseen the restoration of colonial Santo Domingo and, upon his return to the presidency in 1986, he began in earnest the construction of El Faro. The plan was also a part of his stress on *hispanidad* and the Dominican Republic's Spanish heritage. The project had been surrounded by a great deal of controversy. One issue concerned the expensive building costs, which critics estimated at fifty to seventy million dollars, but Balaguer claimed to be fifteen million dollars. Another stemmed from the fact that three thousand squatters had been forced from a razed area for the construction site. In order to cover up the surrounding slum area, a ten-foot high stone wall was built around the lighthouse—dubbed by its detractors as the "Wall of Shame."

Despite the large financial investment and extensive promotional publicity, the celebration turned out to be a disaster.[16] Celebration ceremonies were scheduled to commence on 6 October with the transfer of the *restos* (remains) of Columbus to a mausoleum in El Faro. But Balaguer's sister, a prominent part of the bachelor-president's personal and political life, died of a heart attack before the event, and Balaguer canceled all public appearances while in mourning. In addition, only one of the invited Latin American presidents appeared, and the King of Spain, who was to preside over the ceremonies, rescheduled his visit for December. These personages did not want to legitimate and be associated with Balaguer's unpopular regime and the controversy about the cost of El Faro as well as the V Centenario in general. Instead the Dominican vice president and the Organization of American States (OAS) secretary-general presided. Pope John Paul II, in the country for the Fourth General Conference of Latin American Bishops (CELAM), distanced himself from the events and declined a request to officiate at a mass on 12 October in El Faro. He said an earlier mass in which he canonized a nineteenth-century Spanish priest who had worked in Gran Colombia; on Columbus Day he said a mass in the small town of Higüey, ninety miles from Santo Domingo. Another disappointment was that the tourist industry benefitted much less than expected because of the limited number of foreign visitors. Finally, public protests were directed against the ceremony in general and against the lighthouse in particular both before and during the ceremony.

Relations with Haiti

Two months after his 1990 inauguration, Balaguer responded to the critical 1989 Americas Watch report and made some improvements in dealing with Haitian workers. The government standardized their immigrant status, issued individual contracts to sugarcane workers, and improved the living facilities on the state plantations. Another Americas Watch report acknowledged the improvements but recounted the continuation of other major abuses.[17] The U.S. Lawyers Committee for Human Rights issued its own critical report, which focused on the treatment of Haitian children. In June 1991 Balaguer further responded to the continued bad publicity by ordering the deportation of illegal Haitians who were under sixteen or over sixty years of age. Within a few months fifty thousand Haitians had been deported or left in anticipation of being rounded up. The deportation policy received a mixed reaction in the Dominican Republic; it was supported by the National Defense Organization but opposed in a letter signed by hundreds of Dominican intellectuals.[18]

Balaguer indicated his traditional negative attitude toward Haiti and Haitians when Jean-Bertrand Aristide, a Roman Catholic liberation-theology priest, was elected president in December 1990 in Haiti's first free and honest national elections. Balaguer refused to recognize Aristide's inauguration in February or to condemn the military action that overthrew him in September. In October the OAS approved economic sanctions against the Haitian military government as a means of pressuring it to accept the return of Aristide to office. Balaguer refused to cooperate, although the Dominican Republic voted for the OAS sanctions. He also declined to support United Nations actions in the situation. In June 1993 the UN imposed an oil embargo, which was temporarily suspended in August but reimposed in October, along with a naval blockade to enforce it. The Dominican border remained open for smuggling goods, especially gasoline, to Haiti. The Balaguer government and Dominicans, continuing a long history of exploitation, were happy to take advantage of the situation. Suppliers and border guards enriched themselves. In addition, Balaguer was engaged in a reelection campaign in which his major rival was the PRD's nominee, Peña Gómez, whom his campaigners disdainfully referred to as "Haitian."

In early May the UN imposed a total blockade. At this time President Clinton publicly called for the Dominican-Haitian border to be closed. He later sent a message to Balaguer stressing that his compliance with the UN embargo would be "the test" of the status of Dominican-U.S. relations. Involved in a mounting controversy concerning voting in the 15 May elections, Balaguer felt that he needed to be on good terms with the United States. Consequently, he reluctantly permitted the military presence of a symbolic UN-U.S. force on the Dominican-Haitian border, although he did not order Dominicans to discontinue their smuggling efforts.[19] Balaguer and many Dominicans did not welcome the September 1994 U.S. military intervention in Haiti, approved by the UN Security Council, and the return of Aristide in October.

The 1994 Campaign and Election

The major contenders for the presidency were familiar personalities. Balaguer sought a sixth elected presidential term and Bosch hoped to rectify his narrow defeat in 1990. Peña Gómez was the PRD nominee. Majluta was the candidate of his independent party; otherwise the PRD appeared to be united.

Two campaign issues were the state of the economy and the age of the octogenarian candidates. Balaguer was in the most favored position inasmuch as the economy had recovered. Agricultural production had increased, inflation had been greatly reduced, unemployment had declined, a new Labor Code had been promulgated, tourism had increased, and the IFZs had increased in number as well as the number of foreign companies operating in them.[20] Balaguer took credit for the greatly improved economic situation and stressed the resultant stability. Balaguer dealt with the issue of age—his increasing enfeeblement was obvious—by selecting as his running mate Jacinto Peynado, a young, energetic, and capable administrator.

At the start of his campaign Peña Gómez publicly supported the return of Aristide to the presidential office in Haiti. He called attention to corruption in the Balaguer government, an issue of reduced importance given the August 1991 public trial, and reaffirmed conviction for corruption of former PRD President Jorge,[21] and the maldistribution of the benefits of the greatly improved economy. Once again but even more racist than before, Peña Gómez was the victim of anti-Haitian bigotry, with a vicious rumor campaign saying that since he practiced voodoo he was not a loyal Dominican. Late in the campaign Balaguer denounced these attacks on Peña; they had apparently served their purpose and were in danger of becoming counterproductive.[22]

A twenty-six member delegation organized by the National Democratic Institute (NDI) in the United States observed the May election. It was headed by former Representative Stephen Solarz (D-N.Y.). The NDI had sponsored a similar group to observe the 1990 Dominican election. The OAS also sent an election observation mission, and another private group of observers was present. Balaguer enjoyed a large early lead as the returns started coming in, but Peña Gómez steadily closed the gap to a minuscule difference of less than one percent (only twenty-two thousand votes). Peña charged fraud and demanded a recount. The charge rested on the fact that the JCE had issued two different voter lists, one to the polling site officials and the other to the political parties. Many names on the latter list did not appear on the former one, so that voters with valid identification cards were turned away; this situation appeared to work against the PRD and Peña Gómez. The members of the NDI observer mission supported this charge and issued a critical report two days after the election.[23] At this time most of the presidential candidates signed a Pact of Civility in which they agreed that they would not claim victory before the final official results were announced and would respect those results. The signing of the pact was formally witnessed by a commission of prominent Dominicans organized by the church.

In response to the charges of fraud, the JCE in early June set up an investigatory verification commission. Its report in mid-July was not convincing, however, since it was factually inconsistent and did not deal with all the issues. In fact, the JCE itself ignored the report when on 2 August it announced the official returns. Balaguer was declared the winner over Peña Gómez by 42.3 percent to 41.6 percent, a margin of 22,281 votes; Bosch received 13.1 percent and Majluta 2.6 percent (87 percent of the electorate participated in the voting). In the Senate, the PRSC kept fourteen seats, the PRD and its allies won fifteen, and the PLD took one; in the Chamber of Deputies, the PRSC won fifty seats, the PRD and allies fifty-seven, and the PLD thirteen.[24]

Peña Gómez renewed his charges of fraud and called for a general strike on 15 and 16 August (the latter was inauguration day). The church and the OAS mediated negotiations between the parties. On 10 August, Balaguer and Peña Gómez signed a Pact of Democracy that provided for Balaguer to serve for fifteen months as president, with a new presidential and vice presidential election to be held in November 1995 in which Balaguer would not be a candidate.[25] The Dominican

Congress legislated an alternative scheme, calling for a special election in 1996 to choose a president to serve out the remaining two years of Balaguer's term that had begun in 1994. The Supreme Court upheld its legality. Then, after much opposition and a long struggle and delay, the Dominican Constitution was amended to prohibit a president from serving a second term. Thus Balaguer could not be a candidate in the 1996 special elections.

Neutral analysts and observers generally agreed that fraud was prevalent in the May 1994 elections and that consequently they were not legitimate. Nevertheless, it was not possible to corroborate and document the fraud or to prove that enough of the disenfranchised voters would have voted for Peña Gómez to assure his victory. (The U.S. State Department sent a computer team to work with the U.S. embassy to analyze the election results.) Perhaps the Clinton administration's preoccupation with Aristide's return to the Haitian presidency, and Balaguer's cooperation by closing the Dominican-Haitian border to smuggling, caused it to be less insistent on a recount of the Dominican balloting. Furthermore, Balaguer was a shrewd politician with experience in dealing with both domestic opponents and the United States regarding contested elections.[26] A test would come with elections in May 1996 and whether Balaguer honored his promise not to be a candidate (he would be eighty-nine years old at the time). Another possible test would be the nature of any self-imposed role of the United States as the "guarantor" of Dominican democracy in the event of broken promises or serious irregularities in that election.

The "Dual" Societies and Increasing Transnationalism

After Balaguer's return to office in 1986, the cultural, educational, economic, and social dimensions of the "dual" societies were reinforced. The relatively new drug trafficking linkage was the province of both increasing cooperation and problems between the governments of the United States and the Dominican Republic.

Drug Trafficking

Despite the friction between Clinton and Balaguer over the latter's refusal, until May 1994, to support the OAS and UN sanctions against Haiti, the two countries cooperated closely in efforts to reduce drug trafficking. Efforts had begun in the mid-1980s, when the Dominican Republic became an important transit point for narcotics coming into the U.S. This mounting problem, to which the United States assigned high priority, involved two broad areas: interdicting drug trafficking prior to entering the United States and dealing with Dominican drug sellers, especially those in New York City and Dominican fugitives fleeing back home. Thus problems of crime and violence existed at both ends of the transnational drug-criminal connection, but the most important juncture was in New York. In the late 1980s, Dominican traffickers gained control of the distribution of cocaine, most of it coming from the Cali cartel in Colombia, in the Washington Heights section of Manhattan. This control resulted in increasing crime and violence in drug-dealer battles over territory. In the early 1990s the U.S. and New York City authorities responded by refusing admission to more and more Dominicans at JFK Airport, making more arrests and indictments, and sending more of them to prison.[27] An example of the problem was provided when a Dominican drug dealer was shot by a plainclothes policeman in Washington Heights in July 1992, an event that sparked riots and looting. At the time Balaguer appealed publicly to his "compatriots," advising them to demand respect for their rights without resorting to violence.[28]

The United States also assisted the Dominican government in an array of other measures: preventing Dominican illegals from departing for the United States, especially to Puerto Rico; seizing drugs in the Dominican Republic or in transit; signing treaties to ban drug trafficking; and extraditing Dominican fugitives to the United States. It also assigned three Drug Enforcement Agency (DEA) agents to the Dominican Republic, and provided training and equipment to Dominican National Police, air force, and navy. In July 1990, the Caribbean Basin Radar Network in Baní began operation. Major drug seizures were made in 1991 and 1993; the one in 1991 was the largest in Dominican history.[29] The Dominican Republic and the United States both belonged to the twenty-nine-member OAS Inter-American Drug Abuse Control Commission.

The United States was party to certain UN treaties that it pressed the Dominican Republic to ratify so as to further facilitate their bilateral effort. Those treaties were the 1961 Single Convention on Narcotic Drugs, the 1971 Convention on Psychotropic Substances, and the 1988 Convention Against Illicit Traffic in Narcotic Drugs and Psychotropic Substances. Soon after the U.S. House of Representatives Select Committee on Narcotics Abuse and Control announced that it would hold hearings on "Dominican Drug Trafficking" in late March 1993, Balaguer sent the 1972 protocol and the 1988 convention to the Dominican Senate for approval, which was forthcoming in September. The United States also solicited the renegotiation and updating of the 1909 extradition treaty between the two countries, which did not apply to drug trafficking and left extradition to the discretion of the Dominican president. Although the Dominican constitution and a Dominican law prohibited the extradition of citizens, Balaguer had extradited two Dominican fugitives, one in 1989 and another in 1991, on the ground that international treaties transcended Dominican domestic law.[30]

An important factor on the Dominican side of the transnational drug linkage, related to the extradition of criminal fugitives, was the impact of the money and values of the wealthy drug traffickers who had survived dealing on the streets of New York City and returned to the Dominican Republic. Their wealth prompted a construction boom, and their preferred locale of San Francisco de Macorís was transformed from a traditional Dominican city to one of expensive cars, boutiques, noisy night clubs and discotheques, large satellite dishes, and spectacular show-house suburbs (named "Bronx" and "Manhattan"). Many poor adolescent males envied the former drug dealers and worshipped them as heroes. These young men attended the lavish funerals of the dealers who had been killed in local violence or as part of the New York drug trade (and shipped home for burial) in such numbers as to make them mob scenes. Going to New York to make a fortune in drug dealing became a second "American dream" for such teenagers, in addition to the long-standing one of being recruited by a U.S. major league baseball team.[31] The established residents of San Francisco de Macorís were dismayed by the impact of these developments, which they blamed for inflating prices, introducing a criminal element, changing traditional values, and the increasing incidence of AIDS.[32]

Economic and Cultural Transnationalism

These related economic and cultural dimensions of the "dual" societies were increasingly important after 1986. This importance was illustrated in the economic arena by more of the Section 936 twin plants, increased numbers of IFZs and companies operating in them, multiplying U.S. private investments in the tourist industry and the numbers of tourists themselves, and more Dominicans with companies in both countries.[33] In 1993 the Dominican government expressed concern about the negative impact on jobs and exports if the U.S. approved the North American Free Trade Agreement (NAFTA).[34] In the United States the success and upward mobility of Dominicans in New York City increased its own demand for more migrants.[35] Dominicans in New York increasingly became small entrepreneurs, taking over most of the Spanish bodegas, portions of garment contracting, retail trade, and public transportation. They managed 90 percent of the taxi and limousine services in upper Manhattan, owned three newspapers, three supermarket chains, and two television stations.[36] As a sign of their prosperity as well as link with the Dominican Republic, the *dominicanos ausentes* joined U.S. Anglo investors in supporting joint projects in the IFZs.

On the cultural side, English had clearly become the second language of the Dominican Republic, and Dominicans in the United States placed a high premium on learning English and going to college. This importance was well-illustrated in New York City, where Dominicans were instrumental in the establishment of the Hostos Community College. It was named after a famous Puerto Rican educational reformer who in the 1880s had lived in exile in the Dominican Republic. He advocated new teaching methods, especially in the training of teachers, and was director of the Normal School in Santo Domingo. A Latin American

Writers Institute was located at the community college. The numbers and impetus of Dominican students also resulted in April 1993 in the creation of the Dominican Studies Institute (the only one in the United States) in the City College of the City University of New York—its director is Professor Silvio Torres-Saillant. The purpose of the institute, as stated in a brochure announcing a November 1994 conference on "Dominican Writers in the Context of the Americas: A Dialogue on Literature and Cultural Identity," was to make up for "the current lack of information in the U.S. about the Dominican experience" by organizing scholarly conferences, creating a data bank, publishing a Dominican Studies Research Monograph series, and sponsoring research projects on Dominican life in the United States. This conference, and an earlier one, were cosponsored by the Dominican-American Assistance Fund and La Alianza Dominicana. An example of its work is the preparation of the first *Directory of Dominicanists*, compiled by Dominican poet Norberto P. James. For several years he had kept an unpublished listing of authors and specialists in Dominican affairs from various disciplines and fields. Another example was provided by the 1993 announcement from Lehman College's Puerto Rican Studies Program of a tenure-track faculty position for the comparative study of the Caribbean "with special interest in the Dominican Republic."[37]

Music was an expanding influence in the binational cultural linkage. Dominican musicians achieved considerable success in the United States (and in Europe), after which many of them returned home to alter music in the Dominican Republic. We may mention one leading musician and his famous group—Juan Luís Guerra and the 440. Guerra formed his band in 1984 on his return to the Dominican Republic after studying at Boston's Berklee College of Music. His music drew on Caribbean and African-based folkloric rhythms mixed with poetic lyrics. With the dominance of the meringue, however, Guerra was only modestly popular at home, whereas in 1987 a recording titled "Ojalá que Lleva Café" was an international success.[38] Guerra, contrary to perhaps most Dominican musicians, drew on the African roots of Dominican culture and music. A major success came with an album, "Bachata Rosa," which won a Grammy award in 1992. Guerra also popularized the Dominican merengue but came to lead a movement challenging it by reviving the bachata.[39] With two former members of his 440 group, Víctor José Víctor Rojos ("Víctor Víctor") and Maridalia Hernández, their efforts are marking the end of the dominance of merengue as the Dominican Republic's sole musical export.

The Campaign and Election of 1996

In contrast to previous elections over the past thirty years, incumbent Joaquín Balaguer and his political protagonist, Juan Bosch, did not battle each other in the 1996 election. Balaguer, aged eighty-nine years, was barred from seeking reelection, and Bosch, eighty-seven years old, had retired from public life due to ill health. Their respective parties consequently nominated much younger candidates: the PRSC selected Balaguer's vice president, businessman Jacinto Peynado, fifty-five; and the PLD chose Bosch's 1994 vice presidential nominee and new head of the party, lawyer Leonel Fernández, forty-three. The PRD's candidate was once again José Francisco Peña Gómez, fifty-nine, who was also the nominee of an alliance of small parties.

The campaign revolved around the economic situation and government leadership. The PLD and PRD candidates focused on the declining economy, ineffective and corrupt government, and the need for leaders with new and modern ideas (polls indicated that most Dominicans favored such leaders). The PRSC was on the defensive, mainly because of the way Balaguer had won the 1994 election. PRSC leaders initially ignored the 1994 political agreement and organized a movement to have the election annulled. When this failed and became counterproductive, they focused on defending Balaguer's economic policies. In the spring and summer of 1995, strikes and riots occurred over increased bus fares and limited salary increases. Increasing police suppression resulted in many arrests and injuries. In early 1996, the government aired exaggerated claims about increasing economic growth and declining inflation. Balaguer's supporters again injected the racist-nationalist issue against Peña Gómez—that he was not Dominican but Haitian and favored the unification of the two countries. Three weeks before the election Balaguer ordered the deportation of Haitians, which resulted in a roundup of thousands. Peña Gómez denied the rumors and appealed to his constituency, the poor masses, stressing the slogan *"primero la gente"* ("the people first"). Relative political novice Fernández ran the most U.S.-style of campaign among the candidates. He had lived in New York City for ten years and had attended public schools there. His constituency was mainly the middle and upper classes and he promised an end to protectionism, favored economic competition, and stressed the important "special relationship" with the United States. Although Peynado's campaign presented modern, progressive ideas (his running mate was a young businesswoman with no political experience), he was viewed by the electorate as the status quo candidate—although Balaguer gave him no public support. Some political violence occurred, primarily at PLD and PRD political rallies, resulting in a number of deaths.

In preparation for the 16 May election, which applied only to the presidency, a number of observer groups were present to assure the integrity of the process. Some of them had also been present in 1994—those from the OAS and United Nations, the U.S. Democratic and Republican parties, and the Carter Center, among others. The voter turnout was about 75 percent, in what the OAS observer team certified as a valid, reliable, and representative election. As expected, Peña Gómez received the greatest number of votes with 46 percent, and Fernández won 39 percent. Peynado trailed with only 15 percent of the total.[40]

In keeping with the new election laws, a runoff election was required to be held within forty-five days between the two leading candidates. The runoff election was scheduled for 30 June to decide between Peña Gómez and Fernández. The PRSC met formally soon after the first round election in order to prepare for the second round to decide on which of the two remaining candidates to support. The predictably easy and pragmatic decision was in favor of Fernández over longtime protagonist Peña Gómez; the former needed PRSC backing in order to win the presidency. This decision resulted in a symbiotic agreement signed and alliance formed between the two parties, called the National Patriotic Front. Peña Gómez protested to no avail. The campaign environment was generally peaceful and positive with only isolated incidents; the opposition continued to promote the usual talk about Peña Gómez as Haitian. Again about 75 percent of the electorate turned out to vote in another fair and honest election. The election was verified by the outside observer groups and by the Dominican civic *Red Ciudadana de Observadores Electorales/Participación Ciudadana,* and was praised by former President Jimmy Carter. Fernández won over Peña Gómez by a narrow margin, an outcome clearly made possible by the PRSC. He received 51.25 percent of the vote to Peña Gómez's 48.75 percent.[41] Soon after the Central Electoral Commission (JCE) announced the results on 1 July, Peña Gómez conceded his loss and indirectly admitted the fairness of the election. In a message to Fernández, Peña Gómez declared, "I have no alternative but to admit we, unfortunately, did not win the election. . . . [We] will be a tough opposition, but fair."[42]

On 16 August 1996 Leonel Fernández was inaugurated the one-hundredth and youngest president of the Dominican Republic, and Joaquín Balaguer ended his tenure as the oldest president in Dominican history. In his inaugural address, Fernández stressed his commitment to modernize the country and renovate the government, including the elimination of corruption. President Fernández clearly represents a new generation of Dominican leadership. His effectiveness in carrying out his policies as chief executive, however, will depend on the old generation and ex-President Balaguer, whose party has a veto with its control of the legislative branch.

Conclusion

With the end of the Balaguer era and the beginning of a new period of Dominican politics, the state of democracy in the Dominican Republic presented a mixed picture. Democracy and its development, a combination of political, economic, and social-cultural elements, has particular characteristics in the Dominican context. We must acknowledge that by any definition of democracy—and definitions vary considerably in their specific formulations—any state's concurrence is a matter of degree. It seems that virtually every democracy is, in practice, at least sometimes a messy affair. Nevertheless, if we apply the generally accepted standards of fair and competitive access to political power, open accountability on the part of governors to the governed, basic civil rights and freedoms, and equitable rule of law, the system in the Dominican Republic, as it has emerged from 1978 and continued to evolve into the 1990s, may be fairly called a "partial democracy."

Although the Guzmán and Jorge administrations from 1978 to 1986 were unable to implement their principal economic and social reforms because they faced serious economic problems and at times the opposition of the National Assembly, they made contributions to the furtherance of Dominican democracy. Guzmán released many political prisoners, and both he and Jorge established freedom of expression and of the press. They also made progress in depoliticizing the armed forces. The economic crises, however, tended to exacerbate class and social divisions.

An important political development was that the National Assembly became more active and institutionalized and effectively challenged the president. This situation changed, however, when Balaguer returned to power in 1986 and his party won a majority in both legislative chambers, a situation continuing in 1996 and expected to do so until the elections of 1998.

With regard to the political parties, Rosario Espinal argued that "competitive elections truly began" with the 1978 election, which demonstrated the existence of a two-party system. The situation continued through the elections of 1982 and 1986. But then the tendency developed toward a multiparty system, which was manifested in the 1990, 1994, and 1996 elections. At the same time, Jonathan Hartlyn's characterization of Dominican democracy as "crisis-prone" was apt, demonstrated by the course of the four elections between 1978 and 1994.[43]

Other reasons indicate why Dominican democracy was crisis-prone. One was the personalist nature of politics, which placed leaders above party and resulted in party fragmentation. The PRD was a prime example. The leader of a "tendency" or wing was more interested in winning the party's nomination, even if it divided the party and weakened its ability to compete with Balaguer and his PRSC. This personalist aspect was further demonstrated when Jorge and Majluta as senators opposed their own party's president in order to enhance their personal political positions in the quest for the presidency. In the other two major parties, the PRSC and the PLD, one person dominated—Balaguer and Bosch, respectively—and, despite their advanced ages, refused to prepare successors. Michael Kryzanek calls the lack of successorship "political atrophy."[44] The question of what would happen to their parties and the political process when age finally caught up with the two octogenarian *caudillos* was answered for the PLD in 1995 when Bosch announced his retirement from politics and turned the party over to Fernández. The PRSC was still led by Balaguer; he and his party exercised influence because of the alliance with the PLD that assured Fernández's runoff election victory. Furthermore, the PRSC had a controlling majority in both the Senate and Chamber of Deputies. The next elections are scheduled for 1998.

Another problem stemmed from an important aspect of the "duality" of the Dominican Republic—its economic dependence on the United States. This problem was serious on account of the link between politics and economics, often expressed as the economic "prerequisite" for representative democracy. Two sides to this problem were evident. First, Dominican presidential candidates and presidents felt compelled to go to the United States, making the rounds of executive agencies and legislative committees to lobby for their programs and solicit economic assistance. Second, the United States could cut the Dominican sugar quota or public funds without concern for the devastating economic impact on the Dominican Republic. International agencies in which the United States strongly influenced decisions might engage in the same behavior (such as IMF standby agreements with conditions that when implemented had significant domestic political consequences). Outside advice for Dominican economic diversification without assisting the process was a hollow gesture. Some diversification did occur, however; in the late 1980s, tourism and exports through the Industrial Free Zones (IFZs) together produced more income than sugar exports.

The 1994 election appeared to validate characterizations of the condition of Dominican democracy as fragile and crisis-prone. Yet the election also indicated that the Dominican model was making progress. A competitive party system seemed to have emerged, which was continued in the 1996 special election. The class system had become more flexible, with a steady increase in the size and influence of the middle class. A general consensus existed among Dominicans, indicated by certain groups—the church, labor unions, elements of the military, virtually all classes, students, and the business community—in favor of representative democracy, political party competition, an effective legislature, honest elections, and an end to government corruption. The JCE and government bore the brunt of this consensus in 1994 when the JCE engaged in electoral fraud and a coverup. The JCE appeared to have learned its lesson—its conduct in both rounds of the 1996 special election was open and responsible. The hundreds of outside observers and those of the Dominican *Red Ciudadana* made a significant contribution to the JCE's new professionalism.

Another negative aspect was continuing racism in Dominican society—toward Haitians in general and sugarcane cutters in particular, and toward darker-skinned Dominicans. Balaguer continued to tolerate and even promote these racial attitudes, as evidenced by the attacks on Peña Gómez in the elections of 1990, 1994, and 1996 (plus his deportation of Haitians as a campaign ploy) and by his approach to the problem of Haitian sugarcane cutters in the Dominican Republic. Nonetheless, progress is being made on the racial issue, both toward Haitians and "darker" Dominicans. The church has become socially active, has spoken out about the treatment of Haitian laborers, and has been working to improve racial relations among Dominicans. UCMM has organized seminars and conferences on Dominican-Haitian relations and sponsored research on revisionist views about them. UCMM and the Museo del Hombre Dominicano have sponsored seminars on Dominican and Caribbean identity. The recognition, legitimation, and celebration of Dominicans' African roots and the *cultura criollo* have finally been institutionalized and have become an integral aspect of Dominican culture and society. This accomplishment has been achieved despite Balaguer's earlier resistance.

The various dimensions of the "dual" societies continue to be strengthened. The relatively new and negative dimension of drug trafficking remains highly problematical (President Fernández pledged his cooperation with the United States in controlling it). Those dimensions of an economic and cultural character, however, especially continue to indicate the transnational relations and linkages that bind the two countries together in inseparable and symbiotic ways.

Epilogue

This study has focussed on the evolution of Dominican Republic–United States relations from the mid-nineteenth century to the present in their political, military, economic, and sociocultural dimensions. As indicated in the book's subtitle, those relationships evolved from primarily imperial connections to essentially transnational associations. An intervening period in the course of change was characterized by immense state power asymmetry and complicated by the nature of the long-term Trujillo dictatorship (1930–61). After a chaotic five-year transition period, the next thirty years constituted a politically semidemocratic and personalist era. This era was dominated by President Joaquín Balaguer (1966–78, 1986–96), with an eight-year interregnum (1978–86) in which two leaders of the opposition Dominican Revolutionary Party, Silvestre Antonio Guzmán and Salvador Jorge Blanco, each served as president. Throughout most of the twentieth century, the question of Dominican democracy and the U.S. role accompanied and compounded the complexity of the progression from imperialism to transnationalism.

Imperialism, one of the oldest concepts and phenomena in international relations, was well-known to Dominicans who, from the 1490s to the 1920s, were subject to the imperial policies of great powers. According to Plano and Olton, imperialism was "a superior-inferior relationship in which an area and its people have been subordinated to the will of a foreign state."[1] Colonialism, one of the ways in which classic imperialism was manifested, involved the settling of people from the imperial power in the territory in question and imposition of rule over any local peoples. The colony was a nonsovereign dependent territory, the possession of a sovereign state and completely subject to its rule.

Beginning with Columbus's voyages in 1492, the Americas were absorbed into the evolving new international system, characterized by European conquest, colonization, and commercial domination. What became the Dominican Republic was the first Spanish (and European) colony in the New World and the starting point for the creation of Spain's vast American empire. Spain ruled its colony of Santo Domingo for three centuries; it ceded the western third of Hispaniola to France, laying the basis for the later creation of independent Haiti. For a brief period Spain also ceded the Spanish-speaking portion to France, after which Spain reassumed control. Dominicans declared their independence in 1821 but were immediately subject to further conquest and occupation—not by a European power, but by newly independent Haiti (from 1822 to 1844). The occupation was followed by an enduring enmity between the small neighboring island-states.

Imperialism persisted after the Dominican Republic secured its independence in 1844. Outside actors were certain European states and the United States as well as certain individuals who became deeply involved in the chronic intrigue of Dominican politics while seeking personal gain. The United States did not become a major presence until after the end of its civil war in 1865; it then took an essentially imperialist attitude, characterized by the mixture of a nascent strategic-political calculation, economic motives, and cultural arrogance. For the Dominican Republic itself, from 1844 through the rest of the nineteenth century, international history also followed the fortunes of Dominican individuals who dominated politics.

The involvement of foreigners in Dominicans' affairs aroused their nationalism, yet it also stimulated their acceptance and even willingness to exchange sovereignty for security under a protectorate or with outright annexation. (A protectorate was a treaty-based arrangement of a "semisovereign state" with a relatively powerful outside state, which provided security and exercised certain sovereign powers but without annexing and governing the subordinate entity as a colony.) Certain Dominican leaders, mostly authoritarian military men who feared Haiti and sought personal advantage, disagreed over who should be the foreign protector. They favored and approached, inter alia, Spain, France, the United Kingdom, and the United States. Except for Spain, the European states were not interested in protecting or annexing the chaotic Dominican entity, but neither did they want any other state to do so.

Nevertheless, in 1861, Spain accepted the invitation to reannex the Dominican Republic; at the time the other outside states were unwilling or unable to stop the arrangement. In 1865 Dominicans themselves demanded and (again) received their independence. The Dominican Republic signed a treaty of annexation with the United States in 1869 but the U.S. Senate refused to consent. Dominican presidents made ruinous contracts with European and U.S. financiers.

After 1898 and the clear emergence of the United States as a world power, most of the circum-Caribbean became a U.S. sphere of influence. In the pursuit of imperialism, yet short of colonization, U.S. interests and power dominated the area in a kind of dependent territory arrangement. Other outside states generally recognized and conceded the U.S. sphere of influence.

The Dominican Republic was one of the principal objects of U.S. Caribbean imperialism. From about 1900 to 1924 the United States dominated and directly intervened in Dominican affairs, including political, military, economic, and cultural manifestations of imperialism. U.S. officials sought primarily to prevent further European influence in the area and to maintain political stability in the local states; they were specifically concerned with securing the Caribbean approaches to the Panama Canal. The Dominican Republic's overwhelming financial obligations to European creditors, and the specter of a European military presence to enforce pecuniary claims, was a particular concern. The United States became so involved in the Dominican economy, especially in customs receiverships, that the Dominican government did not make the normally sovereign fiscal and monetary decisions; economic dependency made it risky for Dominican leaders to defy U.S. political preferences. President William Howard Taft (1909–13) added the practice of "dollar diplomacy," which encouraged U.S. entrepreneurs to make capital investments in and extend loans to the Dominican Republic, which in turn led to military intervention during times of default or endangerment to U.S. lives and property. President Woodrow Wilson (1913–21) increased the number of interventions in the Dominican Republic and further justified them in terms of a democratic credo. Periodic U.S. fiscal, electoral, and military intervention culminated in military occupation and governance from 1916 to 1924. U.S. cultural imperialism—the imposition of one nation's values on another—was more subtle and indirect and less developed.

By the mid-1920s imperial policies had fallen into disrepute in the United States, and the orientation and certain allied instruments were incrementally abandoned. The process was completed by the mid-1930s. It coincided with Rafael Trujillo's rise to power in the Dominican Republic and his consolidation of dictatorial power. Elements of a sphere of influence structure persisted, however, in terms of power politics and economic dependency. They were reasserted from time to time throughout the Trujillo dictatorship until its end in 1961 and continued until recent years. The most dramatic use of U.S. police power was the military intervention during the 1965 Dominican civil war. But U.S. policy was not so much a concerted or systematic imperial policy as much as the ad hoc application of instruments to deal with problems as they arose related to perceptions of extrahemispheric threats in the circum-Caribbean.

This interpretation may be disputed. After World War II and the disappearance of classic imperialism, some opponents of U.S. policy in the Dominican Republic and the United States referred to dependency theory and the notion of neocolonialism operating in terms of the international capitalist system. In our view, U.S. policy was better explained in terms of an often exaggerated fear of Soviet expansionism, benign neglect when that fear abated, and vacillating attempts to "democratize" Latin America, all within the context of inherent power disparities. In the Dominican Republic, the concept of neocolonialism reflected ambivalence in seeking assistance from the United States while rejecting its interference in internal affairs. Nor were Dominican governments without at least limited recourse and ways to deal with the United States to their advantage (a matter discussed in the earlier chapters).

Over the years, and especially after 1966 with the end of the Trujillo dictatorship and its turbulent aftermath, Dominican-U.S. governmental relationships were increasingly parallelled by transnational associations. In time the consequences of transnationalization transcended those associated with the vestiges of imperialism and the disparities in state power. That is, unofficial binational relationships came to be more consequential than the bilateral interstate ones; furthermore, the Dominican Republic had a significant impact on the United States in numerous respects.

Transnational relations have elevated the prominence of non-nation-state actors (e.g., multinational corporations, nongovernmental organizations, communications and entertainment media, political party associations, criminal drug groups, and educational and religious networks) and intensified pivotal sets of phenomena that evolve in a manner largely autonomous from and parallel with interstate relations (the political, social, cultural, and economic consequences of cross-national trade and other commercial activity, movement of peoples, traffic in narcotics, religious networks, sports, popular culture, educational interchange, and more). The assumption is that such phenomena have increasingly tied together the multiple elements of Latin America's complex international relations. We argue this has been the case in the Dominican-U.S. instance. The transnationalization of inter-American relations has been accompanied by their globalization—the augmented intertwining of both interstate and unofficial relations on intra-Latin American, inter-American, extra-hemispheric, and global levels. In the case of the Dominican Republic, the primary orientation has continued to center on the United States and its Caribbean neighbors, although the other levels of expansion have been important. Globalization has been evident in the challenges of economic reform and integration, problems of human rights, military relations, arms control and demilitarization, migration of peoples, the narcotics traffic, insurgencies, environmental questions, and other matters. Transnationalization and globalization have also been understood in the context of the new Latin American democracies and partial democracies, a primary element regarding the Dominican Republic.

The dramatically increasing transnational relations between the two countries have been a two-way street. As indicated earlier, analysts have referred to the consequences of U.S. influence as the "Northamericanization" of the Dominican Republic and the reciprocal impact as the "Dominicanization" (a special part of the larger "Caribbeanization") of the United States. It was also pointed out that a third concept arose, in reaction to U.S. cultural influences: the "Dominicanization of the Dominican Republic," which was pursued as policy by President Balaguer. In fact, the process of Northamericanization resulted in divided Dominican views, and sometimes ambivalence, about the United States, with some developing a taste for U.S. products and lifestyle and others an objection to U.S. popular cultural, materialism, and secularism. Balaguer attempted to counteract the process by stressing the Spanish cultural and historical legacy, at the same time resisting the rising popular *cultura criollo* movement that emphasized the country's black African roots.

Some of the elements of transnationalism sprang from what were originally ingredients of the early imperial relationship. Dominicans who have resented or feared foreign influences continued to see them as cultural imperialism, as have some analysts of international relations. Past cultural imperialism may result in extended domination and fundamental changes in the original culture. In fact, Dominicans have widely adopted English as a second language, and combined with their movement between the Dominican Republic and the United States and the proliferation of the U.S. communications and entertainment media in the Caribbean, "foreign" ideas and values have been accepted. But these phenomena have not been concomitant to or a consequence of U.S. state policies, and they have been welcomed by a large number of Dominicans so that, in the traditional sense of power politics, cultural imperialism does not seem to be involved. Frank Moya Pons equates Northamericanization with modernization, seeing it as an inevitable consequence of the societies' proximity, migration, commerce, and cultural contact.[2]

At the end of the 1980s Latin America's ongoing political and economic transformations combined with the end of global East-West conflict to produce a new post-Cold War era in inter-American relations. In that context the traditional U.S. security concerns and their connection to Dominican stability greatly decreased in importance, while such matters as Dominican democracy and economic well-being, movement of peoples as migrants and travelers, and narcotics trafficking rose to top priority. Consequently, the attention and influence of the U.S. government further decreased while those of transnational private and nongovernmental sectors increased.

The 1996 election marked the end of the Balaguer era and the beginning of something new. While we cannot yet determine the new era's characteristics, the election did mark the marriage of Dominican democracy and transnationalism in the sense that new president Leonel Fernández dramatically personifies the transnationalization of Dominican-U.S. relations. The youngest president in Dominican history, Fernández had lived in New York City as a member of the Dominican immigrant community for ten years (almost a quarter of his life at the time he was elected at the age of forty-three). He attended elementary and secondary schools in New York, acquired excellent English as a second language, and became a basketball (not baseball) fan (of the New York Knicks). After finishing high school in the United States he returned to the Dominican Republic and earned his law degree. He ran a U.S.-style electoral campaign in 1996, one of videos, political consultants, advertisements, and constant polling. Some of the videos showed him shooting baskets in a Chicago Bulls uniform, which was in the same colors as those of his political party. As a mulatto Fernández is proud of his African roots. A political and economic pragmatist and realist, he realizes the importance of cooperative and friendly relations with the United States. A majority of the Dominican electorate seemed to signal that it either supported or did not object to transnational realities.[3]

Notes

Introduction

1. These matters regarding general U.S. policy orientations are discussed in detail in G. Pope Atkins, *Latin America in the International Political System*, 3d ed. (Boulder: Westview Press, 1995), chap. 5; and Atkins, "The United States and the Caribbean Basin," chap. 2 in *Regional Hegemons: Threat Perceptions and Strategic Response*, ed. David J. Myers (Boulder: Westview Press, 1991). See also Larman C. Wilson, "Multilateral Policy and Organization of American States: Latin American–U.S. Convergence and Divergence," in Harold E. Davis, Larman C. Wilson, and others, *Latin American Foreign Policies: An Analysis* (Baltimore: Johns Hopkins University Press, 1975), 47–84; and Howard J. Wiarda, *Ethnocentrism in Foreign Policy: Can We Understand the Third World?* (Washington, D.C.: American Enterprise Institute, 1985).

2. See Mariano Baptista Gumucio, *Latinoamericanos y norteamericanos: Cinco siglos de dos culturas* (La Paz: Editorial "Artística," 1987); and John J. Johnson, *Latin America in Caricature* (Austin: University of Texas Press, 1981).

3. P. H. Coombs, *The Fourth Dimension of Foreign Policy: Educational and Cultural Affairs* (New York: Harper and Row, 1964); and J. M. Mitchell, *International Cultural Relations: Key Concepts in International Relations* (London: Allen and Unwin, in association with the British Council, 1986), 1–2, 8–9.

4. Howard J. Wiarda and Michael J. Kryzanek, *The Dominican Republic: A Caribbean Crucible*, 2d ed. (Boulder: Westview Press, 1992), 126; and Jan K. Black, *The Dominican Republic: Politics and Development in an Unsovereign State* (London: Allen and Unwin, 1986).

1. Colonial and Nineteenth-Century Foundations

1. Graham H. Stuart and James Tigner, *Latin America and the United States*, 6th ed. (Englewood Cliffs: Prentice-Hall, 1975), 411. Frank Moya Pons, *The Dominican Republic: A National History* (New Rochelle, N.Y.: Hispaniola Books, 1995), chaps. 2–5, is authoritative on the colonial period.

233

2. Fradique Lizardo Barinas, *Cultura africana en Santo Domingo. Dibujos primarios* . . . [y] *dibujos definitivos* (Santo Domingo: Sociedad Industrial Dominicana en Editora Taller, 1979), 26–27, 72–75; and Moya Pons, *Dominican Republic*, 33–37.

3. Stuart and Tigner, *Latin America and the United States*, 411.

4. See Moya Pons, *Dominican Republic*, chaps. 5–7.

5. Stuart and Tigner, *Latin America and the United States*, 412–13.

6. Rayford W. Logan, *Haiti and the Dominican Republic* (New York: Oxford University Press, 1968), 17–22. Logan points out that hostility was aimed by the mulatto *gens de couleur* and *affranchis* toward the white *grands-blancs*, *bourgeois-gentilshommes*, and *petits blancs*, who in turn were hostile toward the mulattos. See Frank Moya Pons, *La dominación haitiana, 1822–1844*, 2d ed. (Santiago de los Caballeros: Universidad Católica Madre y Maestra, 1972). Bernardo Vega, *Trujillo y Haití (1930–1937)* (Santo Domingo: Fundacíon Cultural Dominicana, 1988), has a section on "El Antihaitianismo" (23–30) that includes quotes from leading Dominican thinkers and historians expressing their racial attitudes during the period 1844–1930.

7. Charles Callan Tansill, *The United States and Santo Domingo, 1798–1873: A Chapter in Caribbean Diplomacy* (Baltimore: Johns Hopkins University Press, 1938).

8. Luis Martínez-Fernández, *Torn between Empires: Economy, Society, and Patterns of Political Thought in the Hispanic Caribbean, 1840–1878* (Athens: University of Georgia Press, 1994), 32–40, 57.

9. Tansill, *United States and Santo Domingo*, presents trade data for the period. Official U.S. and Dominican documents are contained in *Diplomatic Correspondence of the United States: Inter-American Affairs, 1831–1860*, vol. 7, *Dominican Republic, Ecuador, France*, selected and arranged by William R. Manning (Washington, D.C.: Carnegie Endowment for International Peace, 1935), 2–219.

10. John J. Johnson, *A Hemisphere Apart: The Foundations of United States Policy toward Latin America* (Baltimore: Johns Hopkins University Press, 1990).

11. For details see Moya Pons, *Dominican Republic*, chaps. 8 and 9.

12. Harry Hoetink, "The Dominican Republic in the Nineteenth Century: Some Notes on Stratification, Immigration, and Race," in *Race and Class in Latin America*, ed. Max Mörner (New York: Columbia University Press, 1970), 117.

13. Fernando Pérez Memen, "Panorama Histórico de las Emigraciones Dominicanas a Puerto Rico," in *Los Inmigrantes Indocumentados Dominicanos en*

Puerto Rico: Realidad y Mitos, ed. Juan E. Hernández Cruz (San Germán: Universidad Interamericana de Puerto Rico, 1989), 11–12.

14. On the Spanish recolonization, see Moya Pons, *Dominican Republic,* chap. 10.

15. Sumner Welles, *Naboth's Vineyard: The Dominican Republic, 1844–1924* (New York: Payson and Clarke, 1928), 1:311–15.

16. This period of Dominican political history is treated by Moya Pons, *Dominican Republic,* chap. 11.

17. Martínez-Fernández, *Torn between Empires,* 143.

18. For further discussion, see G. Pope Atkins, *Latin America in the International Political System,* 3d ed. (Boulder: Westview Press, 1995), chap. 5; and Atkins, "Reorienting U.S. Policies in the New Era," chap. 1 in *The United States and Latin America: Redefining U.S. Purposes in the Post-Cold War Era,* ed. G. Pope Atkins (Austin: Lyndon B. Johnson School of Public Affairs, University of Texas at Austin, 1992).

19. Frank Moya Pons, *Manual de Historia Dominicana* (Santiago: Universidad Católica de Madre y Maestra, 1977), 403–9; Bruce Calder, *The Impact of Intervention: The Dominican Republic during the U.S. Occupation of 1916–1924* (Austin: University of Texas Press, 1984), 92–98; and Lester D. Langley, *The United States and the Caribbean in the Twentieth Century,* 4th ed. (Athens: University of Georgia Press, 1989), 77–85.

20. Welles, *Naboth's Vineyard,* 1:353.

21. See Tansill, *United States and Santo Domingo,* 230; and Welles, *Naboth's Vineyard,* 1:320. A similar treaty with Haiti had gone into effect in 1865. The United States had for many years refused to recognize the black government there but had nevertheless sent commercial agents to protect the interests of U.S. citizens. After the emancipation of slaves in the United States there was no further reason to refuse to recognize Haiti.

22. Tansill, *United States and Santo Domingo,* 250–56, chronicles the complex negotiations involving a series of proposals and counterproposals.

23. Ibid., 427–64.

24. Ibid., 406. President Grant had transmitted a pro-annexation argument, in U.S. Congress, Senate, Commission of Inquiry to Santo Domingo, *Report of the Commission of Inquiry* (Washington, D.C.: Government Printing Office, 1871).

25. Larman C. Wilson, in Harold E. Davis, Wilson, and others, *Latin American Foreign Policies: An Analysis* (Baltimore: Johns Hopkins University Press, 1975), 202.

26. See details in Moya Pons, *Dominican Republic,* chaps. 11 and 12; and Julio G.

Campillo Pérez, *El Grillo y el Ruiseñor: Elecciones Presidenciales Dominicanas, Contribución a su Estudio* (Santo Domingo: Editora del Caribe, 1966), 73–88. Also of interest are General Gregorio Luperón, *Notas Autobiográficas y apuntes históricas de la República Dominicana, desde de la restauración a nuestros días,* 3 vols. (Ponce, P.R.: 1895–96); his biography by Manuel Rodríguez Obijo, *Gregorio Luperón e Historia de la Restauración,* 2 vols. (Santiago, RD: Editora El Diario, 1939); Padre Fernando A. de Meriño, *Elementos de Geografía Física, Política, e Histórica de la República Dominicana,* 3d ed. (Santo Domingo: Imprenta de García Hermanos, 1898; reprint, Santo Domingo: Editora Taller, 1984); and Ulises Francisco Espaillat, *Escritos de Espaillat: Artículos, Cartas y Documentos Oficiales* (Santo Domingo: Imprenta la Cuna de América, 1909).

27. José del Castillo and Martin F. Murphy, "Migration, National Identity and Cultural Policy in the Dominican Republic," *Journal of Ethnic Studies* 15, no. 3 (fall 1987): 57.

28. This and the following section rely on R. Michael Malek, "The Ulises 'Lilis' Heureaux Regime, 1882–1899: Development and Dictatorship in the Dominican Republic" (paper presented to the 4th annual Caribbean Studies Association convention, Universidad Católica Madre y Maestra, Santiago de los Caballeros, República Dominicana, 12 January 1978), 19ff; Wilfrid Hardy Calcott, *The Caribbean Policy of the United States, 1890–1920* (Baltimore: Johns Hopkins University Press, 1942), 166–91; Moya Pons, *Dominican Republic,* chap. 13; Selden Rodman, *Quisqueya: A History of the Dominican Republic* (Seattle: University of Washington Press, 1964), 91–117; and Welles, *Naboth's Vineyard,* 1:449–96 and 2:497–600.

29. See Campillo Pérez, *El Grillo y el Ruiseñor,* 88–92, on the splitting of the *azul* party and ballot box stuffing in the first election that chose Billini.

30. Merline Pitre, "Frederick Douglass and the Annexation of Santo Domingo," *Journal of Negro History* 62 (October 1977): 390–400.

31. Campillo Pérez, *El Grillo y el Ruiseñor,* 104–7.

32. In 1895 Richard Olney, secretary of state to President Grover Cleveland, had presented one of the first formally stated perceptions of U.S. superiority in terms of both power and culture. Speaking at the time of U.S. arbitration of the British-Venezuela boundary dispute, and dubbed the Olney Corollary to the Monroe Doctrine, it combined the U.S. strategic-cultural views that centered on the circum-Caribbean and resonated with particular relevance for the Dominican Republic. While intended as a warning to the British, it also proclaimed that the United States was "practically sovereign on this continent, and its fiat is law upon the subjects to which it confines

its interposition," partly "by reason of its high character as a civilized state" as well as "its infinite resources combined with its isolated position."

2. United States Imperialism

1. This chapter draws on G. Pope Atkins and Larman C. Wilson, *The United States and the Trujillo Regime* (New Brunswick: Rutgers University Press, 1972), chap. 2.
2. G. Pope Atkins, *Latin America in the International Political System*, 3d ed. (Boulder: Westview Press, 1995), 116–17, 340; and Atkins, "The United States and the Caribbean Basin," chap. 2 in *Regional Hegemons: Threat Perception and Strategic Response*, ed. David J. Myers (Boulder: Westview Press, 1991), 34–39.
3. Of Alfred Thayer Mahan's many writings, see especially *The Interest of America in Sea Power, Present and Future* (Boston: Little, Brown, 1918).
4. Richard D. Challener, *Admirals, Generals, and American Foreign Policy, 1898–1914* (Princeton: Princeton University Press, 1973), chaps. 1, 2, 4 and 5.
5. Bruce J. Calder, *The Impact of Intervention: The Dominican Republic during the U.S. Occupation of 1916–1924* (Austin: University of Texas Press, 1984), xxxi; Sumner Welles, *Naboth's Vineyard: The Dominican Republic, 1844–1924* (New York: Payson and Clarke, 1928), 2:602–4.
6. This paragraph is based on Graham H. Stuart and James L. Tigner, *Latin America and the United States*, 6th ed. (Englewood Cliffs: Prentice-Hall, 1975), 423–24.
7. J. Fred Rippy, "The Initiation of the Customs Receivership in the Dominican Republic," *Hispanic American Historical Review* 17 (November 1934): 419–517; and Selden Rodman, *Quisqueya: A History of the Dominican Republic* (Seattle: University of Washington Press, 1964), 106–21.
8. Lester D. Langley, *The Banana Wars: An Inner History of American Empire, 1900–1934* (Lexington: University Press of Kentucky, 1983), 32–33, 118–19; Frank Moya Pons, *The Dominican Republic: A National History* (New Rochelle, N.Y.: Hispaniola Books, 1995), 278, 286, 292–93, 295–303. Emilio Betances, *State and Society in the Dominican Republic* (Boulder: Westview Press, 1995), 31, 52–56, 57, 71–75, 135–37, offers an interesting revisionist political-sociological interpretation of Cáceres's contribution to Dominican modernization.
9. For text see U.S. Department of State, *Papers Relating to the Foreign Relations*

of the United States, 1905 (Washington, D.C.: Government Printing Office, 1906), 311–12; and of the treaty and proclamation by President Roosevelt, ibid, *1907* (1910), 307–10.

10. Dana G. Munro, *Intervention and Dollar Diplomacy in the Caribbean, 1900–1921* (Princeton: Princeton University Press, 1964), 124.

11. Moya Pons, *Dominican Republic*, 305.

12. This paragraph is based on ibid., chap. 15.

13. See Calder, *Impact of Intervention*, 6–7; Langley, *Banana Wars*, 122; and Moya Pons, *Dominican Republic*, 311–12.

14. Moya Pons, *Dominican Republic*, 311–13.

15. Samuel Flagg Bemis, *The Latin American Policy of the United States: An Historical Interpretation* (New York: Harcourt, Brace, 1943), 157; Lester D. Langley, *The United States and the Caribbean in the Twentieth Century*, 4th ed. (Athens: University of Georgia Press, 1989), 77–78; David Charles Mac-Michael, *The United States and the Dominican Republic, 1871–1940: A Cycle in Caribbean Diplomacy* (Ph.D. diss., University of Oregon, 1964), 503; Munro, *Intervention and Dollar Diplomacy*, 531, 533–35; and Welles, *Naboth's Vineyard* 2:972.

16. Challener, *Admirals, Generals*, 398. Moya, *Dominican Republic*, chap. 16, provides a good synoptic overview of the U.S. military occupation.

17. Calder, *Impact of Intervention*, chap. 1; Stephen M. Fuller and Graham A. Cosmas, *Marines in the Dominican Republic, 1916–1924* (Washington, D.C.: History and Museums Division, Headquarters, U.S. Marine Corps, 1974), 7–24. A contemporary account was by Marine Major Edwin N. McClellan, "Operations Ashore in the Dominican Republic," *U.S. Naval Institute Proceedings* 47 (February 1921): 238.

18. Rodman, *Quisqueya*, 122–23; and Stuart and Tigner, *Latin America and the United States*, 427.

19. Calder, *Impact of Intervention*, 10–11.

20. Fuller and Cosmas, *Marines in the Dominican Republic*.

21. The text of the proclamation is reproduced in U.S. Congress, Senate, Select Committee on Haiti and Santo Domingo, *Inquiry into Occupation and Administration of Haiti and Santo Domingo*, 67th Cong., 1st sess. (1922), 90–94. See also Fuller and Cosmas, *Marines in the Dominican Republic*; and Stuart and Tigner, *Latin America and the United States*, 427–28.

22. Fuller and Cosmas, *Marines in the Dominican Republic*, 52–61, discuss the civil administration. Langley, *United States and the Caribbean*, 81–83, discusses the numerous positive public works and civic improvements.

23. Helen Miller Bailey and Abraham P. Nassatir, *Latin America: The Development of Its Civilization*, 2d ed. (Englewood Cliffs: Prentice-Hall, 1968), 712.

24. Welles, *Naboth's Vineyard*, 2:802–18.

25. Calder, *Impact of Intervention*, xxvii, Introduction, and Epilogue; Fuller and Cosmas, *Marines in the Dominican Republic*, 29; Rodman, *Quisqueya*, 123.

26. Langley, *Banana Wars*, 121.

27. Clyde J. Metcalf, *History of the United States Marine Corps* (New York: G.P. Putnam and Sons, 1939), 355.

28. Harry A. Ellsworth, *One Hundred and Eighty Landings of United States Marines, 1800–1934* (Washington, D.C.: U.S. Navy, Historical Section, 1934), 71.

29. Fuller and Cosmas, *Marines in the Dominican Republic*; Calder, *Impact of Intervention*, chap. 2.

30. Langley, *Banana Wars*, 122.

31. Calder, *Impact of Intervention*, xv, xxi, 22–23, 81–86.

32. MacMichael, *United States and the Dominican Republic*, 457.

33. Marvin Goldwert, *The Constabulary in the Dominican Republic and Nicaragua: Progeny and Legacy of United States Intervention* (Gainesville: University of Florida Press, 1962), 2–3.

34. Ibid., 12; Munro, *Intervention and Dollar Diplomacy*, 317.

35. U.S. Congress, *Occupation and Administration of Haiti and Santo Domingo*; and Carl Kelsey, "The American Intervention in Haiti and the Dominican Republic," *Annals of the American Academy of Political and Social Science* 100 (March 1922): 110–22. See Dana Gardner Munro, "Getting Out of Santo Domingo," chap. 3 in *The United States and the Caribbean Republics, 1921–1933* (Princeton, N.J.: Princeton University Press, 1974).

36. Welles, *Naboth's Vineyard*, 2:819–21.

37. Stuart and Tigner, *Latin America and the United States*, 431–32.

38. Text of the 1924 treaty is in U.S. Department of State, *Treaty Series*, no. 726.

39. Calder, *Impact of Intervention*, 65; chap. 3 is devoted to "The Impact of World War I."

40. Goldwert, *Constabulary in the Dominican Republic and Nicaragua*, vi.

41. Robert D. Crasswell, *Trujillo: The Life and Times of a Caribbean Dictator* (New York: Macmillan, 1966), 22–49; and Goldwert, *Constabulary in the Dominican Republic and Nicaragua*, 20. For this period see Munro, "The Hoover Administration, Central America and the Dominican Republic, 1929–1933," chap. 8 in *United States and the Caribbean Republics*.

42. *Papers Relating to the Foreign Relations of the United States, 1930*, 2:699–717.

43. Ibid., 708.

44. Ibid., 711.
45. Ibid., 704–5, 714–15.
46. Ibid., 718–19.
47. For example, Goldwert, *Constabulary in the Dominican Republic and Nicaragua*; and Noel Henríquez, *La verdad sobre Trujillo: capítulos que se le olvidaron a Galíndez* (Havana: Luz Hilo, 1959).

3. The Trujillo Regime, Nonintervention, and World War II

1. Rafael Leonidas Trujillo Molina, *Message Addressed to his Countrymen on the Tenth Anniversary of Assuming the Political Direction of the Dominican People* (Ciudad Trujillo: Imprenta Listín Diario, 1940), 4.
2. Hubert Herring, "Scandal of the Caribbean: The Dominican Republic," *Current History* 38 (March 1960): 141–42.
3. Bryce Wood, *The Making of the Good Neighbor Policy* (New York: Columbia University Press, 1961), 152.
4. Text of the telegram is in the *New York Times*, 7 July 1939.
5. Charles A. Thomson, "Dictatorship in the Dominican Republic," *Foreign Policy Reports* 12 (15 April 1936): 40.
6. U.S. Department of War, Bureau of Insular Affairs, General Receiver of Dominican Customs, *Report of the Dominican Customs Receivership under the American-Dominican Convention of 1924, together with a Summary of Commerce* (calendar year 1930), 9–11, and (1934), 6; W. E. Dunn, Special Emergency Agent, Dominican Republic, *Report of the Special Emergency Agent for the Period October 23, 1931 to December 31, 1932* (n.p., n.d.), 10–11; and U.S. Department of State, *Press Releases*, 14 November 1931, 454.
7. U.S. Department of War, *Report of the Dominican Customs Receivership . . .* (1934), 7–9.
8. U.S. Department of State, *Papers Relating to the Foreign Relations of the United States, 1936* (Washington, D.C.: Government Printing Office, 1936), 5:444.
9. Texts of some of the proposals submitted by both governments are in ibid., *1937*, 5:444–49, 453–61, 464–65; and *1940*, 5:792–97.
10. Ibid., *1936*, 5:435–58; *1937*, 5:440–67; *1938*, 5:491–508; *1939*, 5:579–95; and *1940*, 5:792–830.
11. Ibid., *1937*, 5:452; and *1939*, 5:588.
12. *New York Times*, 23 September 1939.

13. *Papers Relating to the Foreign Relations of the United States, 1939*, 5:587.
14. Text of the convention is in U.S. Department of State, *Treaty Series*, no. 965 (1941).
15. *Congressional Record* v. 87, pt. 1 (1941): 1027; U.S. Department of State, *Bulletin* 4 (22 March 1941): 345; and Manuel A. Peña Battle, *Contribución a una campaña. Cuatro discursos políticos* (Santiago: Ed. el Diario, 1941).
16. U.S. Department of State, *Bulletin* 17 (17 August 1947): 341, and *Bulletin* 25 (20 August 1951): 299.
17. R. Michael Malek, "Dominican Republic's General Rafael L. Trujillo M. and the Haitian Massacre of 1937: A Case of Subversion in Inter-American Relations," *SECOLAS Annals* 11 (March 1980): 137–55.
18. *New York Times*, 21 November 1937.
19. See Malek, "Trujillo and the Haitian Massacre"; Brenda Gayle Plummer, *Haiti and the United States* (Athens: University of Georgia Press, 1992), 154–57; Bernardo Vega, *Trujillo y Haití (1930–1937)* (Santo Domingo: Fundación Cultural Dominicana, 1988); and T. Fiehrer, "Genocide on the Massacre River: The Haitian View" (paper presented at annual meeting of South Eastern Council on Latin American Studies, Tampa, Fla., 19–21 April 1979). Of interest is René Fortunato, "Trujillo: El Poder del Jefe" (Philadelphia: Disc Makers, 1993), video, part 1. See also Ernesto Sagás, "The Development of Antihaitianism into a Dominant Ideology during the Trujillo Era" (paper presented at International Congress of the Latin American Studies Association, Washington, D.C., 28–30 September 1995).
20. *New York Times*, 22 December 1937.
21. Ibid., 18 December 1937.
22. Fiehrer, "Genocide on the Massacre River"; and Robert D. Crassweller, *Trujillo: The Life and Times of a Caribbean Dictator* (New York: Macmillan, 1966), 160–61.
23. J. Lloyd Mecham, *The United States and Inter-American Security, 1889–1960* (Austin: University of Texas Press, 1961), 175–76.
24. *Papers Relating to the Foreign Relations of the United States, 1938*, 5:196.
25. Ibid., *1937*, 5:135–40.
26. J. Lloyd Mecham, *A Survey of United States–Latin American Relations* (Boston: Houghton Mifflin Company, 1965), 104, covers the background and treaty ramifications.
27. *Congressional Record* 87:2040 and 2043.
28. *Time*, 17 August 1942, 18–19.
29. Malek, "Trujillo and the Haitian Massacre," 142–43.

30. Pan American Union, *Bulletin* 72 (March 1938): 288–304; and U.S. Department of State, *Press Releases*, 19 March 1938.

31. *Papers Relating to the Foreign Relations of the United States, 1938*, 5:197–98.

32. *New York Times*, 21 May 1939.

33. Rayford W. Logan, *Haiti and the Dominican Republic* (New York: Oxford University Press, 1968), 14–16.

34. Ibid., 14; and Malek, "Trujillo and the Haitian Massacre," 151.

35. Frank Moya Pons, *El pasado dominicano* (Santo Domingo: Fundación J. A. Caro Alvarez, 1986), 246.

36. World Peace Foundation, *Documents on American Foreign Relations* 2 (1939): 208–16, and 3 (1940): 134.

37. *Papers Relating to the Foreign Relations of the United States, 1939*, 5:579–80.

38. Mecham, *Inter-American Security*, 195–96.

39. Stetson Conn and Byron Fairchild, *The Western Hemisphere: The Framework of Hemispheric Defense*, vol. 12, pt. 1, of Department of the Army, *United States Army in World War II* (Washington, D.C.: Government Printing Office, 1960), 213.

40. Texts of both agreements are in *Papers Relating to the Foreign Relations of the United States, 1941*, 7:253–55.

41. U.S. Congress, House of Representatives, Committee on Foreign Affairs, *Twenty-Ninth Report to Congress on Lend-Lease Operations*, 81st Cong., 2d sess., 1950, 16–18.

42. *Papers Relating to the Foreign Relations of the United States, 1941*, 6:87; Edwin Lieuwen, *Arms and Politics in Latin America*, rev. ed. (New York: Published for the Council on Foreign Relations by Frederick A. Praeger, Publisher, 1961), 153, 190–91; Mecham, *Inter-American Security*, 201; and Ernesto Vega y Pagán, *Historia de las fuerzas armadas* (Ciudad Trujillo: Imprenta Dominicana, 1955), 2:439.

43. U.S. Department of State, *Executive Agreement Series*, no. 350 (1944) and no. 404 (1944).

44. Philip M. Glick, *The Administration of Technical Assistance: Growth in the Americas* (Chicago: University of Chicago Press, 1957), 10; U.S. Department of State, *Executive Agreement Series*, no. 346 (1943); U.S. Congress, House of Representatives, Committee on Foreign Affairs, *Institute of Inter-American Affairs*, Hearings, 80th Cong., 1st sess., 1947, 11, 49; and U.S. Department of State, *Bulletin* 16 (12 March 1951): 414.

45. Two examples from many are Dominican Revolutionary Party, *Trujillo: A Nazi* (Mayaguëz, P.R.: 1944); and Juan Isidro Jiménez Grullón, *Una gestapo*

en América. Vida, tortura, agonía y muerto de presos políticos bajo la tiranía de Trujillo (Havana: Ed. Lex., 1946).

46. Germán E. Ornes, *Trujillo: Little Caesar of the Caribbean* (New York: Thomas Nelson and Sons, 1958), 272–75; and Bernardo Vega, *Nazismo, Fascismo y Falangismo en la República Dominicana* (Santo Domingo: Fundación Cultural Dominicana, 1985), chaps. 2 and 4. The latter chapter from the Vega book contains an interesting section on "ambivalence in the North American attitude toward European totalitarianism and Latin American dictatorships."

47. From among many examples see U.S. Department of State, *Bulletin* 5 (20 December 1941): 547; *Bulletin* 7 (14 November 1942): 912; and *Bulletin* 10 (10 June 1944): 531.

48. *Papers Relating to the Foreign Relations of the United States, 1944*, 7:1019. See also Ellis O. Briggs's memoirs, *Farewell to Foggy Bottom: The Recollections of a Career Diplomat* (New York: David McKay, 1964), 221–25. Ambassador Briggs confirmed to the present authors in a letter dated 29 April 1968 that the Dominican government had not declared him *persona non grata* in 1945 as some Dominican writers had suggested.

49. *Papers Relating to the Foreign Relations of the United States, 1944*, 7:1015–24; and Briggs, *Farewell to Foggy Bottom*, 221–25.

4. The Trujillo Regime and the Cold War

1. The first half of this chapter draws on G. Pope Atkins and Larman C. Wilson, *The United States and the Trujillo Regime* (New Brunswick: Rutgers University Press, 1972), 62–78, 83–100.

2. See, for example, U.S. Congress, House of Representatives, Committee on Foreign Affairs, *Report on United States Relations with Latin America*, 86th Cong., 1st sess. (1959), 3.

3. Douglas Cater and Walter Pincus, "The Foreign Legion of U.S. Public Relations," *Reporter* (22 December 1960): 15–22.

4. These facts were disclosed in diplomatic documents obtained by the *New York Times* in Santo Domingo after Trujillo's death and corroborated by the newspaper in subsequent interviews at the White House, reported on 22 July 1962.

5. Ibid., 5 December 1963 and 11 January 1964.

6. Arturo R. Espaillat, *Trujillo: The Last Caesar* (Chicago: Henry Regnery, 1963).

7. Pamela Johnson Sybert, "Mutual Admiration: MBS and the Dominican Republic," *Journal of Broadcasting* 24 (spring 1980): 189–97.
8. Antonio V. Menéndez Alarcón, *Power and Television in Latin America: The Dominican Case* (Westport, Conn.: Praeger Publishers, 1992), 10.
9. Ornes, *Trujillo*, chap. 11.
10. Northwestern University, "The Organization of American States," in U.S. Congress, Senate, Committee on Foreign Relations, *United States-Latin American Relations*, 86th Cong., 2d sess., doc. no. 125 (31 August 1960), 216.
11. Edgar S. Furniss Jr., "The Inter-American System and Recent Caribbean Disputes," *International Organization* 4 (November 1950): 593–94.
12. General Secretariat of the Organization of American States, Department of Legal Affairs, *Inter-American Treaty of Reciprocal Assistance, Applications*, vol. 1, 1948–1959, 3d ed. (Washington, D.C., author, 1973). See also J. Lloyd Mecham, "Caribbean Turbulence (1949–1960)," chap. 13 in *The United States and Inter-American Security, 1889–1960* (Austin: University of Texas Press, 1961).
13. Leonard H. Pomeroy, "The International Trade and Traffic in Arms: Its Supervision and Control—II," U.S. Department of State, *Bulletin* 22 (6 March 1950): 357–58.
14. *A Bulletin of the Dominican Embassy*, no. 43 (15 October 1947).
15. Organization of American States, *Second Report of the Inter-American Peace Committee Submitted to the Tenth Inter-American Conference* (Washington, D.C.: Pan American Union, 1954); and Pan American Union, *Bulletin* 82 (October 1948): 591.
16. General Secretariat of the Organization of American States, *Inter-American Treaty of Reciprocal Assistance, Applications*; and Organization of American States, *Second Report of the Inter-American Peace Committee*, 6–7. Text of the joint declaration is in U.S. Department of State, *Bulletin* 20 (26 June 1949), 833.
17. Pomeroy, "International Trade and Traffic in Arms," 357; "The Caribbean Situation: U.S. Memorandum to the Inter-American Peace Committee," U.S. Department of State, *Bulletin* 21 (26 September 1949): 450–54; and Organization of American States, *Second Report of the Inter-American Peace Committee* (1954).
18. U.S. Department of State, *Bulletin* 21 (26 September 1949): 990.
19. U.S. Department of State, *Peace in the Americas: A Resumé of Measures Undertaken through the OAS to Preserve Peace* (pub. no. 3964, International Organization and Conference Series II, American Republics 6, 1950), 3–4.
20. Investigating Committee of the Organ of Consultation, Organization of

American States, *Documents Submitted at the Meeting of March 13, 1950* (Washington, D.C.: Pan American Union, 1950).

21. Department of State, *Peace in the Americas*, 8–18; see Edward Jamison, "Keeping Peace in the Caribbean Area," U.S. Department of State, *Bulletin* 23 (3 July 1950): 18–25.

22. U.S. Department of State, *Inter-American Efforts to Relieve International Tensions in the Western Hemisphere, 1959–1960* (1962), 5–18.

23. U.S. Department of State, *Bulletin* 41 (27 July 1959): 136–37.

24. Ibid., 41 (31 August 1959): 299–305; Organización de los Estados Americanos, *Quinta Reunión de Consulta de Ministros de Relaciones Exteriores, Santiago, Chile, 1959* (Washington, D.C.: Unión Panamericana, 1959), 2–3; and Organization of American States, *Report of the Inter-American Peace Committee to the Fifth Meeting of Consultation of Ministers of Foreign Affairs* (Washington, D.C.: Pan American Union, General Secretariat of the Organization of American States, 1959).

25. Organization of American States, Inter-American Peace Committee, *Special Report on the Relationship between Violations of Human Rights or the Non-Exercise of Representative Democracy and the Political Tensions that Affect the Peace of the Hemisphere* (Washington, D.C.: Pan American Union, General Secretariat of the Organization of American States, 1960).

26. Organization of American States, *Report of the Inter-American Peace Committee to the Seventh Meeting of Consultation of Ministers of Foreign Affairs* (Washington, D.C.: Pan American Union, General Secretariat of the Organization of American States, 1960).

27. Organization of American States, Inter-American Juridical Committee, *Study of the Juridical Relationship between Respect for Human Rights and the Exercise of Democracy* (Washington, D.C.: Pan American Union, General Secretariat of the Organization of American States, 1960), 18.

28. Organization of American States, Council, Committee of Investigation, *Report Submitted by the Committee of the Council, Acting Provisionally as Organ of Consultation in the Case Presented by Venezuela, to Comply with the Provisions of the Third Paragraph of the Resolution of July 8, 1960* (Washington, D.C.: Pan American Union, General Secretariat of the Organization of American States, 1960).

29. Organización de los Estados Americanos, *Sexta Reunión de Consulta de Ministros de Relaciones Exteriores, San José, Costa Rica, 1960: Documents* (Pan American Union, General Secretariat of the Organization of American States, 1960).

30. John C. Dreier, *The Organization of American States and the Hemisphere Crisis*

(New York: Harper and Row, 1962), 98; and Jerome Slater, *The OAS and United States Foreign Policy* (Columbus: Ohio State University Press, 1967), 188–89.

31. Organization of American States, *Sixth Meeting of Consultation of Ministers of Foreign Affairs, Serving as Organ of Consultation in Application of the Inter-American Treaty of Reciprocal Assistance, San José, Costa Rica, August 16–21, 1960: Final Act* (Washington, D.C.: Pan American Union, General Secretariat of the Organization of American States, 1960).

32. U.S. Department of State, *Bulletin* 43 (12 September 1960): 412, and 43 (3 October 1960): 542–43.

33. Organization of American States, *First Report of the Special Committee to Carry Out the Mandate Received by the Council Pursuant to Resolution I of the Sixth Meeting of Consultation of Ministers of Foreign Affairs* (Washington, D.C.: Pan American Union, General Secretariat of the Organization of American States, 1960).

34. Quoted in Robert D. Crassweller, *Trujillo: The Life and Times of a Caribbean Dictator* (New York: Macmillan, 1966), 216.

35. U.S. Department of State, *Bulletin* 22 (26 September 1949): 479–81.

36. "Military Assistance to Latin America," U.S. Department of State, *Bulletin* 28 (30 March 1953): 463–67.

37. Texts of treaties, in the order listed in the text, are in U.S. Department of State, *Treaties and Other International Agreements Series*, no. 2425 (1953), no. 1955 (1950), no. 2143 (1951), no. 3699 (1957), no. 3711 (1957), and no. 3780 (1957).

38. Text in ibid., no. 2777 (1954).

39. Agency for International Development, *U.S. Overseas Loans and Grants and Assistance from International Organizations, Obligations and Loan Authorizations, July 1, 1945–June 30, 1965* (1966), 26.

40. Crassweller, *Trujillo*, 344, 423.

41. Germán E. Ornes, *Trujillo: Little Caesar of the Caribbean* (New York: Thomas Nelson and Sons, 1958), 136.

42. Ibid., 136–37; and U.S. Congress, Senate, Committee on Foreign Relations, *Study Mission in the Caribbean Area*, 85th Cong., 2d sess., 1958, 11–12.

43. John Knape, "Anglo-American Rivalry in Post-War Latin America: The Question of Arms Sales," *Ibero-American Archive* 15 (1989): 319–50.

44. Ernesto Vega y Pagán, *Historia de las fuerzas armadas* (Ciudad Trujillo: Imprenta Dominicana, 1955), 2:405–6, 497–98, and 504.

45. República Dominicana, Secretariado Técnico, Oficina de Planificación, *Bases*

para el Desarrollo Nacional: Análisis de los problemas y perspectivas de la economía dominicana, Diciembre 1965, table 29; and Howard Wiarda, "The Politics of Civil-Military Relations in the Dominican Republic," *Journal of Inter-American Studies* 7 (October 1965): 465–84.

46. Crassweller, *Trujillo,* 346–47.

47. Ibid., 347; and Howard J. Wiarda, *Dictatorship and Development: The Methods of Control in Trujillo's Dominican Republic* (Gainesville: University of Florida Press, 1968), 45.

48. U.S. Department of State, *Bulletin* 24 (12 March 1951): 414; National Planning Association, *Technical Cooperation in Latin America: Recommendations for the Future* (Washington, D.C.: National Planning Association, 1956), 177, 179, 180, and 182; and U.S. Congress, Senate, Special Committee to Study the Foreign Aid Program, *Foreign Aid Program,* 85th Cong., 1st sess., 1957, 1553.

49. *Congressional Quarterly Almanac* 17 (27 January 1961): 121.

50. U.S. Department of Agriculture, Agricultural Stabilization and Conservation Service, Sugar Division, "Sugar Statistics and Related Data," *Statistical Bulletin* 1, no. 293 (1961): 152–53 and 157.

51. U.S. Department of State, *Bulletin* 43 (12 September 1960): 412–13.

52. *Congressional Quarterly* 16 (1960): 214–16.

53. Public Law 87–15 (31 March 1961).

54. Galíndez had recently defended his dissertation and left a copy with a Chilean friend in New York, who had it published in Chile as *La Era de Trujillo: Un Estudio Casuístico de Dictadura Hispanoamericano* (Santiago de Chile: Editorial del Pacífico, 1957). An English edition appeared fifteen years later: *The Era of Trujillo: Dominican Dictator,* ed. Russell H. Fitzgibbon (Tucson: University of Arizona Press, 1973).

55. Porter's speeches before the House are in *Congressional Record* 103:2815–18. See also his articles in *Coronet* (June 1957) and *The New Leader* (7–14 July 1958).

56. U.S. Department of State, *Bulletin* 36 (11 February 1957): 221; 36 (4 March 1957): 610; and 36 (24 June 1957): 1025–28.

57. Germán E. Ornes, *The Other Side of the Coin* (Washington, D.C.: Embassy of the Dominican Republic, 1958).

58. Morris L. Ernst, *Report and Opinion in the Matter of Galindez* (New York: Sidney S. Baron and Co., 1958).

59. *Congressional Record* 154:12860–67.

60. *Address of Hon. William T. Pheiffer, Ambassador of the United States of America*

to the Dominican Republic, at the Luncheon Meeting of the Miami Beach Rotary Club on March 6, 1956 (Ciudad Trujillo: Impresora Dominicana, 1956).

61. *Congressional Record* 103:2817–18 and 11756–57.

62. Ibid., 4944–46, 5935, 5938, 6462, 7793–95.

63. Ibid., 9983–84, 10299–300, and 14349–50; and U.S. Congress, Senate, Committee on the Judiciary, *Communist Problems in Latin America*, 85th Cong., 1st sess., 1957, 3–4.

64. *Congressional Record* 103:8868–69, 9052–53, 9219–20, and 11538–39.

65. Ibid., 104:8620, 8719, 8734, and 11648–50.

66. Embassy of the Dominican Republic in Washington, *A Look at the Dominican Republic* 3 (July 1958): 4–5; and (September 1958): 3–6 and 7–9.

67. *Congressional Record* 102:9983–84, 10299–300, 14348–50; 104: 10267, 10270, and 10273.

68. Ibid., 107:4421.

69. Douglas Cater and Walter Pincus, "Our Sugar Diplomacy," *Reporter* (13 April 1961): 24–28.

70. *New York Times*, 20 December 1963.

71. U.S. Department of State, *Bulletin* 43 (29 August 1960): 312.

72. *UN Security Council Official Records*, 15th Year, Supplement for July, August, and September (S/4471, 5 September 1960 and S/4481/Rev. 1, 8 September 1960) and 15th Year, 895th Meeting, 9 September 1960, p. 5; Inis S. Claude Jr., "The OAS, the UN, and the United States," *International Conciliation*, no. 547 (March 1964): 48–49; and Manuel Canyes, *The Organization of American States and the United Nations* (Washington, D.C.: Pan American Union, General Secretariat of the Organization of American States, 1960), 56–59.

73. Crassweller, *Trujillo*, 425.

5. The Post-Trujillo Aftermath, 1961–1966

1. See Bernard Dietrich, *Trujillo: The Death of the Goat* (Boston: Little, Brown, 1978); and Howard J. Wiarda, *Dictatorship and Development: The Methods of Control in Trujillo's Dominican Republic* (Gainesville: University of Florida Press, 1969), 170–73.

2. Information in this and the succeeding two sections has been drawn from G. Pope Atkins and Larman C. Wilson, *The United States and the Trujillo Regime* (New Brunswick, N.J.: Rutgers University Press, 1972), chap. 6; see

also Atkins, *Arms and Politics in the Dominican Republic* (Boulder: Westview Press, 1981), chap. 3.

3. Fidel Castro was the real father of the Alliance for Progress in the sense that the Cuban Revolution of 1959 inspired its main goal of preventing a political vacuum and instability following the overthrow of a dictator, which could facilitate a communist takeover. It was assumed that bringing about economic, social, and political development, including a series of structural improvements and reforms (agrarian, agricultural, land, governmental, labor, tax, health, education, and so on) would assure stability. Private enterprise and investment were to be stressed. The "Declaration to the Peoples of America" and the "Charter of the Alliance for Progress," both issued at the Punta del Este meeting, identified the goals, ends, and means. The Alliance was established for a ten-year period; one hundred billion dollars would be applied to achieving the proclaimed goals, of which 80 percent was to come from the Latin American states themselves; 10 percent from the United States, mainly in public funds; and the remaining 10 percent from the international financial institutions—the Inter-American Development Bank, World Bank (United Nations Special Fund for Development), and International Monetary Fund. The United States initiated the provision of funds by contributing five hundred million dollars to the Social Progress Trust Fund administered by the Inter-American Development Bank. J. Warren Nystrom and Nathan A. Haverstock, *The Alliance for Progress: Key to Latin America's Development* (Princeton, N.J.: D. Van Nostrand, 1966), 21–25.

4. Organization of American States, *Report Submitted by the Subcommittee to the Special Committee to Carry Out the Mandate Received by the Council Pursuant to Resolution I of the Sixth Meeting of Consultation of Ministers of Foreign Affairs* (Washington, D.C.: Pan American Union, General Secretariat of the Organization of American States, 1961).

5. Organization of American States, *Second Report of the Subcommittee Submitted to the Special Committee to Carry Out the Mandate Received by the Council Pursuant to Resolution I of the Sixth Meeting of Consultation of Ministers of Foreign Affairs* (Washington, D.C.: Pan American Union, General Secretariat of the Organization of American States, 1961).

6. Organización de los Estados Americanos, Comisión Interamericana de Derechos Humanos, *Informaciones sobre el respeto de los derechos humanos en la República Dominicana* (Washington, D.C.: Pan American Union, General Secretariat of the Organization of American States, 1961).

7. Comisión Interamericana de Derechos Humanos, *Informaciones sobre la situación de los derechos humanos en la República Dominicana* (Washington, D.C.: Pan American Union, General Secretariat of the Organization of American States, 1962), 34–40.

8. U.S. Department of State, *Bulletin* 45 (11 September 1961): 447.

9. Ibid., 45 (4 December 1961): 929–32.

10. Ibid., 931.

11. *New York Times*, 19 and 20 November 1961.

12. U.S. Department of State, *Bulletin* 45 (18 December 1961): 1003; 45 (15 December 1961): 1054–55; and 46 (1 January 1962): 34–35.

13. Organization of American States, *Third Report Submitted by the Subcommittee to the Special Committee to Carry Out the Mandate Received by the Council Pursuant to Resolution I of the Sixth Meeting of Consultation of Ministers of Foreign Affairs* (Washington, D.C.: Pan American Union, General Secretariat of the Organization of American States, 1961), 9–12.

14. *New York Times*, 19 January 1962. Among the approximately 560 Peace Corps volunteers who served in the Dominican Republic through the end of the 1970s was Christopher Dodd, who became a U.S. Senator and chair of the Foreign Relations Committee's Subcommittee on the Western Hemisphere. After his assignment to the Dominican Republic, Michael Malek wrote his Ph.D. dissertation on Trujillo and became a professor of history. Howard Wiarda, who trained Peace Corps volunteers, also wrote his dissertation on the Trujillo dictatorship and subsequently pursued an academic career as a political scientist, writing prolifically on the Dominican Republic.

15. Ibid.

16. In addition to numerous literary works, Bosch had authored *Trujillo: causas de una tiranía sin ejemplo* (Caracas: Librería "Las Novedades," 1959).

17. *Primer simposio sobre democracia representativa, Santo Domingo, República Dominicana, 17–22 de diciembre de 1962: informe final* (Washington, D.C.: Unión Panamericana, 1962). Harold E. Davis, to whom this book is dedicated, was one of the thirteen U.S. participants as well as an election observer.

18. *New York Times*, 28 April 1963; and George Sherman, "Nonintervention: A Shield for 'Papa Doc,'" *Reporter* 28 (20 June 1963), 28.

19. General Secretariat of the Organization of American States, Department of Legal Affairs, *Inter-American Treaty of Reciprocal Assistance, Applications* vol. 2, 1960–1972, 3d ed. (Washington, D.C.: General Secretariat of the Organization of American States, 1973).

20. Howard J. Wiarda, "The Politics of Civil-Military Relations in the Dominican Republic," *Journal of Inter-American Studies* 7 (October 1965): 480.
21. Ibid., 477.
22. John Bartlow Martin, *Overtaken by Events* (Garden City, N.Y.: Doubleday, 1966), 358.
23. U.S. Department of State, *United States Treaties and Other International Agreements* 15:701–2.
24. Martin, *Overtaken by Events*, 358.
25. Center for Research in Social Systems, American University, *Area Handbook for the Dominican Republic* (Washington, D.C.: Government Printing Office, 1967), chap. 25.
26. For a detailed account of the background to Reid's overthrow and the civil war, see Jerome Slater, *Intervention and Negotiation: The U.S. and the Dominican Revolution* (New York: Harper and Row, 1970). On the civil war and U.S. intervention, and inter-American actions, see also Theodore Draper, *The Dominican Revolt: A Case Study in American Policy* (New York: Commentary, 1968); Julio C. Estrella, *La revolución dominicana y la crisis de la OEA* (Santo Domingo: Talleres de la "Revista AHORA," 1965); Piero Gleijeses, *The Dominican Crisis: The 1965 Constitutionalist Revolt and American Intervention* (Baltimore: Johns Hopkins University Press, 1978); Abraham F. Lowenthal, *The Dominican Intervention* (Cambridge: Harvard University Press, 1972); Larman C. Wilson, "La intervención de los Estados Unidos de América en el Caribe: la crisis de 1965 en la República Dominicana," *Revista de Política Internacional*, no. 122 (July–August 1972): 37–82; Lawrence A. Yates, *Power Pack: U.S. Intervention in the Dominican Republic, 1965–1966* (Ft. Leavenworth, Kans.: U.S. Army Command and General Staff College, 1988); and René Fortunato y Roberto Hiciano, "Abril: La Trinchera del Honor" (Santo Domingo: Videocine Palau, S.A., 1988).
27. Martin, *Overtaken by Events*, 648.
28. Ibid., 653–54, 658, 705.
29. U.S. Department of State, *Bulletin* 52 (17 May 1965): 738, 742; *New York Times*, 3 May 1965.
30. Bruce Palmer Jr., *Intervention in the Caribbean: The Dominican Crisis of 1965* (Lexington: University Press of Kentucky, 1989), 5. See also Lester D. Langley, *The United States and the Caribbean in the Twentieth Century*, 4th ed. (Athens: University of Georgia Press, 1989), 235–43; and his *The United States in the Western Hemisphere* (Athens: University of Georgia Press, 1989), 209–12.

31. Philip L. Geyelin, *Lyndon B. Johnson and the World* (New York: Frederick A. Praeger Publishers, 1966), chap. 10; and Howard J. Wiarda and Michael J. Kryzanek, *The Dominican Republic: A Caribbean Crucible*, 2d ed. (Boulder: Westview Press, 1992), 44.

32. Michael J. Kryzanek, "The Dominican Intervention Revisited: An Attitudinal and Operational Analysis," in *United States Foreign Policy in Latin America: A Quarter Century of Crisis and Challenge, 1961–1968*, ed. John D. Martz (Lincoln: University of Nebraska Press, 1988), 139; Slater, *The OAS and United States Foreign Policy*, 35; and Larman C. Wilson, "The United States and the Dominican Republic: A Post-Election Assessment," in *The Lingering Crisis: A Case Study of the Dominican Republic*, ed. Eugenio Chang-Rodríguez (New York: Las Américas Publishing Co., 1969), 107–8.

33. Gleijeses, *Dominican Crisis*, 196–97, 217–18, 282; and Michael J. Kryzanek and Howard J. Wiarda, *The Politics of External Influence in the Dominican Republic* (New York and Stanford: Praeger Publishers and Hoover Institution Press, 1988), 46. For a contrary view, see Slater, *Intervention and Negotiation*, 36–43.

34. *New York Times*, 26 May 1965.

35. *Congressional Record* (15 September 1965), 22998–23005.

36. Palmer, *Intervention in the Caribbean*, 139–43. See also Larman C. Wilson, "Estados Unidos y la Guerra Civil Dominicana: El Reto a las Relaciones Interamericanas," *Foro Internacional* 8, no. 2 (October–December 1967), 155–78.

37. Slater, *OAS and United States Foreign Policy*, chaps. 3 and 4.

38. *OAS Chronicle* 1 (August 1965): 5. See James Jose, *An Inter-Peace Force within the Framework of the Organization of American States: Advantages, Impediments, Implications* (Metuchen, N.J.: Scarecrow Press, 1970).

39. Slater, *Intervention and Negotiation*, 104–5; and Palmer, *Intervention in the Caribbean*, 63, 97.

40. Wilson, "United States and the Dominican Republic," 110.

41. Palmer, *Intervention in the Caribbean*, 56–57, 62.

42. *OAS Chronicle* 1 (August 1965): 19.

43. Ibid., 21–22.

44. Organization of American States, *Informe del Secretario General de la Organización de los Estados Americanos en relación con la situación dominicana (desde el 29 de abril de 1965 hasta la instalación del gobierno provisional)* (Washington, D.C.: Pan American Union, General Secretariat of the Organization of American States, 1965), 29–31.

45. See Slater, *Intervention and Negotiation*, 97–99, 108–10.
46. Wilson, "United States and the Dominican Republic," 115–17.
47. Larman Wilson was in the Dominican Republic at the time, his first research trip to the country, and he heard President Balaguer's address on the television set in the lobby of the hotel El Comercial.
48. Frank Moya Pons, *El pasado dominicano* (Santo Domingo: Fundación J. A. Caro Alvarez, 1986), 291–92.
49. Palmer, *Intervention in the Caribbean*, 137.
50. Frank Hernández Marino, "Migration of Talent from Latin America to the United States," in *Cultural Factors in Inter-American Relations*, ed. Samuel Shapiro (Notre Dame, Ind.: University of Notre Dame Press, 1968), 149.

6. The Balaguer Regime, 1966–1978

1. Frank Moya Pons, *El pasado dominicano* (Santo Domingo: Fundación J. A. Caro Alvarez, 1986), 360–61. This concept is roughly the Dominican counterpart of what we have earlier referred to as the "Caribbeanization" of the United States, which will be further discussed.
2. Ibid., 336–37; and Frank Brodhead and Edward S. Herman, *Demonstration Elections: U.S.-Staged Elections in the Dominican Republic, Vietnam, and El Salvador* (Boston: South End Press, 1984), 48–49.
3. G. Pope Atkins, *Arms and Politics in the Dominican Republic* (Boulder: Westview Press, 1981), 30.
4. Moya Pons, *El pasado dominicano*, 341.
5. Irma Tirado de Alonso, *Trade Issues in the Caribbean* (Philadelphia: Gordon and Breach, 1992), 129, 163.
6. Atkins, *Arms and Politics*, 31–32; Jan K. Black, *The Dominican Republic: Politics and Development in an Unsovereign State* (Boston: Allen and Unwin, 1986), 66–68; and Michael J. Kryzanek and Howard J. Wiarda, *The Politics of External Influence in the Dominican Republic* (New York and Stanford: Praeger Publishers and Hoover Institution Press, 1988), 51.
7. Letter from Z. Joseph Campos, Director of Education, AIFLD, Washington, D.C., 9 June 1989. See *Twenty-Five Years of Solidarity with Latin American Workers: 1960s, 1970s, 1980s* (Washington, D.C.: American Institute for Free Labor Development, n.d.).
8. Black, *Dominican Republic*, 95–97.
9. Ibid., 63–64; and Kryzanik and Wiarda, *Politics of External Influence*, 50, 138.

10. See Atkins, *Arms and Politics*, chap. 3.

11. Ibid., 61–65.

12. Michael J. Kryzanek, "Political Party Decline and the Failure of Liberal Democracy: The PRD in Dominican Politics," *Journal of Latin American Studies* 9, no. 1 (May 1977): 121–25. See Latin American Working Group, *La banda* (Toronto: LAWG, Fall 1971).

13. Moya Pons, *El pasado dominicano*, 360.

14. See Kryzanek and Wiarda, *Politics of External Influence*, chaps. 1 and 2.

15. Jonathan Hartlyn, "The Dominican Republic: The Legacy of Intermittent Engagement," in *Exporting Democracy: The United States and Latin America*, ed. Abraham F. Lowenthal (Baltimore: Johns Hopkins University Press, 1991), 55; and Moya Pons, *El pasado dominicano*, 336–37. After his reelection in 1970, Balaguer learned how to manipulate the United States to serve his ends and was especially adept after the elections in 1986 and 1990.

16. During Balaguer's three presidential terms, after 1968 when he created the Oficina de Patrimonio Cultural, several new institutions were inaugurated in Santo Domingo: the Museo del Hombre Dominicano in 1973 and the Galería de Arte Moderno in 1976, both on the Plaza de la Cultura; the Museo de la Familia and the Sala de Arte Prehispánico, both in 1973; and the Museo de las Casas Reales in 1976. In Puerto Plata on the north coast, the restoration of the Fortaleza de San Felipe was completed in 1972. José del Castillo and Martin F. Murphy, "Migration, National Identity and Cultural Policy in the Dominican Republic," *Journal of Ethnic Studies* 15, no. 3 (fall 1987): 65–66. For a complete list of all past historical monuments with illustrations, see Joaquín Balaguer, *Guía emocional de la ciudad romántica* (1944; reprint, Santo Domingo: Ediciones Alpa, 1969). On the colonial restoration, see Pedro Julio Santiago, *Santo Domingo Colonial: Guía Monumental* (Santo Domingo: Mundilibro, 1992).

17. Del Castillo and Murphy, "Migration, National Identity and Cultural Policy," 65; and José Alcántara Almanzar, "Black Images in Dominican Literature," *New West Indian Guide* 61, nos. 3 and 4 (1987): 163–71. See also Bernardo Vega and others, *Ensayos sobre cultura dominicana de hoy* (Santo Domingo: Museo del Hombre Dominicano, 1981); and Alan Cambeira, *Quisqueya la Bella: The Dominican Republic in Historical and Cultural Perspective* (Armonk, N.Y.: M.E. Sharpe, 1997), chap. 23.

18. Howard J. Wiarda, *The Dominican Republic: Nation in Transition* (New York: Frederick A. Praeger, Publishers, 1969), 119–20, 225. The 1965 intervention prompted the formation in 1966 in the United States of the North American Congress on Latin America (NACLA). It was a group of radical critics of

U.S. Latin American policy who adopted a dependency approach; they issued a regular publication called *NACLA Report*.

19. Antonio V. Menéndez Alarcón, *Power and Television in Latin America: The Dominican Case* (Westport, Conn.: Praeger Publishers, 1992), especially 29, 64, 70, 72–73, and 77.

20. José Cabrera, *Crisis de la publicidad y la mercadotecnia en la República Dominicana* (Santo Domingo: Editora Taller, 1980), 108, 154, 258–60.

21. David B. Bray, "The Dominican Exodus: Origins, Problems, Solutions," in *The Caribbean Exodus*, ed. Barry B. Levine (New York: Frederick A. Praeger Publishers, 1987), 153.

22. José del Castillo, "La Inmigración Dominicana en los Estados Unidos," in *Los Inmigrantes Indocumentados Dominicanos en Puerto Rico: Realidad y Mitos*, ed. Juan E. Hernández Cruz (San Germán: Universidad Interamericana de Puerto Rico, 1989), 48–52; and Kryzanek and Wiarda, *Politics of External Influence*, 112–14. See also Glenn Hendricks, *The Dominican Diaspora: From the Dominican Republic to New York City — Villagers in Transition* (New York: Teachers College Press, 1974).

23. Kryzanek and Wiarda, *Politics of External Influence*, 114.

24. Del Castillo, "Inmigración Dominicana," 53.

25. Ibid., 49; and Kryzanek and Wiarda, *Politics of External Influence*, 113.

26. Del Castillo, "Inmigración Dominicana," 49–50.

27. Larman Wilson expresses his thanks to Evelyn Rodríguez, M.A., a Dominican, for her assistance in compiling this list of Dominican musicians.

28. Del Castillo, "Inmigración Dominicana," 48–49; and Kryzanek and Wiarda, *Politics of External Influence*, 114.

29. The authors were present when PRD presidential nominee Salvador Jorge Blanco made a presentation at the American Enterprise Institute in March 1982.

30. In his *La realidad dominicana. Semblanza de un país y de un régimen* (Buenos Aires: Imprenta Ferrari Hermanos, 1947); English edition, *Dominican Reality: Biographical Sketch of a Country and a Regime*, trans. Mary Gilland (Mexico, D.F.: n.p., 1949). Balaguer condemned the degeneration and laziness of Haitians and their negative effect upon Dominicans. He reaffirmed his much earlier critical views of Haiti and Haitians in the 1983 edition of his *La isla al revés: Haití y el destino dominicano* (Santo Domingo: Fundación José A. Caro Alvarez, 1983), 35, 37, 52. It was a revised version of the first edition of 1947, *La realidad dominicano*, which was a public relations justification of the 1937 massacre with highly prejudiced views of Haitians.

31. Moya Pons, *El pasado dominicano*, 248. See also "Mirrors of the Heart: Race

and Identity," *Americas* series, program no. 4 (WBGH Boston and Central TV Enterprises in association with Columbia University's School of International and Public Affairs, Florida University's Latin American and Caribbean Center, and Tufts University, 1992); and Antonio Zaglul, *Apuntes*, 5th ed. (Santo Domingo: Ediciones de Taller, 1982).

32. Moya Pons, *El pasado dominicano*, 249.

33. Ibid., 247. Fradique Lizardo Barinas, *Cultura africana en Santo Domingo. Dibujos primarios . . . [y] dibujos definitivos* (Santo Domingo: Sociedad Industrial Dominicana en Editora Taller, 1979), attempted to tabluate the changes. He notes, among other examples, that Dominican black women began to win beauty contests, resulting in the opportunity to represent the Dominican nation in international events, which several of them won (including the Miss Universe competition in 1977); and that the Ballet Folklórico Dominicano received considerable exposure and general acclaim—in 1978 it won first place at the VII International Folklore Festival in Miami from among forty-four competing countries.

34. Moya Pons, *El pasado dominicano*, 247.

35. Monsignor Hugo Eduardo Brito was the founding rector of the university, holding the position until 1970. He was succeeded by his vice-rector, Monsignor Agripino Núñez Collado, who was widely credited as a leading force in guiding the institutionalization of UCMM. See Agripino Núñez Collado, *La UCMM: un nuevo estilo universitario en la República Dominicana*, 2 vols. (Santiago: UCMM, 1982); and Moya Pons, *El pasado dominicano*, 294–98. UCMM began classes on a limited basis for the academic year 1962–63 with only two faculties—education and philosophy—and approximately seventy students. It remained open during the civil war and U.S. intervention, when for academic year 1965–66 some 350 students were enrolled. While UCMM was little affected politically by the events, its physical construction was slowed. When Larman Wilson made his first research trip to the Dominican Republic in the summer of 1966, he visited Santiago and the campus, which had only a few completed buildings and others under construction. In January 1978, both he and Pope Atkins participated in the annual meeting of the Caribbean Studies Association held on the impressive campus.

36. Raúl González Díaz, Larman Wilson's graduate fellow from 1992 to 1994, analyzed *Quién es Quién en la República Dominicana*, 2d ed. (Santo Domingo: Editora Acca, 1978), in terms of the number of Dominicans in various fields and professions who had studied in the United States. He determined that

increasing numbers of Dominicans, starting in the 1950s and rapidly increasing in the 1960s and thereafter, studied and earned their graduate and professional graduate degrees in the United States. The following fields of study were especially popular (in descending order): business (especially banking), economics, medicine, engineering, and agriculture. The most favored universities, listed by regions, were the University of Texas (Austin), Texas A and M, Georgetown University, George Washington University, Howard University, Penn State University, University of Pennsylvania, Cornell University, Columbia University, Syracuse University, Harvard University, Massachusetts Institute of Technology, University of Wisconsin, University of Michigan, Indiana University, and University of Notre Dame. Numerous other Dominicans chose universities in Spain, France, Switzerland, and England for medicine, and Spain and nearby Latin American countries for engineering. A limited reverse flow occurred as U.S. students who were unable to gain acceptance to U.S. medical schools chose to study in the two medical schools in the Dominican Republic. In 1980 the General Accounting Office presented a highly critical report on the quality of these schools, which received U.S. assistance funds.

37. See Bell, *Dominican Republic*, 179. Moya Pons, *El pasado dominicano*, 299, determined that ten thousand Dominicans left to study abroad, mainly in the United States, during the period from 1965 to 1985, and he observed the important positive impact their return had in the Dominican Republic, particularly upon education and economic development and modernization.

38. C. Lloyd Brown-John, "Higher Education in the Dominican Republic: Background and Evaluation," *North South: Canadian Journal of Latin American and Caribbean Studies* 2, no. 3/4 (1977): 130. The United States had provided one million dollars in aid to Trujillo from 1952 to 1957, mainly for vocational and rural education; it had given some assistance to Bosch and the council of state before the civil war.

39. Ian Bell, *The Dominican Republic* (Boulder: Westview Press, 1980), 177. By this time seven universities existed with almost forty-one thousand students (UASD had more than half of them), in contrast to 1965 when two universities enrolled four thousand students.

40. Ibid., 179.

41. Alan M. Klein, *Sugarball: The American Game, The Dominican Dream* (New Haven: Yale University Press, 1991); and Tony Tedesch, "Play Ball!" *Caribbean Travel and Life* (May–June 1992), 66–71.

42. Quoted in Klein, *Sugarball*, 1. See also Rob Ruck, *The Tropic of Baseball: Base-*

ball in the Dominican Republic (New York: Carroll and Graf Publishers, 1991); and "Headstrong and Head-of-the-Class: Resocialization and Labeling in Dominican Baseball," in *Social Role of Sport in Caribbean Societies*, ed. Michael Malec (Beverly Hills: SAGE Publications, 1995).

43. Klein, *Sugarball*, 107, 152–53, 116–17.

7. Dominican Democratization, 1978–1986

1. On the campaign and election, see G. Pope Atkins, *Arms and Politics in the Dominican Republic* (Boulder: Westview Press, 1981), chap. 4; and Michael J. Kryzanek, "The 1978 Election in the Dominican Republic: Opposition Politics, Intervention and the Carter Administration," *Caribbean Studies* 19, nos. 1 and 2 (April–July 1979): 51–73. See also Larman C. Wilson, "Die Dominikanische Republik am Ende de Ära Balaguer," *Berichte zur Entwicklung in Spanien, Portugal und Lateinamerika*, 3. Jahr., Heft 19 (September–October 1978): 12–18. Pope Atkins was on an extended research visit in the Dominican Republic during this time and witnessed the election and inauguration.

2. Bosch had dedicated his book—*Crisis de la Democracia de América en la República Dominicana* (Mexico, D.F.: Centro de Estudios y Documentación Sociales, 1964); English edition, *The Unfinished Experiment: Democracy in the Dominican Republic* (New York: Frederick A. Praeger, Publishers, 1965)—to "José Peña Gómez, and through him, to the youth of the people, the seed of hope for the Dominican nation."

3. Quoted in Kryzanek, "1978 Election," 54.

4. Congressman Fraser had cited these campaign events in letters to President Carter and National Security Advisor Zbigniew Brzezinski (Kryzanek, "1978 Election," 55–56).

5. Rosario Espinal, "Electoral Politics in the Dominican Republic, 1978–1990" (paper presented at April 1991 meeting of the Latin American Studies Association, Washington, D.C.), 3. See also her book, *Autoritarismo y Democracia en la Política Dominicana* (San José, Costa Rica: CAPEL, 1987). Jonathan Hartlyn has a section on "Balaguer's Authoritarian Period, 1966–1978: Midwife to Democracy?" in his "The Dominican Republic: Contemporary Problems and Challenges," chap. 8 in *Democracy in the Caribbean: Political, Economic, and Social Perspectives*, ed. Jorge Domínguez and others (Baltimore: Johns Hopkins University Press, 1993). In our view, the birth of Do-

minican democracy was more attributable to the concerted midwifery of the United States, Venezuela, and the Dominican electorate in opposition to Balaguer's authoritarianism; otherwise it would have been aborted.

6. *New York Times*, 18 May 1978.

7. Atkins, *Arms and Politics*, 105–6; Kryzanek, "1978 Election," 58–59; and Wilson, "Die Dominikanische Republik," 14.

8. Based on Larman Wilson's later discussions with Gregory Wolfe and with Frank Moya Pons on several occasions, the most recent with the latter on 10 June 1992 in Santo Domingo.

9. Atkins, *Arms and Politics*, 112–13.

10. "Dominican Republic: Remarks of the Newly Appointed Ambassador . . . ," U.S. Department of State, *Press Release* (11 January 1979), 2.

11. This section relies on Atkins, *Arms and Politics*, chap. 5, 123–26, 132–35.

12. Frank Moya Pons, *Empresarios en conflicto: políticas de industrialización y sustitución de importaciones en la República Dominicana* (Santo Domingo: Fondo para la Avance de las Ciencias Sociales, 1992), 257–60. See also Howard J. Wiarda and Michael J. Kryzanek, *The Dominican Republic: A Caribbean Crucible*, 2d ed. (Boulder: Westview Press, 1992), 114–16.

13. Moya Pons, *Empresarios en conflicto*, 360.

14. Rosario Espinal, "Dominican Republic: Electoralism, Pacts, and Clientelism in the Making of a Democratic Regime," in *Democracy in the Caribbean: Myths and Realities*, ed. Carlene J. Edie (New York: Praeger Publishers, 1994), 155.

15. Pablo A. Maríñez, *Democracia y procesos electorales en la República Dominicana* (Santo Domingo: Editora Alfa y Omega, 1994), 152–53.

16. John Nuttall, *Evolution of Sugar Import Policies and Programs, 1981–1988*, Staff Paper no. 8 (Washington, D.C.: U.S. Department of Agriculture, November 1988), 106.

17. Michael J. Kryzanek and Howard J. Wiarda, *The Politics of External Influence in the Dominican Republic* (New York and Stanford: Praeger Publishers and Hoover Institute Press, 1988), 138–39.

18. Atkins, *Arms and Politics*, 129–31.

19. Wiarda and Kryzanek, *Dominican Republic*, 134.

20. Howard J. Wiarda and Michael J. Kryzanek, "Dominican Republic," in *Latin America and Caribbean Contemporary Record*, ed. Jack W. Hopkins (New York: Holmes and Meier, 1976), 2:670.

21. Richard A. Haggerty, ed., *Area Handbook for the Dominican Republic and Haiti*, 2d ed. (Washington, D.C.: Government Printing Office, 1991), 157–58.

22. Martin F. Murphy, *Dominican Sugar Plantations: Production and Foreign Labor Integration* (New York: Praeger Publishers, 1991); Frank Báez Evertsz, *Braceros haitianos en República Dominicana* (Santo Domingo: Instituto Dominicano de Investigaciones Sociales, 1986); and Saskia K. S. Wilhelms, *Haitian and Dominican Sugar Cane Workers in Dominican Bateyes: Patterns and Effects of Prejudice, Stereotypes, and Discrimination* (Boulder: Westview Press, 1995). National Film Board of Canada, "Black Sugar: 200,000 Slaves in the Heart of the Americas" (1987) is a critical documentary film video.

23. Jan K. Black, *The Dominican Republic: Politics and Development in an Unsovereign State* (Boston: Allen and Unwin, 1986), 122.

24. G. Pope Atkins, "The April 1986 Elections in the Dominican Republic," in *The Caribbean After Grenada: Revolution, Conflict, and Democracy*, ed. Scott B. MacDonald, Harald M. Sandstrom, and Paul B. Goodwin Jr. (New York: Praeger, 1988); and Maríñez, *Democracia y procesos electorales*, 186.

25. Black, *Dominican Republic*, 137.

26. Larman Wilson, on his first trip to the Dominican Republic in August 1966, interviewed Jorge in his Santo Domingo law office.

27. Wiarda and Kryzanek, "Dominican Republic," 670–71.

28. Black, *Dominican Republic*, 139. She has an excellent account of the IMF role (138–46), which we rely upon. The United States had the largest share of votes in IMF decisions—in 1994 almost 18 percent.

29. Ibid., 139.

30. Ibid., 67–69; and Kryzanek and Wiarda, *Politics of External Influence*, 120–21. For the famous debate between a Marxist (Cuello) and Gulf + Western's attorney (Peynado) about the fairness of the contracts signed between the Dominican government and the U.S. company, see José Israel Cuello H. and Julio E. Peynado, *La Gulf and Western en la reformismo* (Santo Domingo: Ediciones Taller, 1974).

31. It is a party to only two United Nations conventions: the 1961 Convention on Narcotic Drugs (but not the amending 1972 protocol—that is, not until 1993, shortly after the chair of the House Select Committee on Narcotics Abuse and Control announced a hearing on Dominican drug trafficking) and the 1972 Convention on Psychotropic Substances.

32. Eugenia Georges, *The Making of a Transnational Community: Migration, Development, and Cultural Change in the Dominican Republic* (New York: Columbia University Press, 1990). See also Jorge Duany, "Quisqueya on the Hudson: The Transnational Identity of Dominicans in Washington Heights" (paper presented at the 19th Annual Conference of the Caribbean Studies Association, Mérida, México, 24–27 May 1994).

33. Luís E. Guarnizo, "Los Dominicanyorks: The Making of a Binational Society," in *Trends in U.S.-Caribbean Relations*, ed. Anthony P. Maingot, entire issue of *Annals of the American Academy of Political and Social Science* 533 (May 1994): 77–81, 86.

34. Alan Klein, *Sugarball: The American Game, the Dominican Dream* (New Haven: Yale University Press, 1991), 43.

35. The full title is Convention on the Elimination of All Forms of Racial Discrimination. Its enforcement is unlikely, given the legacy of Dominican attitudes toward race and Haitians.

36. Jonathan Hartlyn, "The Dominican Republic," in *Latin America and Caribbean Contemporary Record*, ed. Abraham F. Lowenthal (New York: Holmes and Meier, 1987), 5:520.

8. The Second Balaguer Regime, 1986–1996, and the Election of Fernández

1. This section relies on G. Pope Atkins, "The April 1986 Elections in the Dominican Republic," in *The Caribbean After Grenada: Revolution, Conflict, and Democracy*, ed. Scott B. MacDonald, Harald M. Sandstrom, and Paul B. Goodwin Jr. (New York: Praeger Publishers, 1988). Atkins was present on research trips in the Dominican Republic during the last part of the campaign and for a period following the election.

2. Rosario Espinal, "Dominican Republic: Electoralism, Pacts, and Clientelism in the Making of a Democratic Regime," in *Democracy in the Caribbean: Myths and Realities*, ed. Carlene J. Edie (New York: Praeger Publishers, 1994), 151.

3. Ibid., 152.

4. Jonathan Hartlyn, "The Dominican Republic," in *Latin America and Caribbean Contemporary Record*, ed. Abraham F. Lowenthal (New York: Holmes and Meier, 1987), 5:514.

5. Pablo A. Maríñez, *Democracia y procesos electorales en la República Dominicana* (Santo Domingo: Editora Alfa y Omega, 1994), 152–53.

6. James Ferguson, *The Dominican Republic: Beyond the Lighthouse* (London: Latin American Bureau, 1992), 35.

7. Jan K. Black, "Democracy and Disillusionment in the Dominican Republic," in *Modern Caribbean Politics*, ed. Anthony Payne and Paul Sutton (Baltimore: Johns Hopkins University Press, 1994), 66–67; and Espinal, "Dominican Republic," 156–57.

8. The Dominican demand for medical care in Cuba resulted in the introduction of a weekly charter flight in 1988. Although the cost was a fraction of that in the United States, Cuba provided some care free of charge. Julie M. Feinsilver, "Cuba as a 'Medical Power': The Politics of Symbolism," *Latin American Research Review* 24, no. 2 (1989): 20–21.

9. Michael J. Kryzanek and Howard J. Wiarda, *The Politics of External Influence in the Dominican Republic* (New York and Stanford: Praeger Publishers and Hoover Institute Press, 1988), 166.

10. Ferguson, *Dominican Republic*, 58, 86–87; Americas Watch, *Haitian Sugar Cane Cutters in the Dominican Republic* (New York: November 1989); and Americas Watch, *Harvesting Oppression: Forced Haitian Labor in the Dominican Sugar Industry* (New York: June 1990).

11. Black, "Democracy and Disillusionment," 64–66; and Ferguson, *Dominican Republic*, 51–53.

12. Section 936 of the U.S. Internal Revenue Code offered tax exemptions to U.S. companies that located and operated in Puerto Rico. In the mid-1980s, an agreement was worked out between the U.S. Treasury and the governor of Puerto Rico whereby the latter's Caribbean Development Program, in support of the Reagan administration's Caribbean Basin Initiative, would permit the Section 936 corporations to invest in Caribbean countries. The Dominican Republic benefitted greatly from the investments of these companies, especially in pharmaceuticals, apparel and textiles, and electronics. See Sara L. Grusky, "The Politics of Development: Puerto Rico's Caribbean Program," *21st Century Policy Review: An American, Caribbean and African Forum* 2, nos. 1–2 (spring 1994): 267–85.

13. Ferguson, *Dominican Republic*, 51.

14. Richard S. Hillman and Thomas J. D'Agostino, *Distant Neighbors in the Caribbean: The Dominican Republic and Jamaica in Comparative Perspective* (New York: Praeger Publishers, 1992), 112, table 5.1. See also National Democratic Institute for International Affairs and the Carter Center of Emory University, *1990 Elections in the Dominican Republic: Report of an Observer Delegation* (Washington, D.C., and Atlanta: National Democratic Institute for International Affairs and the Carter Center of Emory University, 1990), 18–19. Bosch charged fraud and called for two days of "civic mourning." Former President Carter said in the report that the election was "among the most disputed in the country's history," but after a review of "irregularities," the delegation concluded that "the allegations of fraud were not substantiated" (7).

15. Ladislao Brachowicz, "Turnaround in the Dominican Republic: Reforms Pay Off with Growth and Stabilization," in Inter-American Development Bank, *The IDB* (Washington, D.C.: Inter-American Development Bank, December 1993), 6–7.

16. Based on Larman Wilson's long conversation with Martha Ellen Davis, anthropologist, Center for Latin American and Caribbean Studies, Indiana University, Bloomington, who attended and prepared a video of the formal ceremony that began on 6 October. See news reports by Douglas Farah, *Washington Post*, 7 and 13 October 1992. The building of the lighthouse, first proposed just prior to Dominican independence in 1844 and officially endorsed in the 1870s, had been authorized by the Fifth International Conference of American States in 1923. A competition was held for the design in 1929 and in 1931 an international jury selected the design of British architect J. L. Gleave from among the seven hundred plans submitted. Balaguer actively pursued its building and completion in time for the V Centenario and provided a burial place for himself in El Faro—reminding his detractors of the late Francisco Franco of Spain who built his own burial site as part of El Valle de los Caídos. For the history of El Faro, see Fernando Pérez Memen, "Faro a Colón: Ideal y realidad," *Listín Diario*, 3 de Octubre de 1993.

17. Americas Watch, *Half Measures: Reform, Forced Labor and the Dominican Sugar Industry* (New York: March 1991).

18. Ferguson, *Dominican Republic*, 88–91.

19. Georges A. Fauriol and Andrew S. Failoa, "Prelude to Intervention," in *Haitian Frustrations: Dilemmas for U.S. Policy*, ed. Georges A. Fauriol (Washington, D.C.: Center for Strategic and International Studies, 1995), 111.

20. Brachowicz, "Turnaround." See also Dale Mathews, "Export Processing Zones in the Dominican Republic" (paper presented at the annual conference of the Caribbean Studies Association, San Juan, Puerto Rico, 27–31 May 1996).

21. In 1987, Jorge and other PRD officials had been indicted for corrupt practices in the use of public funds and military purchases. After collapsing in court while being tried and convicted, Jorge was permitted to go to the United States for medical treatment. In 1991 he returned to the Dominican Republic, and the original sentence was reaffirmed.

22. *Listín Diario*, 13 de abril de 1994. See also Howard J. Wiarda, "Out with the Old, but Not too Fast," *North-South* (September/October 1994), 10–11. This article and others about the campaign were supplied by Larman Wilson's

former student, Amanda Fernández, M.A., who was working for Catholic Relief Services in the Dominican Republic at the time. For a biographical study of the PRD nominee, see Osvaldo Santana, *Peña Gómez: sus orígines* (Santo Domingo: Alfa y Omega, 1981).

23. This preliminary report noted that the "pattern of disenfranchisement—which affected predominantly votes for opposition parties—suggested the real possibility that a deliberate effort was made to tamper with the electoral process" (4). In its final report, the NDI concluded that "the legitimacy of the . . . elections must be called into question" (1). See also Jonathan Hartlyn, "Crisis-Ridden Elections (Again) in the Dominican Republic: Neo-patrimonialism, Presidentialism, and Weak Electoral Oversight," *Journal of Interamerican Studies*, no. 3 (winter 1994): 122–34. Hartlyn was a member of the NDI delegation. Solarz testified before the House Committee on Foreign Affairs, Subcommittee on Western Hemisphere Affairs, on 24 May and 13 July 1994.

24. Ibid., 122, 132; and National Democratic Institute, *1990 Elections*, 1–3, Appendix A.

25. National Democratic Institute, *1990 Elections*, 5–7, Appendix C.

26. Wiarda, "Out with the Old," 16.

27. José de Córdoba, "Nouveau Riche: New York Drug Link Enriches a Poor City in Dominican Republic," *Wall Street Journal*, 8 July 1992; and U.S. Congress, House of Representatives, Select Committee on Narcotics Abuse and Control, *Dominican Drug Trafficking: Hearing*, 103rd Cong., 1st sess., 24 March 1993 (Washington, D.C.: Government Printing Office, 1993), 55–56.

28. "Balaguer pide a dominicanos que protestan pacificamente en Nueva York," *Diario las Américas*, 11 de julio de 1992.

29. Ivelaw L. Griffith, "Drugs and World Politics: The Caribbean Dimension, *The Round Table*, no. 332 (October 1994): 426.

30. Ibid., 428–30; and U.S. Congress, *Dominican Drug Trafficking*, 48–49.

31. M. McAlary, "To Die in New York: Exclusive Report from Drug Capital of the Dominican Republic," *New York Post*, 16 September 1992.

32. De Córdoba, "Nouveau Riche." Blaming the "Domyorks" for bringing back AIDS did not lessen the Dominican inclination to place the onus on Haitians.

33. Luis E. Guaranizo, *One Country in Two: Dominican-owned Firms in New York and the Dominican Republic* (Ph.D. diss., Johns Hopkins University, 1992).

34. In October 1993, the Dominican ambassador to the United States warned

that one hundred thousand Dominicans would lose their jobs under NAFTA unless it included a provision to encompass the circum-Caribbean along the lines of the Caribbean Basin Initiative. The signatories (Canada and Mexico along with the United States) approved NAFTA and the market began to function in January 1994.

35. Sherri Grasmuck and Patricia R. Pessar, *Between Two Islands: Dominican International Migration* (Berkeley: University of California Press, 1991), chap. 6. The second island referred to in the title is Manhattan. See also Jorge Duany, "Quisqueya on the Hudson: The Transnational Identity of Dominicans in Washington Heights" (paper presented at the 19th Annual Conference of the Caribbean Studies Association, Mérida, México, 24–27 May 1994).

36. Alejandro Portes and Ramón Grosfoguel, "Caribbean Diasporas: Migration and Ethnic Communities," in *Trends in U.S.-Caribbean Relations,* ed. Anthony P. Maingot, entire issue of *Annals of the American Academy of Political and Social Science* 533 (May 1994): 63.

37. The announcement appeared in *LASA Forum* 24 (spring 1993): 11. An important example of Dominican academic influence is the presence of Dominicans who earned their graduate degrees in the United States and are now professors at U.S. institutions, where they teach and write on Dominican and Caribbean history, politics, international relations, literature, and other subjects, and participate in professional societies such as the Caribbean Studies Association, Latin American Studies Association, and those serving specific disciplines. Among them are Emilio Betances (Gettysburg College), Rosario Espinal (Temple University), Norberto James (Boston College), and Frank Moya Pons (formerly visiting at the University of Florida and City University of New York).

38. Jordan Levin, "People in Paradise: Juan Luis Guerra," *Caribbean Travel and Life* (July-August 1992), 30, 32–33. See also Dario Tejeda, *La historia escondida de Juan Luis Guerra y 4–40* (Santo Domingo: Amigos del Hogar, 1993).

39. See Deborah Pacini Hernández, *Bachata: A Social History of Dominican Popular Music* (Philadelphia: Temple University Press, 1995); Pacini Hernández, "Cultural Politics and Popular Music in the Dominican Republic: Bachata and *nueva canción* in the 1990s" (paper presented at International Congress of the Latin American Studies Association, Washington, D.C.: 28–30 September 1995; and Mark Holston, "Music is Big Business in the Dominican Republic but Bachata now Challenges the Monopoly of Merengue," *Caribbean Week*, 25 December 1993 to 7 January 1994, 49. The leading promoter

of Latin musical concerts and groups in Washington, D.C., is a Dominican, Daniel Bueno—report by Patrick Symes, *Washington Post*, 9 October 1994.

40. Howard J. Wiarda, *The 1996 Dominican Republic Elections: Post-Election Report* (Washington, D.C.: Western Hemisphere Election Study Series, CSIS Americas Program, 8 July 1996), 1, 16; Appendix 3.

41. Ibid., 18, Appendix 4.

42. *Washington Post*, 2 July 1996. See also Council of Freely Elected Heads of State and National Democratic Institute for International Affairs, "Preliminary Statement, July 1, 1996" (Atlanta and Washington, D.C.: Council of Freely Elected Heads of State and National Democratic Institute for International Affairs, 1996).

43. Espinal, "Dominican Republic." 151, 159–61; Rosario Espinal, "Electoral Politics in the Dominican Republic, 1978–1990" (paper presented at the April 1991 meeting of the Latin American Studies Association, Washington, D.C.), 5–6, 11–12, 18; Hartlyn, "Crisis-Ridden Elections (Again)," 122–34.

44. Michael J. Kryzanek, "The Waiting Game: Opposition and Political Atrophy in the Dominican Republic" (paper presented at the 18th Annual Meeting of the Caribbean Studies Association, Ocho Rios, Jamaica, 28 May 1993).

Epilogue

1. Jack C. Plano and Roy Olton, *The International Relations Dictionary*, 4th ed. (Santa Barbara: ABC-CLIO, 1988), 26–33, provides solid definitions of imperialism and its constituent elements that are used in this discussion.

2. Frank Moya Pons, *El pasado dominicano* (Santo Domingo: Fundación J. A. Caro Alvarez, 1986), 360–61.

3. Max J. Castro, "Dominican Republic: The Long Transition: Dilemmas of Democracy and Development," *North-South Focus* 5, no. 2 (1996): 4–5. For the first biography of the new president, see Marcelino Ozuna, *Leonel: su historia* (Santo Domingo: Editora Alfa y Omega, 1996).

Bibliographical Essay

This essay lists and evaluates the salient works—books, monographs, articles, chapters, and public documents—consulted and used in the preparation of this volume. It is organized in terms of general, thematic, and time-specific categories. Some bibliographic sources and other guides are also included. Readers are directed to the chapter notes for more specific items such as news and information sources, statistics, texts of treaties and other international instruments, interviews, correspondence, brief quotations, and other relatively technical matters.

The most useful bibliography in terms of the greatest number of categories and entries (annotated), as well as recency, is Kai Schoenhals, *Dominican Republic*, World Bibliographic Series, vol. 3 (Santa Barbara: CLIO Press, 1990). Deborah S. Hitt and Larman C. Wilson, *A Selected Bibliography of the Dominican Republic: A Century after the Restoration of Independence* (Washington, D.C.: Center for Research in Social Systems, American University, 1968), is a thorough monograph-length annotated work. Wolf Grabendorff, *Bibliographie zu Politik und Gesellschaft der Dominikanischen Republic: Neuere Studien, 1961–1971* (Munich: Weltforum Verlag, 1973), by a German political scientist, now director of the Institute of European-Latin American Relations in Madrid, stresses U.S. intervention, without annotations. Bernardo Vega, *Bibliografía de asuntos económicos dominicanos* (Santiago: Asociación para el Desarrollo, 1955), is dated but still useful. Howard J. Wiarda, *Materials for the Study of Politics and Government in the Dominican Republic, 1930–1966* (Santiago: Universidad Católica Madre y Maestra, 1968), is organized by time periods, with brief comments.

A good analytic treatment of the principal sources by a political scientist is Michael J. Kryzanek, "The Dominican Republic," chap. 5 in *Handbook of Political Science Research on Latin America: Trends from the 1960s to the 1990s*, ed. David W. Dent (Westport: Greenwood Press, 1990), 99–107. Shorter, annotated, and recent studies are H. Hoetink, "Dominican Republic: Economy, Society, Politics, c. 1870–1930," 423–26; and Frank Moya Pons, "Dominican Republic: Economy, Society, Politics, 1930 to c. 1990," 734–41, in *The Cambridge History of Latin America: Latin America Since 1930, Mexico, Central America, and the Caribbean*, ed. Leslie Bethel (Cambridge: Cambridge University Press, 1995).

Helpful guides to official sources are Library of Congress, *A Guide to the Official Publications of the other American Republics*, vol. 8, *Dominican Republic*, comp. John de Noia (Washington, D.C.: Library of Congress, 1947); National Archives, *List of Records of the Bureau of Insular Affairs Relating to the Dominican Customs Receivership, 1905–1940*, comp. Kenneth Munden (Washington, D.C., 1943); National Archives, *Materials in the National Archives Relating to the Dominican Republic*, comp. Seymour J. Pomrenze (Washington, D.C.: U.S. Government Printing Office, 1948). Of special interest is Pablo A. Maríñez, *Relaciones dominico-haitianas y raíces histórico culturales africanas en la República Dominicana: bibliografía básica* (Santo Domingo: Editora Universitaria—UASD, 1986), by a Dominican sociologist.

A number of works were called on to provide a general international relations background, as well as for U.S. policy calculations: G. Pope Atkins, *Latin America in the International Political System*, 3d ed. (Boulder: Westview Press, 1995); Atkins, "Reorienting U.S. Policies in the New Era," chap. 1 in *The United States and Latin America: Redefining U.S. Purposes in the Post-Cold War Era*, ed. G. Pope Atkins (Austin: Lyndon B. Johnson School of Public Affairs, University of Texas at Austin, 1992); Atkins, "The United States and the Caribbean Basin," chap. 2 in *Regional Hegemons: Threat Perceptions and Strategic Response*, ed. David J. Myers (Boulder: Westview Press, 1991); Mariano Baptista Gumucio, *Latinoamericanos y norteamericanos: Cinco siglos de dos culturas* (La Paz: Editorial "Artística," 1987); Samuel Flagg Bemis, *The Latin American Policy of the United States: An Historical Interpretation* (New York: Harcourt, Brace, 1943); P. H. Coombs, *The Fourth Dimension of Foreign Policy: Educational and Cultural Affairs* (New York: Harper and Row, 1964); John J. Johnson, *A Hemisphere Apart: The Foundations of United States Policy toward Latin America* (Baltimore: Johns Hopkins University Press, 1990); Johnson, *Latin America in Caricature* (Austin: University of Texas Press, 1981); J. Lloyd Mecham, *The United States and Inter-American Security, 1889–1960* (Austin: University of Texas Press, 1961); J. M. Mitchell, *International Cultural Relations, Key Concepts in International Relations* (London: Allen & Unwin, in association with the British Council, 1986); and Larman C. Wilson, "Multilateral Policy and Organization of American States: Latin American–U.S. Convergence and Divergence" in Harold E. Davis, Larman C. Wilson, and others, *Latin American Foreign Policies: An Analysis* (Baltimore: Johns Hopkins University Press, 1975), 47–84.

Three leading works by historians with a Caribbean policy focus are Wilfrid Hardy Calcott, *The Caribbean Policy of the United States, 1890–1920* (Baltimore: Johns Hopkins University Press, 1942); Lester D. Langley, *The United States and the Caribbean in the Twentieth Century*, 4th ed. (Athens: University of Georgia Press, 1989); and Dana G. Munro, *Intervention and Dollar Diplomacy in the Caribbean, 1900–1921* (Princeton: Princeton University Press, 1964). An excellent work is Luis Martínez-Fernández, *Torn between Empires: Economy, Society, and Patterns of Political Thought in the Hispanic Caribbean, 1840–1878* (Athens: University of Georgia Press, 1994).

Several general treatments of the Dominican Republic describe and assess numerous domestic and international historical, political, economic, and social elements. American University, Center for Research in Social Systems, *Area Handbook for the Dominican Republic*, ed. T. D. Roberts (Washington, D.C.: Government Printing Office, 1967), and *Area Handbook for the Dominican Republic and Haiti*, ed. Richard A. Haggerty (Washington, D.C.: Government Printing Office, 1991), provide considerable information; the latter work is more up to date but the former has broader coverage. Ian Bell, *The Dominican Republic* (Boulder: Westview Press, 1980), is a basic introduction by a former British Ambassador to Santo Domingo. Jan K. Black, *The Dominican Republic: Politics and Development in an Unsovereign State* (London: Allen & Unwin, 1986), written by a former Peace Corps volunteer in Chile who is now a professor of political science, is concerned with U.S. economic and military influence. Julio G. Campillo Pérez, *El Grillo y el Ruiseñor: Elecciones Presidenciales Dominicanas, Contribución a su Estudio* (Santo Domingo: Editora del Caribe, 1966), is an original electoral guide. James Ferguson, *The Dominican Republic: Beyond the Lighthouse* (London: Latin America Bureau, 1992), is by a British specialist on the Caribbean. Howard J. Wiarda, *The Dominican Republic: Nation in Transition* (New York: Frederick A. Praeger, Publishers, 1969), is a basic introduction to the country by a prolific writer. Michael J. Kryzanek and Howard J. Wiarda, *The Politics of External Influence in the Dominican Republic* (New York and Stanford: Praeger Publishers and Hoover Institution Press, 1988), is a provocative application of the concepts of dependence, independence, and interdependence of domestic and international systems to the Dominican case. Wiarda and Kryzanek also collaborate on *The Dominican Republic: A Caribbean Crucible*, 2d ed. (Boulder: Westview Press, 1992).

Three works by Frank Moya Pons, a leading Dominican historian and social scientist, are authoritative: *The Dominican Republic: A National History* (New Rochelle, N.Y.: Hispaniola Books, 1995); *Manual de Historia Dominicana* (Santiago: Universidad Católica de Madre y Maestra, 1977); and *El pasado dominicano* (Santo Domingo: Fundación J. A. Caro Alvarez, 1986). Selden Rodman, *Quisqueya: A History of the Dominican Republic* (Seattle: University of Washington

Press, 1964), is a balanced account by a long-time observer, art collector, poet, and former resident of Haiti. *The Dominican Republic: Social Change and Political Stagnation*, entire issue of *Latin American Perspectives* 22 (summer 1995), contains numerous chapters authored by historians and social scientists.

Two works present valuable data concerning the Dominican armed forces: Bernardo Vega, *Historia de las Fuerzas Armadas Dominicanas* (Santo Domingo: Fundación Cultural Dominicana, 1992); and Ernesto Vega y Pagán, *Historia de las fuerzas armadas*, 2 vols. (Ciudad Trujillo: Imprenta Dominicana, 1955). See also Howard Wiarda, "The Politics of Civil-Military Relations in the Dominican Republic," *Journal of Inter-American Studies* 7 (October 1965): 465–84; and G. Pope Atkins, *Arms and Politics in the Dominican Republic* (Boulder: Westview Press, 1981)—published in Spanish in the Dominican Republic as *Los Militares y la Política en la República Dominicana* (Santo Domingo: Fundación Cultural Dominicana, 1987).

Several of the above works contain sections on Dominican foreign policy and international relations as part of their "overviews" of the country. Standard sources that deal directly with these subjects in a general way are J. Lloyd Mecham, *A Survey of United States–Latin American Relations* (Boston: Houghton Mifflin Company, 1965); and Graham H. Stuart and James L. Tigner, *Latin America and the United States*, 6th ed. (Englewood Cliffs: Prentice-Hall, 1975). Official U.S. diplomatic papers can be traced through the serial U.S. Department of State, *Papers Relating to the Foreign Relations of the United States* [1870– 1931; title varied prior to 1907] (Washington, D.C.: Government Printing Office, 1870–1946), retitled, *Foreign Relations of the United States, Diplomatic Papers* [1932–1961/63] (1947–1993)—see specific vols. for Latin America; coverage of the Dominican Republic varies.

On the specific subject of Dominican relations with Haiti, see the classic work by Rayford W. Logan, *Haiti and the Dominican Republic* (New York: Oxford University Press, 1968); Larman C. Wilson, "The Dominican Republic and Haiti," chap. 10 in Harold E. Davis, Larman C. Wilson, and others, *Latin American Foreign Policies: An Analysis* (Baltimore: Johns Hopkins University Press, 1975), examines domestic factors affecting relations between the two countries and their relations with the United States.

A number of scholarly and other sources taken together provide coverage of the complex nineteenth century events that spilled over into the early twentieth. Charles Callan Tansill, *The United States and Santo Domingo, 1798–1873: A Chapter in Caribbean Diplomacy* (Baltimore: Johns Hopkins University Press, 1938), is a highly detailed and heavily documented study with many references to papers from the foreign offices of France, Germany, and the United Kingdom. Frank Moya Pons, *La dominación haitiana, 1822–1844*, 2d ed. (Santiago de los Caballeros: Universidad Católica Madre y Maestra, 1972), is the leading work on the Haitian occupation. Sumner Welles, *Naboth's Vineyard: The Dominican Republic, 1844–1924*, 2 vols. (New York: Payson & Clarke, 1928), was until recently the only comprehensive treatment of the period indicated in the title. The author, who revealed his racial biases in the book, was sent by President Harding in 1922 to the Dominican Republic to arrange elections and U.S. troop withdrawal and was a key figure in President Roosevelt's Good Neighbor Policy of the 1930s.

Diplomatic Correspondence of the United States: Inter-American Affairs, 1831– 1860, vol. 7, *Dominican Republic, Ecuador, France*, selected and arranged by William R. Manning (Washington, D.C.: Carnegie Endowment for International Peace, 1935), 2–219, provides official papers for the era of Haitian occupation and the early national period. U.S. Congress, Senate, Commission of Inquiry to Santo Domingo, *Report of the Commission of Inquiry* (Washington, D.C.: Government Printing Office, 1871), is a pro-annexation document, transmitted by President Grant, that reports on economic, political, and social conditions in the Dominican Republic.

A number of works regarding Dominican leaders during the chaotic decade from 1882 provide some insight into their foreign policy making: Ulises Francisco Espaillat, *Escritos de Espaillat: Artículos, Cartas y Documentos Oficiales* (Santo Domingo: Imprenta la Cuna de América, 1909); General Gregorio Luperón, *Notas Autobiográficas y apuntes históricas de la República Dominicana, desde de la restauración a nuestros días*, 3 vols. (Ponce, Puerto Rico: 1895–96); Manuel Rodríguez Objío, *Gregorio Luperón e Historia de la Restauración*, 2 vols. (Santiago, RD: Editorial del Diario, 1939); Padre Fernando A. de Meriño, *Elementos de Geografía Física, Política, e Histórica de la República Dominicana*, 2d ed. (Santo Domingo: Imprenta de García Hermanos, 1898; reprint, Santo Domingo: Editora Taller, 1984). R. Michael Malek, "The Ulises 'Lilis' Heureaux Regime, 1882–1899: Development and Dictatorship in the Dominican Republic" (paper presented to the 4th annual Caribbean Studies Association convention, Universidad Católica Madre y Maestra, Santiago de los Caballeros, República Dominicana, 12 January 1978), is a thorough handling of the subject. Harry Hoetink, "The Dominican Republic in the Nineteenth Century: Some Notes on Stratification, Immigration, and Race," in *Race and Class in Latin America*, ed. Max Mörner (New York: Columbia University Press, 1970), is an important study by a leading anthropologist. Merline Pitre, "Frederick Douglass and the Annexation of Santo Domingo," *Journal of Negro History* 62 (October 1977): 390–400, is of particular interest regarding the activities of the famous black leader. J. Fred Rippy, "The Initiation of the Customs Receivership in the Dominican Republic," *Hispanic American Historical Review* 17 (November 1934): 419–517, details the beginnings of the receivership that was to be a major Dominican-U.S. issue until World War II.

The principal studies of the U.S. intervention and military occupation from 1916–24 are highly critical ones. Bruce Calder, *The Impact of Intervention: The Dominican Republic during the U.S. Occupation of 1916–1924* (Austin: University of Texas Press, 1984), is an excellent analysis and description. Harry A. Ellsworth, *One Hundred and Eighty Landings of United States Marines, 1800–1934* (Washington, D.C.: U.S. Navy, Historical Section, 1934), is a by-and-large objective official history that devotes attention to the Dominican Republic. Stephen M. Fuller and Graham A. Cosmas, *Marines in the Dominican Republic, 1916–1924* (Washington, D.C.: History and Museums Division, Headquarters, U.S. Marine Corps, 1974), is a generally nonjudgmental and detailed official chronicle of the Marines' military operations and administration; the authors view the United States as provoked into intervention and accept the official strategic rationale. Edwin N. McClellan, "Operations Ashore in the Dominican Republic," *U.S. Naval Institute Proceedings* 47 (February 1921) is a contemporary treatment by a Marine major. U.S. Congress, Senate, Select Committee on Haiti and Santo Domingo, *Inquiry into Occupation and Administration of Haiti and Santo Domingo*, 67th Cong., 1st sess. (1922), is a hard-hitting revelation and condemnation of Marine maltreatment of and even atrocities against Dominicans. Marvin Goldwert, *The Constabulary in the Dominican Republic and Nicaragua: Progeny and Legacy of United States Intervention* (Gainesville: University of Florida Press, 1962), is a classic study that reveals how all recruitment was from the lower classes because of the boycott of the service by the upper class/elite.

Of use and interest are Carl Kelsey, "The American Intervention in Haiti and the Dominican Republic," *Annals of the American Academy of Political and Social Science* 100 (March 1922); David Charles MacMichael, *The United States and the Dominican Republic, 1871–1940: A Cycle in Caribbean Diplomacy* (Ph.D. diss., University of Oregon, 1964); Clyde J. Metcalf, *History of the United States Marine Corps* (New York: G. P. Putnam and Sons, 1939); Dana G. Munro, *Intervention and Dollar Diplomacy in the Caribbean, 1900–1921* (Princeton: Princeton University Press, 1964); and Sumner Welles, *Naboth's Vineyard: The Dominican Republic, 1844–1924*, 2 vols. (New York: Payson & Clarke, 1928).

The following sources relating to the era of Rafael Trujillo cover the dictator's rise to and consolidation of power and the nature of his dictatorship. Juan Bosch, *Trujillo: causas de una tiranía sin ejemplo* (Caracas: Librería "Las Novedades," 1959), is a severe condemnation by a future Dominican president and major political figure into the 1990s. Robert D. Crassweller, *Trujillo: The Life and Times of a Caribbean Dictator* (New York: Macmillan, 1966), is the foremost biography in English. Bernard Diedrich, *Trujillo: The Death of the Goat* (Boston: Little, Brown, 1978), a highly colorful account by a journalist resident in Haiti, contains a great deal of information in minute detail. René Fortunato, "Trujillo: El Poder del Jefe" (Philadelphia: Disc Makers, 1993), video, part 1, is a dramatic presentation of images, covering the years 1916–37 with stress on the U.S. occupation and the Haitian massacre, and part 2 (1994) covers the years 1938–52. Jesús de Galíndez, *La Era de Trujillo: Un Estudio Casuístico de Dictadura Hispanoamericano* (Santiago de Chile: Editorial del Pacífico, 1957), and English edition, *The Era of Trujillo: Dominican Dictator*, ed. Russell H. Fitzgibbon (Tucson: University of Arizona Press, 1973), presents a detailed analysis that raised Trujillo's brutal ire in an internationally publicized case of murder. Morris L. Ernst, *Report and Opinion in the Matter of Galindez* (New York: Sidney S. Baron and Co., 1958), is a disappointing, paid whitewash by a well-known U.S. civil rights lawyer. Arturo R. Espaillat, *Trujillo: The Last Caesar* (Chicago: Henry Regnery, 1963), is an admiring biography and anti-U.S. statement by the head of Trujillo's secret police. Juan Isidro Jiménez Grullón, *Una gestapo en América. Vida, tortura, agonía y muerto de presos políticos bajo la tiranía de Trujillo* (Havana: Ed. Lex., 1946), is by one of Trujillo's surviving prisoners.

The nature of the regime is also indicated in Noel Henríquez, *La verdad sobre Trujillo: capítulos que se le olvidaron a Galíndez* (Havana: Luz Hilo, 1959); Germán E. Ornes, *Trujillo: Little Caesar of the Caribbean* (New York: Thomas Nelson and Sons, 1958); and Manuel A. Peña Battle, *Contribución a una campaña. Cuatro discursos políticos* (Santiago: Ed. el Diario, 1941). Also of interest are two books by Joaquín Balaguer: *La isla al revés: Haití y el destino dominicano* (1949; reprint Santo Domingo: Fundación José A. Caro Alvarez, 1983); and *La realidad dominicana. Semblanza de un país y de un régimen* (Buenos Aires: Imprenta Ferrari Hermanos, 1947). Charles A. Thomson, "Dictatorship in the Dominican Republic," *Foreign Policy Reports* 12 (15 April 1936), was an early recognition of the consolidation of the Trujillo dictatorship. Bernardo Vega, *Nazismo, Fascismo y Falangismo en la República Dominicana* (Santo Domingo: Fundación Cultural Dominicana, 1985) and *Los Trujillo se Escriben* (Santo Domingo: Fundación Cultural Dominicana, 1987), are devastating documentary-archival collections. Vega, a Dominican economist and historian, former governor of the Dominican Central Bank, former director-general of the Museo del Hombre Dominicano, and director of the Fundación Cultural Dominicana, has edited an indispensable series of documents on Dominican internal and foreign affairs, of which these and others cited elsewhere in this essay are a part, drawn from original and official sources (including the U.S. National Archives). Howard J. Wiarda, *Dictatorship and Development: The Methods of Control in Trujillo's Dominican Republic* (Gainesville: University of Florida Press, 1969), is an important scholarly study.

Trujillo's relations with the United States and the Inter-American System are addressed by G. Pope Atkins and Larman C. Wilson, *The United States and the Trujillo Regime* (New Brunswick: Rutgers University Press, 1972), which covers the subject in detail and is drawn on in this volume. Specifically on U.S. policy, see Ellis O. Briggs, *Farewell to Foggy Bottom: The Recollections of a Career Diplomat* (New York: David McKay, 1964), 221–25, by the U.S. ambassador to the Dominican Republic in the middle of World War II who had a strong aversion to the brutality of the dictatorship and unsuccessfully sought changes in U.S. policy; Douglas Cater and Walter Pincus, "The Foreign Legion of U.S. Public Relations," *Reporter* (22 December 1960), 15–22, excellent journalism about Trujillo's extensive propaganda efforts in the United States; Stetson Conn and Byron Fairchild, *The Western Hemisphere: The Framework of Hemispheric Defense*, vol. 12, pt. 1, of Department of the Army, *United States Army in World War II* (Washington, D.C.: Government Printing Office, 1960), an exceptionally good official history; Bryce Wood, *The Making of the Good Neighbor Policy* (New York: Columbia University Press, 1961), the definitive study of the 1930s. Pamela Johnson Sybert, "Mutual Admiration: MBS and the Dominican Republic," *Journal of Broadcasting* 24 (spring 1980): 189–97, is a revealing treatment of the subject. *U.S. Congressional Record* carries many of the congressional speeches during the debate at the time over U.S. policy toward Trujillo. Bernardo Vega contributes *Kennedy y los Trujillo* (Santo Domingo: Fundación Cultural Dominicana, 1991); and *Trujillo y las Fuerzas Armadas Norteamericanos* (Santo Domingo: Fundación Cultural Dominicana, 1992)—in 1997 President Leonel Fernández appointed Vega the Dominican ambassador to Washington.

On the post-World War II Caribbean conflict in which Trujillo played a central role and related activities by the Inter-American System, see John C. Dreier, *The Organization of American States and the Hemisphere Crisis* (New York: Harper and Row, 1962), by a U.S. ambassador for ten years to the Council of the Organization of American States; Edgar S. Furniss Jr., "The Inter-American System and Recent Caribbean Disputes," *International Organization* 4 (November 1950): 593–94; J. Lloyd Mecham, "Caribbean Turbulence (1949–1960)," chap. 13 in

The United States and Inter-American Security, 1889–1960 (Austin: University of Texas Press, 1961); and Jerome Slater, *The OAS and United States Foreign Policy* (Columbus: Ohio State University Press, 1967).

U.S. Department of State publications on the same subject include *Peace in the Americas: A Resumé of Measures Undertaken through the OAS to Preserve Peace* (pub. no. 3964, International Organization and Conference Series II, American Republics 6, 1950); *Inter-American Efforts to Relieve International Tensions in the Western Hemisphere, 1959–1960* (1962). See also Edward Jamison, "Keeping Peace in the Caribbean Area," Department of State, *Bulletin* 23 (3 July 1950): 18–25 (the author's last name, Jameson, is misspelled).

A set of publications issued by the Organization of American States thoroughly documents the "Dominican situation" that occupied a great deal of the organization's attention from 1950 to 1961: *Inter-American Treaty of Reciprocal Assistance, Applications,* General Secretariat, Department of Legal Affairs, vol. 1, 1948–1959, 3d ed. (Washington, D.C., 1973); *Documents Submitted at the Meeting of March 13, 1950,* Investigating Committee of the Organ of Consultation (Washington, D.C.: Pan American Union, 1950); *Second Report of the Inter-American Peace Committee Submitted to the Tenth Inter-American Conference* (Washington, D.C.: Pan American Union, 1954); *Quinta Reunión de Consulta de Ministros de Relaciones Exteriores, Santiago, Chile, 1959* (Washington, D.C.: Unión Panamericana, 1959); *Report of the Inter-American Peace Committee to the Fifth Meeting of Consultation of Ministers of Foreign Affairs* (Washington, D.C.: Pan American Union, General Secretariat of the Organization of American States, 1959); *Sexta Reunión de Consulta de Ministros de Relaciones Exteriores, San José, Costa Rica, 1960: Documents* (Washington, D.C.: Pan American Union, General Secretariat of the Organization of American States, 1960); *Sixth Meeting of Consultation of Ministers of Foreign Affairs, Serving as Organ of Consultation in Application of the Inter-American Treaty of Reciprocal Assistance, San José, Costa Rica, August 16–21, 1960: Final Act* (Washington, D.C.: Pan American Union, General Secretariat of the Organization of American States, 1960); *First Report of the Special Committee to Carry Out the Mandate Received by the Council Pursuant to Resolution I of the Sixth Meeting of Consultation of Ministers of Foreign Affairs* (Washington, D.C.: Pan American Union, General Secretariat of the Organization of American States, 1960); *Report Submitted by the Committee of the Council, Acting Provisionally as Organ of Consultation in the Case Presented by Venezuela, to Comply with the Provisions of the Third Paragraph of the Resolution of July 8, 1960* (Washington, D.C.: Pan American Union, General Secretariat of the Organization of American States, 1960); *Study of the Juridical Relationship between Respect for Human Rights and the*

Exercise of Democracy, Inter-American Juridical Committee (Washington, D.C.: General Secretariat of the Organization of American States, Pan American Union, 1960); *Report of the Inter-American Peace Committee to the Seventh Meeting of Consultation of Ministers of Foreign Affairs* (Washington, D.C.: Pan American Union, General Secretariat of the Organization of American States, 1960); and Inter-American Peace Committee, *Special Report on the Relationship between Violations of Human Rights or the Non-Exercise of Representative Democracy and the Political Tensions that Affect the Peace of the Hemisphere* (Washington, D.C.: Pan American Union, 1960).

Trujillo's relationship with Haiti is a special subject. T. Fiehrer, "Genocide on the Massacre River: The Haitian View" (paper presented at annual meeting of South Eastern Council on Latin American Studies, Tampa, Fla., 19–21 April 1979), deals with a little-studied perspective. R. Michael Malek, "Dominican Republic's General Rafael L. Trujillo M. and the Haitian Massacre of 1937: A Case of Subversion in Inter-American Relations," *SECOLAS Annals* 11 (March 1980): 137–55, is the best source in English on the subject. Ernesto Sagás, "The Development of Antihaitianism into a Dominant Ideology during the Trujillo Era" (paper presented at International Congress of the Latin American Studies Association, Washington, D.C., 28–30 September 1995), places Trujillo's views in a broad social-political context. Bernardo Vega, *Trujillo y Haití (1930–1937)* (Santo Domingo: Fundacíon Cultural Dominicana, 1988), is a collection of documents providing a chronology of events, identification of personalities involved, estimates of the casualties, and theories of the causes.

The Dominican civil war of 1965, the U.S. intervention, and subsequent inter-American actions have been well-researched and analyzed. On the background to the civil war, see Theodore Draper, *The Dominican Revolt: A Case Study in American Policy* (New York: Commentary, 1968), a sharp rejection of President Johnson's policy based on articles written at the time, to be read with his follow-up article, "The Dominican Intervention Reconsidered," *Political Science Quarterly* 86, no. 1 (March 1971): 1–36; Philip L. Geyelin, *Lyndon B. Johnson and the World* (New York: Frederick A. Praeger, Publishers, 1966), chap. 10, also a critical analysis by a prominent journalist; and John Bartlow Martin, *Overtaken by Events* (Garden City, N.Y.: Doubleday, 1966), by a journalist and President Kennedy's ambassador to the Dominican Republic.

The leading works on the civil war and U.S. intervention, often in disagreement with one another, are Julio C. Estrella, *La revolución dominicana y la crisis de la OEA* (Santo Domingo: Talleres de la "Revista AHORA," 1965), a balanced work by a Dominican journalist; Piero Gleijeses, *The Dominican Crisis: The 1965*

Constitutionalist Revolt and American Intervention (Baltimore: Johns Hopkins University Press, 1978), sharply critical of U.S. policy, presenting a thorough analysis of the Dominican left with documentation not available in other studies; Abraham F. Lowenthal, *The Dominican Intervention* (Cambridge: Harvard University Press, 1972), focusing on the U.S. decision-making process that led to the intervention; and Jerome Slater, *Intervention and Negotiation: The U.S. and the Dominican Revolution* (New York: Harper and Row, 1970), and his *The OAS and United States Foreign Policy* (Columbus: Ohio State University Press, 1967), in which chapters 3 and 4 are especially critical of the United States for losing opportunities to head off the intervention and being trapped by false assumptions.

Bruce Palmer Jr., *Intervention in the Caribbean: The Dominican Crisis of 1965* (Lexington: University Press of Kentucky, 1989), gives an insider's view of decision making and an authoritative account of military operations from the commander of the U.S. interventionary forces. James Jose, *An Inter-American Peace Force within the Framework of the Organization of American States: Advantages, Impediments, Implications* (Metuchen, N.J.: Scarecrow Press, 1970), is the best scholarly source on the subject.

See also Michael J. Kryzanek, "The Dominican Intervention Revisited: An Attitudinal and Operational Analysis," in *United States Foreign Policy in Latin America: A Quarter Century of Crisis and Challenge, 1961–1968*, ed. John D. Martz (Lincoln: University of Nebraska Press, 1988). V. Shiv Kumar, *U.S. Interventionism in Latin America: Dominican Crisis and the OAS* (New Delhi: Radiant Publisher, 1987), is a critical analysis by an Indian professor. Larman C. Wilson, "La intervención de los Estados Unidos de América en el Caribe: la crisis de 1965 en la República Dominicana," *Revista de Política Internacional*, núm. 122 (July–August 1972), is an international legal analysis of intervention and the role of the OAS and the UN. René Fortunato y Roberto Hiciano, "Abril: La Trinchera del Honor" (Santo Domingo: Videocine Palau, S.A., 1988), is a dramatic video produced by two Dominicans sympathetic to and generally representing the views of the pro-Bosch Constitutionalists.

Relevant documents published by the Organization of American States include *Inter-American Treaty of Reciprocal Assistance, Applications*, vol. 2, 1960–1972, 3d ed. (Washington, D.C.: General Secretariat, Department of Legal Affairs, 1973); *Informe del Secretário General de la Organización de los Estados Americanos en relación con la situación dominicana (desde el 29 de abril de 1965 hasta la instalación del gobierno provisional)* (Washington, D.C.: Pan American Union, General Secretariat of the Organization of American States, 1965); Comisión Interamericana de Derechos Humanos, *Informaciones sobre el respeto de los derechos humanos en la República Dominicana* (Washington, D.C.: Pan American Union, General Secretariat of the Organization of American States, 1961); Comisión Interamericana de Derechos Humanos, *Informaciones sobre la situación de los derechos humanos en la República Dominicana* (Washington, D.C.: Pan American Union, General Secretariat of the Organization of American States, 1962); *Primer simposio sobre democracia representativa, Santo Domingo, República Dominicana, 17–22 de diciembre de 1962: informe final* (Washington, D.C.: Unión Panamericana, 1962); *Report Submitted by the Subcommittee to the Special Committee to Carry Out the Mandate Received by the Council Pursuant to Resolution I of the Sixth Meeting of Consultation of the Sixth Meeting of Consultation of Ministers of Foreign Affairs* (Washington, D.C.: Pan American Union, General Secretariat of the Organization of American States, 1961); *Second Report of the Subcommittee Submitted to the Special Committee to Carry Out the Mandate Received by the Council Pursuant to Resolution I of the Sixth Meeting of Consultation of Ministers of Foreign Affairs* (Washington, D.C.: Pan American Union, General Secretariat of the Organization of American States, 1961); and *Third Report Submitted by the Subcommittee to the Special Committee to Carry Out the Mandate Received by the Council Pursuant to Resolution I of the Sixth Meeting of Consultation of Ministers of Foreign Affairs* (Washington, D.C.: Pan American Union, General Secretariat of the Organization of American States, 1961).

The themes of Dominican politics, democratization, and U.S. policy from 1966 to the mid-1990s have been undertaken with increasing scholarly attention. G. Pope Atkins, *Arms and Politics in the Dominican Republic* (Boulder: Westview Press, 1981), based primarily on extensive interviews conducted in the Dominican Republic, discusses the subject from Balaguer's first elected term in 1966 to the middle of Guzmán's presidency in 1980; see also Atkins, "The April 1986 Elections in the Dominican Republic," in *The Caribbean After Grenada: Revolution, Conflict, and Democracy*, ed. Scott B. MacDonald, Harald M. Sandstrom, and Paul B. Goodwin Jr. (New York: Praeger, 1988). Jan K. Black, "Democracy and Disillusionment in the Dominican Republic," in *Modern Caribbean Politics*, ed. Anthony Payne and Paul Sutton (Baltimore: Johns Hopkins University Press, 1994), makes a good case for her disappointment; see also Black, *The Dominican Republic: Politics and Development in an Unsovereign State* (London: Allen & Unwin, 1986). Frank Brodhead and Edward S. Herman, *Demonstration Elections: U.S.-Staged Elections in the Dominican Republic, Vietnam, and El Salvador* (Boston: South End Press, 1984), is critical of the process.

Some of the most incisive work on Dominican politics and elections is by the

Dominican political sociologist Rosario Espinal, who teaches in the United States. Works by Espinal include: *Autoritarismo y Democracia en la Política Dominicana* (San José, Costa Rica: CAPEL, 1987); "Dominican Republic: Electoralism, Pacts, and Clientelism in the Making of a Democratic Regime," in *Democracy in the Caribbean: Myths and Realities*, ed. Carlene J. Edie (New York: Praeger Publishers, 1994); and "Electoral Politics in the Dominican Republic, 1978–1990" (paper presented at April 1991 meeting of the Latin American Studies Association, Washington, D.C.), which is presented in terms of a realistic theoretical background.

Jonathan Hartlyn's studies of Dominican politics are particularly perceptive: "The Dominican Republic: Contemporary Problems and Challenges," chap. 8 in *Democracy in the Caribbean: Political, Economic, and Social Perspectives*, ed. Jorge Domínguez and others (Baltimore: Johns Hopkins University Press, 1993); "The Dominican Republic: The Legacy of Intermittent Engagement," in *Exporting Democracy: The United States and Latin America*, ed. Abraham F. Lowenthal (Baltimore: Johns Hopkins University Press, 1991); and "Crisis-Ridden Elections (Again) in the Dominican Republic: Neo-patrimonialism, Presidentialism, and Weak Electoral Oversight," *Journal of Interamerican Studies*, no. 3 (winter 1994): 122–34.

Especially insightful are the realistic assessments of Dominican political parties and elections by Michael J. Kryzanek: "The 1978 Election in the Dominican Republic: Opposition Politics, Intervention and the Carter Administration," *Caribbean Studies* 19, nos. 1 and 2 (April–July 1979): 51–73; "Political Party Decline and the Failure of Liberal Democracy: The PRD in Dominican Politics," *Journal of Latin American Studies* 9, no. 1 (May 1977); and "The Waiting Game: Opposition and Political Atrophy in the Dominican Republic" (paper presented at the 18th Annual Meeting of the Caribbean Studies Association, Ocho Rios, Jamaica, 28 May 1993). Pablo A. Maríñez, *Democracia y procesos electorales en la República Dominicana* (Santo Domingo: Editora Alfa y Omega, 1994), is by a Dominican sociologist who teaches at the Universidad Nacional Autónoma de México in México City. National Democratic Institute for International Affairs and the Carter Center of Emory University, *1990 Elections in the Dominican Republic: Report of an Observer Delegation* (Washington, D.C., and Atlanta: National Democratic Institute for International Affairs and the Carter Center of Emory University, 1990), is an important statement by the team led by former President Jimmy Carter. See also Howard J. Wiarda, "Out with the Old, but Not too Fast," *North-South* (September/October 1994); and Larman C. Wilson, "The United States and the Dominican Republic: A Post-Election Assessment," in *The Lingering Cri-*

sis: A Case Study of the Dominican Republic, ed. Eugenio Chang-Rodríguez (New York: Las Américas Publishing Co., 1969).

Works by and about certain of the principal political figures are of interest. While president, Joaquín Balaquer published *La marcha hacía el capitolio: Discursos, temas políticos. Dos campañas electorales 1966–1970 y 1970–1974* (México, D.F.: Fuentes Impresores, 1973). From among the substantial writings of Juan Bosch, long-time anti-Trujillist and Balaquer's perennial political opponent, of special interest are his *Trujillo: causas de una tiranía sin ejemplo* (Caracas: Librería "Las Novedades," 1959) and *Crisis de la Democracia de América en la República Dominicana* (Mexico, D.F.: Centro de Estudios y Documentación Sociales, 1964); English edition, *The Unfinished Experiment: Democracy in the Dominican Republic* (New York: Frederick A. Praeger Publishers, 1965). Osvaldo Santana, *Peña Gómez: sus orígines* (Santo Domingo: Alfa y Omega, 1981) is a biography of the PRD leader.

Some aspects of economics, economic development and relations, the role of economic actors, and the relationship between Dominican economics and politics are covered in the following works: Ladislao Brachowicz, "Turnaround in the Dominican Republic: Reforms Pay Off with Growth and Stabilization," in Inter-American Development Bank, *The IDB* (Washington, D.C.: Inter-American Development Bank, December 1993); José Cabrera, *Crisis de la publicidad y la mercadotecnia en la República Dominicana* (Santo Domingo: Editora Taller, 1980); José Israel Cuello H. and Julio E. Peynado, *La Gulf and Western en la reformismo* (Santo Domingo: Ediciones Taller, 1974); Luis E. Guaranizo, *One Country in Two: Dominican-owned Firms in New York and the Dominican Republic* (Ph.D. diss., Johns Hopkins University, 1992); Frank Moya Pons, *Empresarios en conflicto: políticas de industrialización y sustitución de importaciones en la República Dominicana* (Santo Domingo: Fondo para la Avance de las Ciencias Sociales, 1992), in part an economic history that examines the long struggle between Santo Domingo and Santiago and the Cibao Valley; Martin F. Murphy, "The International Monetary Fund and Crisis in the Dominican Republic," in *Crises in the Caribbean Basin*, ed. Richard Tardonico (Newbury Park, Calif.: Sage Publications, 1987); John Nuttall, *Evolution of Sugar Import Policies and Programs, 1981–1988*, Staff Paper no. 8 (Washington, D.C.: U.S. Department of Agriculture, November 1988); and Irma Tirado de Alonso, *Trade Issues in the Caribbean* (Philadelphia: Gordon and Breach, 1992), chap. 4, "Industrialization and Trade in the Dominican Republic and Haiti," and chap. 8, "Economic Policy, Free Zones and Export Manufacturing in the Dominican Republic." From the voluminous literature on the Alliance for Progress, a good summary is J. Warren Nystrom and Nathan A. Haverstock,

The Alliance for Progress: Key to Latin America's Development (Princeton: D. Van Nostrand, 1966).

Dominican relations with Haiti and attitudes toward Haitians in the past three decades form a discrete category of analysis, a complex mixture of elements related to economics, politics, nationalism, society and culture, and race relations. The human rights group Americas Watch observed and reported on the unconscionable situation of Haitian laborers in the Dominican Republic: *Haitian Sugar Cane Cutters in the Dominican Republic* (November 1989); *Harvesting Oppression: Forced Haitian Labor in the Dominican Sugar Industry* (June 1990); and *Half Measures: Reform, Forced Labor and the Dominican Sugar Industry* (March 1991). In a similar vein, the National Film Board of Canada prepared "Black Sugar: 200,000 Slaves in the Heart of the Americas" (1987), a critical documentary film video.

Important analyses of the problem are Frank Báez Evertsz, *Braceros haitianos en República Dominicana* (Santo Domingo: Instituto Dominicano de Investigaciones Sociales, 1986); Martin F. Murphy, *Dominican Sugar Plantations: Production and Foreign Labor Integration* (New York: Praeger Publishers, 1991). See also Saskia K. S. Wilhelms, *Haitian and Dominican Sugarcane Workers in Dominican Bateyes: Patterns and Effects of Prejudice, Stereotypes, and Discrimination* (Boulder: Westview Press, 1995); and "Mirrors of the Heart" (below). Of particular interest are the attitudes revealed by President Joaquín Balaquer in *La isla al revés: Haití y el destino dominicano* (1949; reprint, Santo Domingo: Fundación José A. Caro Alvarez, 1983).

The major sources of information on numerous aspects concerning culture, society, and Dominican-U.S. relations are among the following citations. Luis Martínez-Fernández, *Torn between Empires: Economy, Society, and Patterns of Political Thought in the Hispanic Caribbean, 1840–1878* (Athens: University of Georgia Press, 1994), is especially good on U.S. pre-Civil War racial views and the slavery question. On race and ethnicity, including elements of *hispanidad* and *cultura criollo*, see José Alcántara Almanzar, "Black Images in Dominican Literature," *New West Indian Guide* 61, no. 3 (1987); "Mirrors of the Heart: Race and Identity," *Americas* series, program no. 4 (WBGH Boston and Central TV Enterprises in association with Columbia University's School of International and Public Affairs, Florida University's Latin American and Caribbean Center, and Tufts University, 1992), deals with Dominican racial views, especially toward Haitians and experiences in the United States, and stresses Dominicans' unwillingness to acknowledge African roots, instead identifying their ancestors as Indian; Joaquín Balaquer, *Guía emocional de la ciudad romántica* (1944; reprint,

Santo Domingo: Ediciones Alpa, 1969); Balaquer, *Historia de la literatura dominicana* (Santo Domingo: J. D. Postigo, 1983); Alan Cambeira, *The Dominican Republic in Historical and Cultural Perspective* (Armonk, N.Y.: M.E. Sharpe, 1997); Fradique Lizardo Barinas, *Cultura africana en Santo Domingo. Dibujos primarios . . . [y] dibujos definitivos* (Santo Domingo: Sociedad Industrial Dominicana en Editora Taller, 1979); and Antonio Zaglul, *Apuntes*, 5th ed. (Santo Domingo: Ediciones de Taller, 1982); Pedro Andrés Pérez Cabral, *La comunidad mulata: El caso socio-político de la República Dominicana* (Caracas: Gráfica Americana, 1967); Fernándo Pérez Memen, "Faro á Colón: Ideal y realidad," *Listín Diario*, 3 de Octubre de 1993; and Bernardo Vega and others, *Ensayos sobre cultura dominicana de hoy* (Santo Domingo: Museo del Hombre Dominicano, 1981).

U.S. influence by way of television is critically examined by Antonio V. Menéndez Alarcón, *Power and Television in Latin America: The Dominican Case* (Westport, Conn.: Praeger Publishers, 1992). For the direct and indirect influence of the U.S. educational model, see C. Lloyd Brown-John, "Higher Education in the Dominican Republic: Background and Evaluation," *North South: Canadian Journal of Latin American and Caribbean Studies* 2, no. 3/4 (1977); and Monsignor Agripino Núñez Collado, *La UCMM: un nuevo estilo universitario en la República Dominicana*, 2 vols. (Santiago: UCMM, 1982), by the second rector of UCMM. The subject of Dominican music is interestingly covered by Mark Holston, "Music is Big Business in the Dominican Republic but Bachata now Challenges the Monopoly of Merengue," *Caribbean Week*, 25 December 1993 to 7 January 1994; Deborah Pacini Hernández, *Bachata: A Social History of Dominican Popular Music* (Philadelphia: Temple University Press, 1995), and her "Cultural Politics and Popular Music in the Dominican Republic: Bachata and *nueva canción* in the 1990s" (paper presented at International Congress of the Latin American Studies Association, Washington, D.C., 28–30 September 1995); and Dario Tejeda, *La historia escondida de Juan Luis Guerra y 4–40* (Santo Domingo: Amigos del Hogar, 1993).

The international movement of people, migration, the transnational communities developed in both the United States and the Dominican Republic, and the consequent symbiotic economic and cultural relationship are described and explained in the following works: David B. Bray, "The Dominican Exodus: Origins, Problems, Solutions," in *The Caribbean Exodus*, ed. Barry B. Levine (New York: Praeger, 1987); José del Castillo, "La Inmigración Dominicana en los Estados Unidos," in *Los Inmigrantes Indocumentados Dominicanos en Puerto Rico: Realidad y Mitos*, ed. Juan E. Hernández Cruz (San Germán: Universidad Interamericana de Puerto Rico, 1989); José del Castillo and Martin F. Murphy,

"Migration, National Identity and Cultural Policy in the Dominican Republic," *Journal of Ethnic Studies* 15, no. 3 (fall 1987): 65–66; Jorge Duany, "Quisqueya on the Hudson: The Transnational Identity of Dominicans in Washington Heights" (paper presented at the 19th Annual Conference of the Caribbean Studies Association, Mérida, México, 24–27 May 1994); Eugenia Georges, *The Making of a Transnational Community: Migration, Development, and Cultural Change in the Dominican Republic* (New York: Columbia University Press, 1990); Sherri Grasmuck and Patricia R. Pessar, *Between Two Islands: Dominican International Migration* (Berkeley: University of California Press, 1991), chap. 6; Luis E. Guarnizo, "Los Dominicanyorks: The Making of a Binational Society," in *Trends in U.S.-Caribbean Relations*, ed. Anthony P. Maingot, entire issue of *Annals of the American Academy of Political and Social Science* 533 (May 1994); Glenn Hendricks, *The Dominican Diaspora: From the Dominican Republic to New York City — Villagers in Transition* (New York: Teachers College Press, 1974); Fernando Pérez Memen, "Panorama Histórico de las Emigraciones Dominicanas a Puerto Rico," in *Los Inmigrantes Indocumentados Dominicanos en Puerto Rico: Realidad y Mitos*, ed. Juan E. Hernández Cruz (San Germán: Universidad Interamericana de Puerto Rico, 1989); and Alejandro Portes and Ramón Grosfoguel, "Caribbean Diasporas: Migration and Ethnic Communities," in *Trends in U.S.-Caribbean Relations*," ed. Anthony P. Maingot, entire issue of *Annals of the American Academy of Political and Social Science* 533 (May 1994). For Trujillo's policies, see C. Harvey Gardiner, *La política de inmigración del dictador Trujillo* (Universidad Nacional Pedro Henríquez Ureña, 1979).

Baseball in the Dominican Republic constitutes a sports culture unto itself, largely the result of several forms of the U.S. presence in the country. The subject requires separate commentary in view of the obsession Dominicans have for the sport and their impact on professional baseball in the United States. See Alan M. Klein, *Sugarball: The American Game, the Dominican Dream* (New Haven: Yale University Press, 1991), a sociological study of the place of baseball in Dominican society and how the game reflects Dominican ambivalence toward the United States, i.e., a passion for a game that is U.S. exported and controlled; Michael Malec, ed., *Social Role of Sport in Caribbean Societies* (Beverly Hills: SAGE Publications, 1995), has a chapter titled "Headstrong and Head-of-the-Class: Resocialization and Labeling in Dominican Baseball"; Rob Ruck, *The Tropic of Baseball: Baseball in the Dominican Republic* (New York: Carroll & Graf Publishers, 1991); and Tony Tedesch, "Play Ball!" *Caribbean Travel & Life* (May–June 1992), 66–71.

The illicit international traffic between the Dominican Republic and the

United States and movement of people involved in the drug trade especially from the mid-1980s had significant economic and social impacts on bilateral relations and the respective domestic scenes. Two good news articles are José de Córdoba, "Nouveau Riche: New York Drug Link Enriches a Poor City in Dominican Republic," *Wall Street Journal*, 8 July 1992, and M. McAlary, "To Die in New York: Exclusive Report from Drug Capital of the Dominican Republic," *New York Post*, 16 September 1992. Ivelaw L. Griffith, "Drugs and World Politics: The Caribbean Dimension, *The Round Table*, no. 332 (October 1994), is insightful; and U.S. Congress, House of Representatives, Select Committee on Narcotics Abuse and Control, *Dominican Drug Trafficking: Hearing*, 103d Cong., 1st sess., 24 March 1993 (Washington, D.C.: Government Printing Office, 1993) is informative.

Index